The New Woman and Technologies of Speed in *Fin-de-Siècle* Literature

The New Woman and Technologies of Speed in *Fin-de-Siècle* Literature

EVA CHEN

OXFORD
UNIVERSITY PRESS

OXFORD
UNIVERSITY PRESS

Great Clarendon Street, Oxford, OX2 6DP,
United Kingdom

Oxford University Press is a department of the University of Oxford.
It furthers the University's objective of excellence in research, scholarship,
and education by publishing worldwide. Oxford is a registered trade mark of
Oxford University Press in the UK and in certain other countries

Published in the United States of America by Oxford University Press
198 Madison Avenue, New York, NY 10016, United States of America

British Library Cataloguing in Publication Data
Data available

Library of Congress Control Number: 2024946917

ISBN 9780198922254

DOI: 10.1093/9780198922285.001.0001

Printed and bound by
CPI Group (UK) Ltd, Croydon, CR0 4YY

Acknowledgments

The section on cycling romance in Chapter 3 is a revised version of an earlier article entitled "'The Hate That Changed': Cycling Romance and the Aestheticization of Women Cyclists in the 1890s," published in *Victorian Periodicals Review*, vol. 52, no. 3, 2019, pp. 489–517. ©The Research Society for Victorian Periodicals (2019).

Parts of Chapter 4 are based on my article entitled "Its Beauty, Danger, and Feverish Thrill: Speed and Cycling Women in *Fin-de-siècle* Fiction," published in *MFS: Modern Fiction Studies*, vol. 63, no. 4, pp. 607–27.

Contents

List of Figures

Introduction

"Fast Women"

The New Woman and Speed

> Such change you must have witnessed, most venerable! ... Your hour-glass is sadly out of date. We have advanced beyond its wasp-like waist now, and its imitator woman—lovely woman—works a typewriter, reads scientific papers, rides astride on bicycle, and does not wear corsets—or little else—sometimes!
>
> "To Time: An Apostrophe." *Pick-Me-Up* Oct. 1, 1892

In this 1892 piece addressed to "Time" in the London penny paper *Pick-Me-Up* (1888–1909), the anonymous writer laments the passing of the good old times and the advent of a new age accelerated by modern commerce and technology. Slow "scythes" are now replaced by "two-horse reaping machines" purchased cheap "at a mortgagee's sale," "Society beauties" write testimonials for a famous soap to make "honest" money, and poets turn to magazine writing and are content with frothy and easily forgotten pieces (2). Amid this scene of fast obsolescence and unsettling disruption, the modern woman is seen to ride the wave of change with great ease and dexterity, her provocative "newness" best exemplified by her adroit use of two new technologies of speed: the bicycle and the typewriter. Long gone is the outdated hourglass, meaning both the corseted body of Victorian womanhood and the venerable time device. In comes the flying bicycle and the fast typewriter, mastered to perfection by the liberated New Woman.

This image captures neatly the strong correlation between the New Woman and these two machines of speed in *fin-de-siècle* Britain. Appearing at around the same time as middle-class women in Britain began to enter en masse the public spheres of work, business, and social life, the bicycle and the typewriter are often hailed as twin machines of emancipation that contributed enormously to women's financial autonomy and personal freedom. The typical New Woman of the period is invariably a young lady cycling around without a chaperone, often in her short, controversial Rational cycling costume, and making an independent living as a typewriter girl. Women's rights activists of the time, including Agnes Amy Bulley and Margaret Whitley, welcomed the invention of the typewriter and called it working women's "El Dorado" (41). Others, such as Olive

The New Woman and Technologies of Speed in Fin-de-Siècle *Literature*. Eva Chen, Oxford University Press.
© Eva Chen (2024). DOI: 10.1093/9780198922285.003.0001

Schreiner, Rebecca West, and Elizabeth Banks, credited typewriting with broadening women's employment opportunities and offering "serious work" in what used to be a man's world of business and office (qtd. in Banks 585). The leading manufacturer—Remington—claimed that the typewriter "opened the door for the emancipation of women" (qtd. in Srole 87), and the trade journal *The Practical Phonographer* praised typewriting for raising women's "independence, comfort, and consequent self-respect" ("Self-Supporting Women" 190). As late as 1914, an Underwood typewriter ad prided itself on helping women's suffrage, and asked "Every Prospective Woman Voter" to "raise her right hand in favor of the writing machine generally," because "[t]he soulless little typewriter has done as much toward gaining 'Women's Rights' as all the arguments and agitation of centuries" (qtd. in Olwell, "Typewriters and the Vote" 55). The bicycle is viewed as even more liberating. Feminists celebrated the bicycle for having "done more to emancipate women than anything else in the world" ("Champion of Her Sex" 10). "I stand and rejoice every time I see a woman ride by on a wheel," gushes the suffragette Susan B. Anthony, for it is "the picture of free, untrammeled womanhood" (qtd. in Anthony and Bly 10). Other commentators joined in the chorus, including John Galsworthy, chronicler of the mores and manners of *fin-de-siècle* life:

> The bicycle ... has been responsible for more movement in manners and morals than anything since Charles the Second. Under its influence, wholly or in part, have wilted chaperones, long and narrow skirts, tight corsets, hair that would come down, black stockings, thick ankles, large hats, prudery and fear of the dark; under its influence, wholly or in part, have blossomed weekends, strong nerves, strong legs, strong language, knickers, knowledge of make and shape, knowledge of woods and pastures, equality of sex, good digestion and professional occupation—in four words, the emancipation of women. ("On Forsyte Change")

Critics have pointed out that a plethora of complex structural changes, such as the escalation of urbanization and industrialization, the spread of compulsory education since the 1870 Education Act, and the entrance of middle-class women into the urban public sectors opened up by mass commodity culture, contributed to the rise of the New Woman and the improvement of prospects for women in general.[1] The New Woman is both a sociohistorical phenomenon and also a discursive product constructed by journalists and writers. Many of the conflicting political, moral, and cultural attitudes in late-nineteenth-century Britain over

---

[1] For more recent studies on middle-class women's life and work in the modern city, see Adams, Greenslade and Rogers, Liggins 2006, Richardson and Willis, Shiach 2004, Spiers, and Young. For more specific studies on the New Woman's use of the typewriter and the bicycle, also see Bathurst, Davies, Gray, Hallenbeck, Heilmann, Keep, Ledger, Marks, Mackintosh and Norcliffe, Olwell 2003, Srole, Wånggren, Wosk, Zimmeck.

issues like the Woman Question, female suffrage, inequality in marriage, social and moral purity, and education and employment possibilities for women are embedded in the heated discussions about the New Woman. The concept also moves beyond a predominantly political image to include the vast army of less politically conscious middle-class and lower-middle-class British women, who departed from traditional norms of domesticity to seek greater freedom and self-supporting employment, often in an increasingly commodified modern city. These women are a brand new phenomenon, embodying a hitherto unprecedented range of more liberated feminine roles in terms of spatial mobility, financial independence, and heterosexual interaction—roles aided and accelerated by the bicycle and the typewriter. "[T]he emancipation of women," as Rita Felski points out, is "inseparably linked to their movement into the workplace and the public sphere' (151). The bicycle carries the woman rider far and away to unknown destinations free from supervision. The typewriter offers white-collar office work to women, which often leads to the need to live alone in big cities and go to work alone. This, as claims the female social investigator Clementina Black in 1889, "compels the world to recognize their freedom ... and made it possible for all women to do so" ("Organization" 696).

The bicycle and the typewriter are indeed twin machines of emancipation for women, but it must be noted that they are also machines of speed enabling women to be faster and more physically embroiled in modern speed culture. As technologies that greatly speed up women both in work and in daily movement, they demand from their women operators a response and adaptation to speed right from the beginning. The first thing that confronts women cyclists and typists is the shock of speed and how to catch up with, imitate, adjust to, and finally master this mechanized speed if they hope to be adequate operators. Operating these two machines thus exposes the New Woman to the constraints and possibilities of machine-accelerated speed. The wide popularity of the bicycle and the typewriter in the *fin-de-siécle* period is a sign of an accelerating speed culture and its further infiltration into more aspects of everyday life. Even the daily experience of negotiating the modern city's bustling crowds and adjusting to the fast pace of life is a part of this modern speed culture. For out-and-about, working women, a large part of their enlarged freedom comes about after they have learnt to adapt to this new speed and thrive in the fast-paced modern city. Speed and the ability to use speed is therefore what differentiates these women from their traditional, stay-at-home sisters. The 1892 *Pick-Me-Up* piece quoted earlier pinpoints the typing and cycling New Woman, not just because she embodies the disruptions to traditional gender norms, but also because, in an article addressed to "Time," she represents a new type of faster and more up-to-speed modern women who best embody the disorientating spatial–temporal compression of the time.

Accelerated speed, typically through the help of machines, is, according to Paul Virilio, a phenomenon of industrial modernity. Virilio writes that there is no industrial revolution but a "dromocratic revolution" (*Speed and Politics* 47), by which he means race, derived from the original Greek noun "dromos." Technological innovations, as Daniel Headrick points out, have been "essential to the European conquests of the nineteenth century," (2) aiding and accelerating imperial expansion.[2] Technologies of speed, in particular, have been the driving force of modern Western military–industrial supremacy (Virilio, *Speed and Politics* 47). After the invention of combustion engines that brought about the transportation revolution, accelerated industrial and technological development leads to the pursuit of faster speed and maximum efficiency in all areas of modern life. Walter Benjamin likens the nervous stimulation undergone by the modern city-dweller, in response to a congregation of fast-moving traffic, people, and things, to that of the worker by the factory assembly line, both subject to "the rhythm of production on a conveyer belt" (132). The last years of the nineteenth century see the further rise of personal technologies of speed, including the telephone, typewriter, wireless telegraph, cinema, and bicycle. These technologies, allowing for what Jeffrey T. Schnapp calls the "seculariz[ation]" or democratization of speed to a large public (4), create sweeping changes in concepts and experiences of time and space, and promise the breaking down of traditional boundaries and limitations. But they also demand greater efficiency in information transmission and everyday life, heralding a deeper penetration of mechanized speed into further corners of human life.

Middle-class women in Britain have long been constrained by the bourgeois ideology of separate spheres and alienated from this public world of work and mechanized speed. Working-class women are, of course, exposed to fast-moving machines on the factory floor, but middle-class women's sedentary domesticity is often a symbol of the respectability of their family and their difference from working-class women (Liggins xiii). With the rise of the typewriter and the bicycle, however, a significant number of these women are propelled, for the first time, to the forefront of modern speed culture, with drastic consequences on their subjectivities. This book moves beyond the familiar image of the revolutionary, iconoclastic New Woman cyclist-cum-typist, and focuses instead on her interaction with techno-aided speed. By examining literary and journalistic representations of the New Woman in *fin-de-siècle* Britain, I argue that this interaction is of paramount importance to the New Woman's "newness." All discussions on her possible victimization or empowerment as an iconic figure of the *fin-de-siècle* scene need also to be filtered through the lens of speed culture. The New Woman is new, significantly because she is fast (literally and symbolically). Being fast, having

---

[2] The bicycle, for instance, may be a machine of emancipation for women in Britain and the West, but it also stands for the technological progress and superiority of the West, which could be used to justify colonial conquests of "backward," "uncivilized" nations. In Grant Allen's *Hilda Wade* (1899), for instance, the New Woman Hilda's bicycle-riding in South Africa strikes a male English friend as a sign of "[c]ivilization indeed" in "these remotest wilds of Africa!" (192).

speed, and adjusting to the shocks as well as excitement of techno-aided speed is a key part of her new identity.

Speed offers an exciting new perspective to study the phenomenon of the New Woman. The New Woman, at the same time, is also a suitable subject for a study of modern speed culture. Speed in the *fin-de-siécle* period functions as tightened discipline and subjects labor to greater pressures of efficiency. With the escalation of modern commodity culture, speed, when used in personal, recreational areas of modern life outside of the work place, further translates into a coveted commodity and functions as spectacle and display. The New Woman's typewriting and cycling reflect the increasingly complex working of speed along different lines. While her typewriting work subjects the New Woman to the discipline of industrial speed, her cycling body, made fashionable and glamorous during the mid-1890s "bicycle craze," reflects the commodification of speed as it infiltrates beyond the area of production into that of consumption. The New Woman's fast body is indeed structured and constrained by these disciplinary and commodifying forces of speed, but this also fuels the birth of a rejuvenated, speed-expanded female subjectivity as women stake a claim to modern speed culture as new players.

Women, Technology, and Speed

Typewriting and cycling offer techno-aided speed. Both are technologies produced in the Second Industrial Revolution that are more portable and more tailored to individual needs than the huge machinery of manufacturing and railway transport in the First Industrial Revolution. The typewriter makes a great improvement of speed over handwriting. According to Otto Burghagen, author of the first book-length study of the typewriter in 1889, it could complete office work and the transmission of information in a third of the time one would need with the pen (qtd. in Kittler, *Gramophone, Film, Typewriter* 191). The Safety bicycle of the mid-1890s, with its equal-sized wheels and pneumatic tires, was the fastest vehicle on the road before the arrival of the automobile, and a most visible emblem of modernity's preoccupation with speed, progress, and mobility (Herlihy 252). The typewriter may engender information speed while the bicycle engenders locomotive speed, but typing's words-per-minute speed evokes the same associations of limitless progress, technological optimism, and kinetic dynamism as cycling's miles-per-hour speed. In the last years of the nineteenth century when both machines became popular, typewriter racing competitions were as much of a riveting spectator sport as bicycle races, both triggering huge public passion and wide press coverage because of the thrills of speed. Typewriter speed queens and kings became "celebrities of a minor luminosity," as the typewriter historian Bruce Bliven points out (116), just in the same way that cycling champions were adored as heroes. All major manufacturers of typewriters and bicycles took part in this international craze for racing contests, keeping their own stable of champion racers and coaches, and intent on setting ever-faster records of speed in a bid to transcend human limitations (Wershler-Henry 234; Smith 127). From the very start, these two are machines of speed, offering accelerated velocity and a prosthetic extension of power to their human operators.

Technology and mechanized speed have long had masculine associations. Sociological studies of the history of technology have pointed out that technology is a product of industrialization, when the focus of production moved away from the rural, large, and self-sustaining household where women played a crucial role, to the factory and the marketplace where technological inventions worked to accelerate production and profit-making (Cowan 69).[3] This reduction of the role of the family, and by extension that of women, to that of consumption and the socialization of small children parallels the rise at the same time of the bourgeois ideology of separate spheres, which naturalizes women's domesticity as reflecting their innate qualities of passivity, emotionality, and nurturing, reproductive roles. Feminist critics have pointed out that because both modern technology and hegemonic masculinity are historically associated with industrial capitalism, they are linked symbolically by themes of control and domination (Faulkner 82). Technology takes on masculine associations not just because of the tenacious links between masculinity and abstraction and objectivity—two qualities essential to science and technology—but also because technology as part of the Baconian project sets out to achieve control and domination over organic nature, which has always had feminine associations (82). Women's reproductive roles have long connected them, since the time of classical mythology, to nature's life cycles of fertility, seasons, and reproduction. When *Punch* magazine published a series of cartoons depicting British scientific explorations between 1870 and 1890, the "woman-as-nature" image is carried on with Nature embodied as a female, waiting for the exploration of British men and British Empire (Sheffiled 17–18). When an opposing antimachine tradition gained ground in Victorian literature and culture in the aftermath of the Industrial Revolution, and called for a return to nature and to an organic, preindustrial way of life, this further confirmed women's exclusion from technology as the private home, where women's power lies, was set up as a shelter from the mechanizing impact of what Mark Seltzer calls the modern body–machine confrontation (10).[4]

---

[3] Feminist science and technology studies, informed by a combination of cultural studies, anthropology, and postmodern philosophy, have widened the meaning of technology to more than the application of science to industrial or commercial objectives. Instead, technology is a fusion of the material and the cultural, and a communication medium implicated in the construction of subjective gender identities. For more, see Wajcman 457.

[4] The body–machine relationship has a long history in science and philosophy and could be traced at least to the mid-seventeenth century. Andreas Huyssen points out that in Enlightenment ideas the human and the machine was not particularly polarized, as the body itself was often compared to a machine: a series of pistons, levers, and cogs (72). This body–machine harmony ultimately rests on the

Because women are linked to "cycles, gestation, the eternal recurrence of a biological rhythm which conforms to that of nature" (16), women's time is, as Julia Kristeva points out, characterized by repetition and eternity. This feminine time is outside of the masculinist "time as project teleology, linear and prospective unfolding; time as a departure, progression and arrival ... inherent in the logical and ontological" (17). Kristeva views this as a positive means for the feminine to construct a space for itself, but for many this equates women with passivity, immobility, and inaction. This inherent stasis, perceived as located in the naturalized female body, couples with women's exclusion from technology to further alienate women from techno-aided speed. In "The Foundation and Manifesto of Futurism," published on the front page of *Le Figaro* on February 20, 1909, Filippo Marinetti unequivocally equates modern techno-aided speed with a penetrating, explosive masculinity, celebrating this speed, which he sees as incarnated in the motorcar, as linear, aggressive, dynamically progressive, and adrenaline-packed: "We want to hymn the man who holds the steering-wheel and whose ideal spear passes through the earth that speeds along its orb" (*Critical Writings* 13). The many other products of modern techno-aided speed Marinetti enthuses over—including the "gliding flight of aeroplanes," "adventurous steamers," "great-breasted locomotives" "puffing" "like enormous steel horses," factories "vibrat[ing]" under their "violent electric moons," "gluttonous railway stations devouring smoking serpents"—all radiate masculinist power and aggression. Such speed valorizes dynamic progress and the future, and works to the "despise of women" and static tradition (14).

Marinetti excludes women from modern speed culture, but already in the last decade of the nineteenth century, years before his 1909 manifesto, an increasing number of women were leaving domesticity and breaking free from this long exclusion by using the typewriter and the bicycle. Tens of thousands of middle-class and lower-middle-class women entered the public world of business as typists, contributing to the rapid feminization of low-ranked clerks in the modern office (Fleissner 66). Women office workers in British government agencies numbered only 15 in 1851, but 279 in 1861 and 1,446 by 1871, constituting by then 1.1 percent of all clerks employed in England and Wales (Young, *From Spinster to Career Woman* 104). But the number multiplied more than 80 times between 1850 and 1914 (Price and Thurschwell 4), rising to nearly 25,000 in 1901, and women employed in private companies rose to 60,000 by the same year (Richardson and Willis 5). By 1914, women clerks, mostly of low ranks, constituted 20 percent of the

belief in the transcendence of the God-like soul. By the nineteenth century this idea was reconceptualized as the body as motor, the site of energy conversion and conservation conceived in electro-chemical and thermodynamic terms (Rabinbach 2). As industrialization intensified, an antimachine discourse led by writers like Carlyle, Ruskin, Arnold, Dickens, and Gaskell gained ground, which decried the machine's dehumanizing impact on the body and led to a radical break between the body and the machine. See Sussman 38. For more contemporary views, see Peter Gaskel.

total number of British clerical workers (Price and Thurschwell 4). In the *fin-de-siècle* office, the typewriter came to be seen primarily as a woman's machine, and for a certain period of time until the early years of the twentieth century, the word "typewriter" referred to both the machine and the woman operator ("Things Not to Dwell On" 136, "Is Type-Writing a Successful Occupation" 82). Many middle-class women also took to cycling in the mid-decade bicycle craze, constituting about a third of the 1.5 million cyclists in the height of the bicycle fad (Rubinstein 51). The bicycle was a luxury commodity at that time, but the tapping of the women's market was instrumental for the popularity of the Safety bicycle. During the height of the bicycle boom, the image of the fashionable woman cyclist appeared everywhere: in posters, ads, postcards, cartoons, press reports, and literary works of the period. These two machines were offering women an early taste of what it means to be sped up by mechanized speed.

By now women in Britain had already experienced the locomotive speed offered by the train, a First Industrial Revolution technology of speed, since the mid-nineteenth century. The expansion of railway lines in the "railway mania" of the 1860s had brought a larger number of the paying public, including middle-class women, to the novelty and expanded freedom of rail travel (Martin 132). Women rail passengers particularly aroused conservative anxiety over their invasion into the masculine public space and the sexual danger caused by the close proximity of male and female bodies in the confined space of the railway compartment. In *Lady Audley's Secret* (1862), for instance, Lady Audley's crime of bigamy and her deception of her country-squire husband are at least partially attributable to women's increased mobility through the railway, which allows her to travel great distances from London to a remote village and completely disguise her old identity. When Robert, the best friend of her first husband, chases her around by train, his efforts at exposing her are often thwarted because she beats him to it and escapes in an earlier or faster train. As Daniel Martin points out, her final imprisonment at the end of the novel in a French mad-house, which Robert specifically insists must be far away from any railway line and "out of the track of all railway traffic" (*Lady Audley's Secret* 382), underlines the engrained fear by the dominant masculine order over the sexual danger caused by women's use of rail speed (Martin 149).

But when the bicycle came around as a new, personal speed machine, it offered women a more direct, visceral, and agentic interaction with modern speed culture. Rail travel certainly entails traversing into the masculine public space, but the enclosed and semiprivate railway compartment amounts to what Amy G. Richter calls a "hybrid sphere" of "public domesticity" (8, 6), which railway developers and advertisers actively promoted in order to stress that "a respectable woman's place expanded to include the railroad" (33). The bicycle, however, offers no such semblance of domesticity, as it is ridden by women in full public view, in the streets or country lanes, leading to a more transgressive use of mechanized speed. More importantly, the bicycle entails a more active interaction between the female body and the machine of speed. The train already offers its mostly middle-class customers a chance to be "brought ... up to speed" (Daly 20), in order to adjust to the thrills and shocks of the train's "annihilation" of time and space (Schivelbusch 62). But this is a speed over which the railway passenger has little control. The passenger is both stimulated by speed yet also sits passive and stationary, a fragmentary experience which Lynne Kirby characterizes as a simultaneity of motion and stillness (2).

The bicycle, by contrast, allows the human subject to experience machine-aided speed as a rider rather than as a passenger. Learning to cycle does involve bruises and accidents, awakening fears of the maiming machine on the factory floor. In H. G. Wells's 1896 novel *The Wheels of Chance: A Bicycling Idyll*, for instance, the London shop-hand Hoopdriver, after trying unsuccessfully to learn cycling, looks down at his bruised legs and feels "as if he had been sitting with his nether extremities in some complicated machinery, a threshing-machine, say, or one of those hay-making furies" (2). But mastering the bicycle also renders possible for the first time a more direct, individualized control of velocity and direction, and the possibility of accelerating or decelerating at will. Unlike the fragmentary experience of train speed, bicycling demands both physical exertion and heightened alertness from the New Woman, and a greater somatic and psychic synthesis.

Since the New Woman is often both a cyclist and a typist, her body becomes the site of intimate contact with not just locomotive speed, but also information speed. This latter, located in the context of the late-nineteenth-century Taylorite office where the typewriter girl has to work for long hours, offers a less sanguine picture. The last decade of the nineteenth century saw an expansion in the range of employments available to what the Victorians would call ladies, including nursing, teaching, and office work (which generally entailed typewriting). This is evidenced in a series of interviews with professional women conducted in 1893 by the women's employment editor of *The Queen*, Margaret Bateson, who later published the interviews in *Professional Women upon Their Professions*. Of these professions, typewriting, which offered a major source of work for women because of the rapid expansion of modern business, demands the most direct and prolonged daily interaction with mechanized speed. While all forms of women's work in the public domain are subject to the increasingly time-oriented demands of modern economy, typewriting exerts the greatest pressure because of its nature as a speed machine, and because of its central role in the Taylorite, efficiency-oriented modern office. The typewriter girl learns to be faster and more alert, but to attain speed she has to subject her muscles and nerves to long hours of repetitive, rhythmic straining. This exposes the New Woman to the same body–machine encounter that has defined the lives of the working-class on the factory floor.

The characteristic "blind" dimension of typewriting technology further aggravates fears of mechanization. The typewriter was originally designed for the blind and deaf back in the eighteenth century (Beeching 7). Of the many early models, one writing machine that prints in many ways like a modern typewriter was invented by Pellegrino Turri in 1808, for Countess Carolina Fantonio da Fivizzono who was blind. To provide ink for the machine, Turri also invented carbon paper. Around the same time an Englishman, Ralph Wedgwood, invented carbon paper for his own patented writing machine for the blind (Wershler-Henry 45–46). By the late nineteenth century, even when better models were later developed for general use both in the office and at home, many early models still wrote invisible lines, and what was typed became visible only several lines down. After 1898, when the first Underwood "view typewriters" were developed, allowing the typist to see every letter being typed, fastest speed was still achieved by not looking at the lines but working purely from memory and the triggering of appropriate muscles and nerves (Bukatman 634). This distinct trait further threatens to turn the typewriter girl's body into what Keep calls the passive, "disciplined body" coerced by industrial speed ("Blinded by the Type" 151).

Typewriting is not the only technology of speedy information available to women in the nineteenth century. Electric telegraphy, an earlier technology improved by Samuel Morse in 1840 and adopted as the international standard in 1865, began to offer employment to women operators in Britain, first in some private telegraph companies and then in the British General Post Office after the latter took over the telegraph service in 1870 (Jeffrey 39). About a third of operators in 1870, or 1,535 out of 4,913, were women (85).

As noisy, information-processing technologies, the typewriter and the telegraph have, as Hazel Hutchison points out, "a closely shared history" (150). Thomas Edison, who improved telegraphy by inventing automatic machinery to transmit messages at much higher speed than Morse telegraph operators, was trying to invent his own typewriter in 1870. Edison managed to persuade the Automatic Telegraph Company of New York not to back Christopher Sholes, who had invented the first prototype typewriter two years earlier, in 1868 (Wershler-Henry 69). Scholes, of course, later turned to Remington and developed the first commercial typewriter in 1873. In this competition to design a fast writing technology, the telegraph works best for long distances while the typewriter, which transmits words rather than codes, is more portable and widely used on a daily basis inside offices across a range of business settings. The telegraph did not compete well with the letter post on price and went into decline from 1920, after competition from the telephone removed its speed advantage. But the typewriter proved enormously popular and became the most widely used office technology. It facilitates a greater number of middle-class and lower-middle-class women to find white-collar work, and attracts more prominent press attention and public discussions, thus warranting its position as the most visible writing technology to be associated with the New Woman.

This book focuses on the typewriter and the bicycle not just because they are iconic symbols of the rebellious New Woman, but also because their usage necessitates one of the earliest direct, visceral encounters between mechanized speed and the female body. The New Woman uses cycling and typewriting for different purposes: one for recreation, and one for work. But both amount to a mechanistically enmeshed process that purports to acclimatize her body to a faster pace of life and work. Women are disciplined by speed, but also achieve higher levels of concentration, efficiency, and technological knowledge not commonly required in their more traditional sedentary life.

In recent years, scholarship on literary and cultural representations of the New Woman has moved beyond an emphasis on emancipation and focuses on the technological dimension. In *Gender, Technology and the New Woman* (2017), the first book-length study on the New Woman and technology, Lena Wånggren examines a number of *fin-de-siècle* literary and journalistic writings to challenge the view of technological determinism, arguing instead that women have used the typewriter, the bicycle, and medical examination and diagnostic tools in ways that subvert traditional gender expectations. In Leah Price and Pamela Thurschwell's edited volume *Literary Secretaries/Secretarial Culture* (2005), the focus is on the turn-of-the-century female typist as she appears in literature, and on her role in the mediation of information transmission, writing, and mechanical reproduction. Victoria Olwell's chapter "The Body Types: Corporeal Documents and Body Politics Circa 1900," in particular, questions the conflation of the bodily and the mechanical in *fin-de-siècle* discourses on the typewriter girl, arguing instead that the reduction of the female typist to a mere automaton reveals "so much about the interlocking ideologies of labor, wiring, gender, and citizenship" (60). Christopher Keep points out, in his illuminating work on the typewriter girl, that though the exigencies of the typewriter machine may threaten to empty out the female subject and turn her into an "instrument of speed," the latter would "always interpose a layer of resistance" and leave her signature "in the circuit of transmission" ("Blinded by the Type" 168).

My book, while inspired by this fascinating body of work, further pinpoints the role of techno-aided speed. By studying the New Woman's interaction with speed and her efforts to construct a new, speed-accelerated identity, this book locates itself in the intersection between scholarship on the New Woman and technology, and another expanding body of work on women and modern speed culture. Georgine Clarsen's *Eat My Dust: Early Women Motorists* (2008) and Deborah Clarke's *Driving Women: Fiction and Automobile Culture in Twentieth-Century America* (2007) are representative works in this second body of critical studies. Both analyze women motoring pioneers in the early years of the twentieth century, and how speed and automobility enable the construction of a new, technology-savvy female subjectivity. Inspired by Judy Wacjman's ideas on women's agentic use of motoring technologies, they further resonate with recent work in mobility and speed studies that emphasizes the exhilarating energy of speed, typically epitomized by the automobile. This latter includes Gijs Mom's *Atlantic Automobilism: Emergence and Persistence of the Car, 1895–1940* (2014) and Enda Duffy's *The Speed Handbook: Velocity, Pleasure, Modernism* (2009). My book highlights the bicycle, which has yet to receive detailed analysis in speed studies. I argue that the bicycle, coming to the public ten years earlier than the automobile, already harbors speed's rejuvenating potential. More importantly, I look beyond this emphasis on speed as excitement, and point out the crucial, complex functions of speed as discipline and consumerist display, all incarnated in the cycling and typewriting body of the New Woman. An examination of this prominent *fin-de-siècle* figure promises to add new insight into the study of speed culture.

Speed as Coercive Discipline

The chapters in this book are arranged to analyze these manifold functions of speed as they interact with the New Woman. Each chapter addresses one aspect of this speed, and asks in what ways writers, journalists, and opinion leaders respond to and represent the sped-up New Woman, how their responses resonate with wider social and cultural backgrounds, and how they reflect the ways in which interaction with speed inhibits or facilitates women's agency.

Chapter 1 reads the image of the typewriter girl as she joins the modern work force and becomes exposed to the first function of speed: its use for tightened regimentation and greater efficiency. This crucial function of speed has had a long history. Virilio writes that the modern city has evolved from medieval settlements built around a crossroads and traffic intersection. The "control of traffic," or the speed and rate of movement of people and goods, is a crucial means through which the city-state and later the nation-state exerts social control (*Speed and Politics* 41). While the movement of these people is policed and controlled by the state, the same people are also coerced and persuaded into becoming speeding armies that march swiftly to wars in order to gain more territory and greater power for the state. Social control could be achieved by both regulating and deciding on who gets access to speed and free movement, and also by speeding up the masses when it suits the military needs of the state. Virilio has always argued for the importance of military conquests and strategies in fueling Western industrial and technological development. Machines of speed, to him, are intricately linked with warfare in modern history. War and logistics require increased speed and efficiency, and the latter, in turn, create a more dynamic industrial system that obliterates distances in time and space through the development of technologies of transportation, communication, and information. The speed of the military–industrial complex, with its associations of the blinding prowess of the machine and the violent intensities of the battlefield, is the driving force of industrial modernity (47). Capitalist production further ordains the recruitment of the public to use machines of speed, so as to generate profit gains and capital accumulation for what Duffy calls the "empowered bourgeoisie" (45). In this way, regimes of speed use new, more intense "mechanisms of interpellation" instead of the explicit use of military force to impact on the public and escalate speed's role for social control (44).

The typewriter, patented in America in 1868 and commercially developed into the Remington machine in 1873, became popular as an office machine after the mid-1880s and soon spread to Britain and other countries in Europe. As the most crucial technological innovation in the office before computerization, the typewriter is an integral part of the wider trends toward greater efficiency and productivity in modern business and industry, the "apotheosis of the Taylorist vision" in which every movement is designed to maximize profit (Bukatman 638). The modern office, with its multidepartmental bureaucracies and new organizational hierarchies, aims for "precision, speed, unambiguity, knowledge of the files, continuity, discretion, unity, strict subordination, reduction of friction and of material and personal cost" (Weber 973). The typewriter, which according to Otto Burghagen would "produce a complete letter" with one strike of a key while the pen "has to undergo about five strokes" (qtd. in Kittler 191), is both the product and the ultimate symbol of this profit-driven pursuit of speed.

When middle-class women leave domesticity and work for long hours as typists in the modern office, the strain to keep up with this speed exerts heavy somatic and psychic tolls on their body. To be marketable and get a typewriting job, she has to reach and maintain a highly competitive speed of typing. In 1888, when *The Girl's Own Paper* of London made one of the earliest mentions of the typewriter, it celebrated "forty words per minute" by "a competent operator" as the stunning advantage of the typewriter over the pen ("The Type-Writer and Type-writing" 745). By 1893, when typewriting started to be adopted by more businesses in the UK, George Gissing's New Woman character Rhoda advises her students that a speed of at least "fifty words" per minute is necessary to get typing work (*The Odd Women* 36). Copying at speed all the paperwork that used to be done by pen, the typewriter girl and her ceaselessly clicking machine symbolize the efficiency and productivity of the Taylorite office. Typing to the dictation of her boss and obeying his every order, she also epitomizes that office's demand for "strict subornation" and "discretion" (Weber 973). Typewriting speed has therefore disciplined women and "moulded" them "into a form amenable to the needs of the corporate environment" (Wershler-Henry 88).

When the typewriter girl's body is disciplined and brought up to speed, she evokes a whole variety of responses from *fin-de-siècle* discourses. As Chapter 1 points out, the popular masculine press finds her quicker body alarming, but soon seeks to tame its threat by stressing her increased sexual allure. Fastness in work is equated with fastness in moral standards, as many satirical writings eroticize the typewriter girl while at the same time dismissing her perceived passivity and complete domination by the machine of speed. Women's press retaliates by setting up speed and office work as a source of positive rejuvenation, which propels women into the public masculine world and endows them with much-needed knowledge and skills. This is an attitude which early literary works like George Gissing's *The Odd Women* (1893) also embraces. Literary texts that were published after the mid-1890s, when typewriting became more widespread, turn their focus to the disciplinary costs of this speed. Often penned by women writers with first-hand knowledge of typewriting work, these works, like Geraldine Edith Mitton's *A Bachelor Girl in London* (1898), adopt a tone of somber realism and foreground the painful struggles of the typewriter girl. When these texts pore over the gnawing poverty suffered by the genteel girl clerk and the harsh tolls of mechanized speed on her body and natural instincts, certain echoes of the mid-Victorian industrial novel are discernible, thus linking this *fin-de-siècle* female character to the plight of the industrial subject so much represented in mid-Victorian literature.

Typewriting disciplines the female body, but Chapter 2 points out that women's interaction with typing speed is not all one-sided oppression. This chapter looks at the two examples of piano-playing and literary creation to further argue that a more complicated interplay is possible which allows for mutual accommodation between agentic and mechanical powers. Piano-playing is often compared with typewriting as they work in a similar way and are both undertaken by middle-class women in the nineteenth century. Literary creation plays an opposite role, since the creative writer is often seen as the polar antithesis of the mindless typewriter girl. Both examples, however, serve to shed more light on the relationship between the mechanical and the organic, and automation and creative agency.

Chapter 2 first considers *fin-de-siècle* media reports which often assert that typewriting is ideal for middle-class women as they are already accomplished in piano-playing. Both skills, declare these reports, need nimble fingers and bodily dexterity, as well as long hours of patient practice in the enclosed setting of a private parlor or business office. The intent of such reports, often supported by manufacturers and business owners, is to feminize typewriting and increase public acceptance of the typewriter girl. However, the similarity of the two instruments does make it meaningful to examine whether human agency is totally emptied out by prosthetic machine power.

The typewriter was initially dubbed the "literary piano" because, like the piano, early models used a keyboard of black and white piano keys representing different letters which the human operator presses down with both hands (qtd. in Current, "Original Typewriter Enterprise" 392). The piano, of course, produces music and is equated with art and expressive emotion, but it is also a machine of sound that works on the human sensation with mechanical energies. As Tamara Ketabgian points out in her illuminating study of Victorian machine culture *The Lives of Machines*, the operation of the piano is the consummate manifestation of agentic creativity, but the latter is also expanded and accelerated by the mechanical power of the piano (148). The pianist's creativity, moreover, is best fueled only after long, punitive hours of repetitive practice and disciplined training. To a lesser extent, a similar coexistence and collaboration of agentic and mechanical powers is possible in the typewriting process, where the typewriter girl, sped up and disciplined by mechanized speed, is enlivened into new levels of alertness and new coordinated skills of eye, ear, hand, and brain.

Chapter 2 then moves to consider the perceived polarity between the type-writer girl and the creative writer. Late nineteenth-century cultural discourses often insist on this polarity, as the creative profession is increasingly threatened by the mechanical reproduction of typewriting and popular culture. Julian Hux-ley, for instance, when asked to explain natural selection and evolution, compared typists to millions of monkeys striking keys on the typewriter who could never ever reach the height of Shakespeare (qtd. in Price, "Grant Allen" 130). Genius is to typist as man is to monkey, and their insuperable gap is between one who cre-ates and one who blindly copies. This chapter reads some *fin-de-siècle* stories that point to a different interpretation, where the typewriter girl seems better able to maneuver the fast-paced modern life than the alienated male writer. In some cases she is the one who actively guides him, thus blurring the lines between mechani-cal copy and organic creativity. Grant Allen's *The Type-Writer Girl* (1897) gives a further twist to this polarity by unveiling the creative writer as an "artificial" hack while portraying the typewriter girl as an aspiring writer who uses her own expe-riences as creative inspiration (63). These narratives shed light on another side of typewriting speed that is less pessimistic or over-determined, affirming room for some agentic maneuver.

Speed as Status and Conspicuous Consumption

Speed enforces discipline and tightened control, but, with the escalation of mod-ern commodity culture, speed takes on a new role as commodity and conspicuous display. This function of speed as commodity, spectacle, and status display, reflected in the cycling body of the New Woman during the mid-1890s "bicycle craze," is the focus of Chapter 3.

The bicycle is one of the many personalized technologies of speed of the Second Industrial Revolution that are designed for individual use in daily aspects of life outside the sphere of work. As a result, their use is more than the practical and often laden with symbolic meanings. Capitalism demands speed in production, and also produces speed as products and commodities for consumption. Enda Duffy's insightful study on modern speed uses the example of the automobile as "the ultimate fetish of the commodity age" (8), but this book argues that the bicycle of the mid-1890s, pursued mostly by the middle class for novelty, recreation, and leisure, already offers a highly exclusive and publicly visible consumption of speed.

As Chapter 3 points out, since middle-class women have long assumed the role of conspicuous consumption in the bourgeois gendered ideology whereby they display the status and wealth of their family (Veblen 132), a role that has been further escalated into "a familial and civic duty" with the advent of modern commodity culture (Felski 65), speed's function as privileged commodity sees its best incarnation in the displaying body of the fashionable New Woman cyclist. This is an important development, as women, traditionally alienated from mechanized speed, now play a prominent role at the forefront as modern speed culture expands into areas of consumption. Perhaps more than the early motorcar, which was driven mostly by a small number of elite men until its popularization after the First World War, the mid-1890s bicycle acts as an even more widely visible "fetish of the commodity age," since it counts among its patrons tens of thousands of stylishly dressed middle-class women.[5] The New Woman's access to bicycle speed does liberate her from confining domesticity, but her speeding body, so transgressive and scandalizing to conservative eyes in the early years, is soon subsumed under a consumerist framework where it becomes the best advertisement for bicycle manufacturers. Many New Women worked with such forces of commodification, joining the efforts of manufacturers, advertisers, and commentators to glamorize the woman cyclist in order to effect greater public acceptance of women's cycling. As cyclist, the New Woman uses her speeding body to display not just her social iconoclasm but also her status, glamor, and a commodified form of progressive modernity.

The bicycle was one of the first durable luxury products in modern history to be marketed to the public, and a most desired commodity in those years (Garvey 69; Hanlon 90). Costing between £10 and £30 in the UK, between $100 and $150 in the US in 1895, and almost $80 by 1897, it was used mostly by the middle class for pleasurable recreation rather than as a practical means of transport, often as a welcoming escape from repetitive urban routines (Rush 2).Though by the end of the 1890s over-production and fierce competition had driven the price down, making the bicycle available to working-class people, in the mid-decade "bicycle craze" when the New Woman cyclist was a celebrated symbol, the bicycle and its visible speed was highly sought after and used as a marker of status. About 1.5 million people in Britain took up cycling at the height of the "bicycle craze," testifying to the enormous public enthusiasm that left "[f]ew corners of British society ... untouched" (Rubinstein 71), but these cyclists constituted only 4 percent of the total British population of 35 million (51). The bicycle remained firmly within the province of the rich and fashionable.

The pleasure of cycling, however, does not just lie in ownership of the commodity, but more in its speed and public visibility. In the modern scene of ceaseless change and consumerist stimulation, speed as manifested in the fast, merrily cruising bicycle becomes a spectacle and display, and consumption of speed amounts to a new visible symbol of power and status. As a form of locomotive speed, cycling

---

[5] Very much like the early bicycle, the early motorcar was pursued mostly by young affluent men for adventure and racing. But its prohibitively high price (about £800 apiece) and difficulties of operation limited ownership to a small group of wealthy people. See Richardson, p. 14. Some early women cycling pioneers also took up motoring. See "Notes," p. 835.

speed is not just temporal but also spatial, displayed in full public view on urban streets or country lanes. Cycling speed's high visibility is one major reason why the New Woman cyclist seems to incur greater public outcry than the typewriter girl. While women's use of both machines of speed encounters initial public resistance, typewriting work is mostly carried out inside the office, often as a perceived extension of women's roles in traditional domesticity. Cycling, however, is done in public, forcing attention on the cyclist and subjecting women to an "unseemly display" of themselves (qtd. in Curry and Bingham 45). The mannish, fast, immodest New Woman cyclist horrified a large number of the public, and was the subject of much caricature and criticism by the masculine satirical press (Marks 184, 200).

With so much initial hostility to the "fast" New Woman cyclist, it is therefore quite a surprise that, during the mid-1890s "bicycle craze," public perception dramatically changed from initial opposition to general acceptance within just a few years. The bicycle quickly became very popular with middle-class women, and sales figures bear the best witness to this rather rapid transformation. By 1896, one year into the "bicycle craze," ladies' cycles constituted one-third of all new bicycle orders in Britain, whereas merely three years previously (in 1893) the number was only one in fifty (Hanlon 63). An 1895 entry in the *Cassell's Family Magazine* confirms this sudden change in public attitude: "It would hardly be too much to say that in April of 1895 one was considered eccentric for riding a bicycle, whilst by the end of June eccentricity rested with those who did not ride" (456). Lady Colin Campbell, famous journalist and cyclist, writes in *Lady Cyclist* in 1896 that "[c]ertainly one of the most striking changes in the attitude of the public mind over the recent years, both in rapidity and extent, is that in regard to bicycling, "especially so far as women are concerned ... the tables have completely turned" (9).

This shift in public attitude is at least partially attributable to a commodification of the image of the New Woman cyclist, who is now seen as progressive and modern, but most of all glamorous and fashionable. The role of an accelerating commodity culture is prominent, but so is speed's new function as commodity and status display. A certain form of speed is glamorized: a restrained, elegant, controlled speed prescribed, approved of, and urged on the woman cyclist by manufacturers, etiquette books, cycling manuals, and press reports. This speed acknowledges the pleasure of mobility, but assuages the threat of "fast" and unfeminine speed by turning cycling into the "best public platform" for the display of fashion and status (Mackintosh and Norcliffe 25). Cycling's public visibility, initially a source of impropriety and destabilizing threat, becomes instead the best means of blending the elegantly riding New Woman into a modern urban street scene where spectacle and status display is increasingly important.

It is thus clear that the general public came to accept the woman cyclist in those boom years not because of direct support for the New Woman or her radical calls for social change, but because they had come to equate the New Woman cyclist with fashion, glamor, and status display. Bicycle-aided speed has become the ultimate symbol of conspicuous display for the rich, and of upward mobility for the less privileged. Bicycle historians have tended to credit technological innovation with the bicycle's popularity in the mid-1890s (Beeley; McGurn), but its quick positioning as a conspicuous commodity is also instrumental, particularly where women's cycling is concerned. The New Woman's speeding body is now integrated into a consumerist framework where speed becomes a key marker of status and privilege. But while this has certainly helped to bring more freedom and independence to middle-class women, such conspicuous speed also leads to many exclusions and the formation of a new hierarchy.

Chapter 3 examines how the popular press, bicycle manufacturers and advertisers, and even New Woman activists all joined in to glamorize the woman cyclist, turning her cycling body into the best platform for consumerist display. Special attention will go to the ad-laden, product-specific cycling press which popped up and prospered in the mid-1890s, including cycling magazines, pamphlets, manuals, ads, posters, etiquette books, and cycling romance stories, which sold for extraordinary numbers and helped to advance the image of the woman cyclist as fashionable, elegant, and safely middle class. Cycling romance, a short-lived, ad-supported literary genre that mushroomed during the boom, particularly proved effective. By featuring a new type of out-and-about, freely mobile heroine and stressing her youth, beauty, and elegant fashion, cycling romance manages to convey the message that cycling speed enhances, rather than detracts from, a woman's desirability and actually makes her more marriageable.

With cycling a most visible means of conspicuous speed, a new form of hierarchy is in place to differentiate those who are fast and rich from those who are slow and poor. Chapter 3 moves on to discuss literary representations of the New Woman cyclist, because these more perceptively unveil the hidden class exclusions behind her touted progressiveness. Gissing's story "A Daughter of the Lodge" (1901), for instance, reveals that access to bicycle speed becomes a crucial marker differentiating the New Woman from her poorer, wannabe imitators. In Wells's *The Wheels of Chance*, the London drapery clerk Hoopdriver rides his old, battered bicycle because "all the best people rode" (85). In his attempt to help the New Woman cyclist Jessie during his cycling trip, he does so not just because he imagines himself to be a knight-errant saving a lady in distress, but also because cycling allows him to claim an equal footing with the normally "inaccessible" New Woman, and get a glimpse of her elevated "social altitudes" (112).

Speed as Rejuvenation and Thrill

Speed disciplines and commodifies the New Woman, but Chapter 4 argues that speed's prosthetic extension of human faculties also offers a source of rejuvenation to the New Woman and compensates for these constraints. This regenerative, energizing potential ultimately helps navigate the New Woman toward a better adjustment to modern speed culture.

Speed, as Jeffrey T. Schnapp indicates, is fundamentally a dynamic, adrenaline-packed force, an "*excitant modern*" that energizes and stimulates the human subject (3). Speed as rejuvenation is long embedded in human history, as the pursuit of speed has been associated, through the trope of flying, with angelic or godly power since antiquity. By the time of industrial modernity, accelerated speed, typically through the help of machines, is available for the first time to the mass public on a wide scale. The bicycle's locomotive speed is the most visceral manifestation of modernity's obsessive pursuit of progress and ceaseless movement, allowing the public to "feel modernity in their bones" (Duffy 4). By compressing space and time, cycling offers speed as a new source of stimulation and excitement, and triggers a thrilling fantasy of transcendence and power.

In "The Foundation and Manifesto of Futurism," Marinetti declares that "the world's magnificence has been enriched by a new beauty: the beauty of speed," with its "danger, the habit of energy and fearlessness" (*Critical Writings* 13). Marinetti is referring to the modern phenomenon of machine-accelerated speed, best exemplified in the racing motorcar. The motorist, intensified with the adrenaline power of speed and fertilized by the man–machine interplay, is a quintessential modern subject, "who hurls the lance of his spirit across the Earth, hurtling at breakneck speed along the racetrack of its orbit" (13). In this religion of pure speed, Marinetti does not include the bicycle. In fact, he is annoyed by a couple of cyclists who, "wobbling like two equally convincing but nevertheless contradictory arguments" along the road (12), nearly collided with his car and forced him to swerve and crash into a ditch.

Four years later, however, Marinetti changed his opinion and included the bicycle as one of the new technologies of speed shaping the modern sensibility, alongside the telegraph, the telephone, the train, the motorcar, the ocean liner, the airplane, and the cinema (*Critical Writings* 120). In "The New Ethical Religion of Speed," published in 1916, Marinetti further names the bicycle and the motorcycle as "divine" examples of this religion of speed (*Critical Writings* 256). This change of heart is likely prompted, as argues Deborah Longworth, by the influence of several key members of the European avant-garde, particularly Umberto Boccioni, who was fanatical about bicycle racing and used competitive cycle racing as a favorite subject for his paintings (Longworth 3). Marinetti met Boccioni in 1910, and was impressed with his theories of "plastic" or geometrical dynamism in art, which would give "pictorial shape to Futurist axioms about speed as the defining quality of ... modernity" (3). The racing cyclist in Boccioni's art captures the dynamism, energy, and sensation of speed, and underlines the fact that the bicycle, a product of modern speed culture like the motorcar, demands a similar rush of adrenaline, body and mind instantaneousness, and a stimulated anticipation for danger.

Speed, as a new, adrenaline-packed modern sensation, allows individual control of movement and compensates the modern subject for the time-addled, oppressive speed of the industrial system. Even for the non-racer, the bicycle of the mid-1890s already offers a taste of this active, thrilling, and compensatory use of speed. In the mid-1890s "bicycle craze," many women, aided and accelerated by the speed of the bicycle, are initiated into this rejuvenating aspect of speed. They may be constantly urged to ride erect and slow and restrain from reckless speeding or scorching, but there seems no dearth of women who loved cycling for the "beauty," "danger" and feverish thrill of its speed (Marinetti 13).

Reports of such women are scattered in some magazines, and some literary works also touch upon this significant, though much frowned upon, part of women's cycling. In Allen's *Miss Cayley's Adventures*, Mrs. Edward Kennard's *The Golf Lunatic and His Cycling Wife*, and Gissing's story "The Schoolmaster's Vision" (1896), women's excitement at mastering speed and forging a new speed-expanded self is palpable. These works weave a more nuanced picture of women's foray into modern speed culture, whereby women defy the taming by mainstream discourses, and instead relish speed and its potential for rejuvenation and pleasurable thrill. Speed as a crucial site of modernity does not operate to the exclusion of women, but is rather enriched and complicated by the addition of gender and sexual difference. With the entry of women, a new sexual energy is further unleashed that eroticizes speed, an active, aggressive, speed-liberated sexual energy that is traditionally linked with men but is now available to women.

This dimension of speed, together with other, multifaceted ways in which the New Woman's body interacts with modern speed culture, will be explored in detail in the following chapters. Through this discussion, my book acknowledges the heavy costs of women's exposure to mechanized speed, but also argues for the potential to build a new, sped-up, and energized female subjectivity capable of navigating a fast-paced modern life. If encountering and adapting to speed is the quintessential trait in becoming the new modern subject, then the New Woman stakes as much claim as men to this modern means of individuation.

Scope of the Study

Because this book uses predominantly literary and journalistic materials to study the New Woman, some explanation is called for to justify the scope of the study. The New Woman produces a whole variety of responses in the *fin-de-siècle* period and is the subject of heated literary and journalistic discussions. In the many different forms of representations examined in this book, we will find an effort to articulate and comment on her interaction with speed, comments expressed in varying ideas of stultification, passivity, or vitality and agency. Like the recent critical scholarship examined above, this book uses literary and journalistic sources because these play a crucial role in shaping the meaning of the New Woman, while also raising her visibility as one of the most representative figures of the time.

The very birth of the name "New Woman" came from press debates, as journalists, literary writers, opinion leaders, business owners, manufacturers, feminist activists, and readers all argued over her meaning. Sally Ledger points out that the New Woman's textual configurations are "as significant historically as the day-to-day lived experience of the feminists of the late Victorian women's movement" (Ledger 3). Writing about how media attention heightens public awareness of the New Woman's rebellion against gender norms, the *Westminster Review* claims in 1895 that "it is not possible to ride by road or rail, to read a review, a magazine or a newspaper, without being continually reminded of the subject which lady-writers love to call the Woman Question" (Sykes 396). The *Humanitarian* concurs when it declares in 1896 that of all social revolutions of the late nineteenth century, nothing is "more discussed, debated, newspaper-paragraphed, caricatured, howled down and denied, or acknowledged and approved" than "the new woman ... immeasurably the first in importance, the most abounding in potentialities and in common interest" (Morgan-Dockrell 339–40).

The New Woman is an equally ubiquitous presence in *fin-de-siècle* literary works. Many New Woman novels were bestsellers. Sarah Grand's *The Heavenly Twin* (1893), for example, ran to six editions in the first year of its publication and sold well over 20,000 copies within England alone after just one year (A. Cunningham 179). If novels published in the 1880s and dealing with the Woman Question are included, more than 100 New Woman novels were published in the seventeen years between 1883 and 1900 (Ardis 4). Such density of media and literary coverage by both the conservatives and feminist writers forces attention on the Woman Question to an unprecedented extent, thus allowing literature and journalism to reflect and reproduce, as well as shape and produce, history.

The women's press, for instance, has been especially instrumental in impacting on changing attitudes toward women's work, and has inspired real-life women's activism. An 1883 leader in *The Queen* writes that Jessie Boucherett's Society for Promoting the Employment of Women, which has done so much for expanding women's work (including typewriting), "owes its existence" to Harriet Martineau's *Edinburgh Review* article "Female Industry" on the need to enlarge women's sphere of work ("The Employment of Women" 261). Women's press also worked hard to exert pressure on business owners and government agencies, hoping to improve pay and working conditions for women typists ("Parliamentary Nottings" 475; "Society of Typists 1891" 584). An early positive result was seen in 1894, when the Treasury, citing considerable "adverse criticism" from the "Public Press," agreed to raise women typists' weekly pay scale from 14-2-24 shillings (starting salary of 14 shillings raised to 24 shillings after 2 years) to 16-17-2-25 shillings in 1894 (Zimmeck 80). In 1908, following a campaign by the Civil Service Typists' Association, the rate was raised further, to 20-2-26 shillings (80).

Literature, in its turn, impacts on evolving public opinions. While writers such as Gissing are known to have consulted the feminist press before writing their novels, the latter is also often used as references for feminist social investigators like Clementina Black.[6] Contemporary reviews of Gissing's novel *The Odd Woman*, for instance, called it "the Woman question made flesh" (qtd. in Coustillas and Partridge 219), and praised the book for turning a "grim" social question of "real" and "painful" interest to "clever and original purpose" ("Review of *The Odd Women*" 667). By highlighting the dire situation of the "odd women" who could no longer count on marriage and have to work for a living, literary works like Gissing's novel lends a powerful voice to *fin-de-siècle* debates about the New Woman. As *The Woman's Herald* wrote in 1892, "ideals of womanhood are largely originated by heroines in real life, and by heroines in fiction, as well as by the unconscious but powerful interaction of these two factors" ("Ideals of Womanhood" 3). The New Woman and what she means is therefore heavily influenced by the recordings and representations by writers and journalists, as they both interact with real historical events to form a mosaic of the richly complicated *fin-de-siècle* sociocultural landscape.

In seeking to supplement literary representations with sources from the popular press, I use discussions of the New Woman typist and cyclist from mainstream media like *The Times* or *The Nineteenth Century*, popular masculine satirical press like *Punch*, product-specific commercial magazines like *Lady Cyclist*, and women's press like *Women's Penny Paper*. These journalistic materials, together with other historical sources like ads, posters, manuals and guides, and etiquette books, are in constant dialogue with the literary representations. The popular press and ads, being a more commodified form of mass culture and often supported by advertising entrepreneurs, offer a less nuanced and more complicit view. But they provide a set of narratives which literary writings, more versed in the portrayal of contrasting voices and conflicting perspectives, seek to reinforce, modify, interrogate, and often subvert. Both are what culture studies critics call "culture in action" (Veeser xi), as they become, in a sense, social documents engaged in an ongoing interaction with their historical situations to mold and shape the meanings of the period.

The rise of the New Woman represents a key period in middle-class women's history in the last years of the nineteenth century, when out of necessity or by choice women have to leave domesticity and adapt to what Judith Walkowitz calls the "new urban female style of 'being at home' in the city" (46). Whether this is for the purpose of pursuing paid work in the public domain, or to generally move around freely and without supervision, the New Woman constitutes a major challenge to established ideas of femininity. Literary and journalistic representations

---

[6] Liggins writes that Clementina Black "would make the comparison between the results of her research into the conditions of shop-girls and the representation of their exploitation in naturalist fiction" in Black's 1907 study *Sweated Industry and the Minimum Wage* (xv-xvi).

constitute leading voices about the freedoms and dangers brought by this major change, and actively shape and contribute to *fin-de-siècle* debates about women's place in society.

This book has chosen the New Woman literature by George Gissing, Grant Allen, H. G. Wells, Geraldine Edith Mitton, and Mrs. Edward Kennard, as well as the short stories published in literary and family magazines, because these give thematic importance to women's typewriting and cycling. Many canonical New Woman writers also use the bicycle and the typewriter, but the two machines do not often figure importantly in their works. Instead, they are more concerned with marriage and sexuality, moral and social purity, and political activities waged in the privacy of the domestic home. Even Sarah Grand, an avid cyclist herself, does not devote much narrative space to women's cycling in her fiction. In George Egerton's short story "Her Share" (1894), Alice Meynell's "A Woman in Grey" (1896), and Kate Chopin's "The Unexpected" (1895), the New Woman protagonist is briefly mentioned as a cyclist. But apart from signaling that the heroine is a New Woman, the bicycle plays little role in the stories' thematic focus on marriage and love. One reason for this neglect is that New Women writers, as Elaine Showalter points out, have rarely focused on the city and its outdoor life as a subject for their work, unless in terms of interior spaces like the upper-class drawing-room (*Daughters of Decadence* viii).[7]

In this sense, the stories and novels chosen in this book are valuable because they all feature typewriting and cycling as a crucial plot device, which drives the narrative forward and shapes the development of the protagonists. These works have a wide range and are diverse in nature, including serious, mature works like Gissing's "Women's Problem" novel *The Odd Women* (1893), which contemporary critics praise for being much "stronger" and "more striking" than anything Gissing has written before ("Review of *The Odd Women*" 667). Also included are more light-hearted, satirical novels about the New Woman cyclist-cum-typist like Allen's *The Type-Writer Girl* (1897) and *Miss Cayley's Adventures* (1899). Critics were more dismissive, calling the former amusing to the "ten-thousand type-writer girls" who "crowd London today," but not of enough "features of interest" to the "critics" ("Review of *The Type-Writer Girl*," *Athenaeum* 348). Geraldine Edith Mitton's *A Bachelor Girl in London* (1898) embodies the gritty realism of an increasing number of female-penned working-girl literature, while Mrs. Edward Kennard's *The Gold Lunatic and His Cycling Wife* (1902) captures women's restless desire to break free from sedentary domesticity and find release and rejuvenation in cycling. The female-penned narratives are more first-hand and emotionally charged, often drawing from the authors' own experience as typist and cyclist. Gissing, Wells, and Grant, writing profusely on the subject in journals as well as in their literary creations, tend to reflect a masculine unease over the disruptions to home and

---

[7] For more, see Gail Cunningham 2–3, 104–26.

society signaled by the rise of the New Woman. But they also demonstrate through their naturalistic portrayals an "extraordinary knowledge of the social and moral condition of our great cities—more particularly of London," as one 1897 reviewer finds of Gissing's fiction.[8] These narratives by male and female writers all seek to shed focused light on how modern women tackle the trials and hopes of negotiating the fast-paced life of big cities like London, while attempting to forge a new speed-structured and speed-expanded subjectivity.

[8] Fred Dolman, *National Review*, no. 30, 1897, pp. 258–66. Quoted in Coustillas and Partridge, p. 311.

1

A Woman's Machine

Typewriting and Disciplinary Speed

On September 15, 1894, "Three Young Lady 'Typists'" wrote to *Cycling: An Illustrated Weekly* to "roast" a Mr. Whitwell for using the word "typewriter" for the lady operator and calling her cheap ("Whitwell Roasted" 137). In a short play published in the journal one week earlier, Mr. Whitwell had claimed that "only shopgirls and cheap typewriters" and not ladies would wear the Rational costume when cycling ("The Stranger" 128). The three young lady typists, in their retort, insist that the typewriter is the machine, not the lady, and that this conflation is "the ignorance of the end of the 19th Century" ("Whitwell Roasted" 137). They challenge him to produce a sketch of a "typewriter (and a cheap one, too) careering about on a bicycle in Rationals" (137). A typist, they point out, does not "cease to be a lady" or become a "cheap typewriter," because typewriting is a calling which "does not necessarily imply either want of brains or want of breeding, and in which ladies are the rule, and not the exception" (137).

Mr. Whitwell is not alone in conflating the machine with the woman operator, suggesting that by the 1890s the typewriter was widely viewed as a woman's machine and closely associated with women office workers. His response, however, also underlines the problematic nature of public perceptions of the typewriter girl in *fin-de-siécle* Britain. The three young lady typists, like much of the women's press, try to emphasize the serious nature of typewriting work and the intelligence of the woman typist, but their angry protest points to the prevalence of perceptions of the typewriter girl as dumb, in want of "brains" or skills, and mechanical. They take great offence at being called cheap, not only because women typists are paid cheaper than male clerks, but also because the typewriter girl occupies a precarious social position, having somehow lost her lady status by having to sell her labor for money. More importantly, the typewriter girl is often viewed as morally "fast" and sexually available for the benefit of the male boss. When Mr. Whitwell chastises a typewriter girl for cycling, he is not just askance at her fast speed but *particularly* at her supposedly loose morality.

In the *fin-de-siècle* years, when an expanding army of women typists and stenographers entered into the modern office, the typewriter girl becomes a crucial cultural icon in the Victorian imagination of a new type of working, independent young women. Offering her labor for a weekly payment that sustains an independent living, often at modest boarding houses in large cities away from home, she

The New Woman and Technologies of Speed in Fin-de-Siècle *Literature*. Eva Chen, Oxford University Press.
© Eva Chen (2024). DOI: 10.1093/9780198922285.003.0002

lays claim to a financial autonomy that answers to no one. Working for long hours in a modern office in close proximity to male colleagues, she learns to use technology and new skills of information processing, while also accessing a more relaxed code of heterosexual interaction. This allows her, as the *London Phonographer* claims in 1891, to be one of the "pioneers of progress in this very progressive country" (13).

At the same time, the typewriter girl is also part of the labor force in a modern business culture which makes the pursuit of profit, hyper-productivity, and streamlined control its primary goal. The typewriter may be a personalized machine of speed, but because it is primarily used for work in the Taylorite office, it becomes a major manifestation of the increased regime of speed in modernity and a tightened means of socioeconomic control. More than other modern technologies of speed, the typewriter triggers graver anxiety over its perceived threat to human psychic depth, because its predominant use in a context of repetitive, unrelenting labor awakens memories of the dehumanizing machines of the First Industrial Revolution. When women leave domesticity and enter office work as low-end typists, they become frontline workers bearing the direct brunt of a newly rationalized modern office. All the widely differing responses by *fin-de-siècle* reporters and writers on her perceived sexual allure, lack of brains, or radical progressiveness are also inevitably commentaries on the impact of mechanized speed on her body.

This chapter will first trace how the typewriter evolved as a machine of speed, and particularly how it became a woman's machine that facilitated women's en masse entrance into office work. It will then study the three main images of the typewriter girl in journalistic and literary representations, and how these representations view her interaction with disciplinary speed. The popular masculine press and some early magazine stories portray her as a sexy but dumb machine woman, constructing her disciplined and sped-up body first as disruptive but then as sexually alluring. This is the polar opposite to the emancipated, active professional celebrated in the women's press, an image further consolidated in literary works like Gissing's *The Odd Women*. Typewriting is hailed as a socially transformative solution to the Woman Question, and speed's disciplinary impact energizes women to become active "invaders" into the traditional male world "which men have always forbidden us to enter" (*The Odd Women* 54, 135).

As the decade moves on, the third image is the toiling urban worker portrayed in literary texts published after the mid-1890s. These stories, mostly penned by women writers, continue to refute the trivialization of the popular masculine press, but they also modify the optimism of women's press by focusing on the harsh costs of life as a typewriter girl. In the same way that the concept of the New Woman has broadened beyond its early political, privileged image, the typewriter girl portrayed in these works is no longer the "honorary girl" of the early years (Zimmeck 80)[1], but increasingly lower-middle-class women of reduced circumstances struggling to make a living through typewriting. In Geraldine Edith Mitton's *A Bachelor Girl in London*, and in many short stories published in literary and family magazines, the typewriter girl is neither Gissing's militant, energetic feminist activist, nor the jolly, morally "fast" "female bachelor" decried in much of the satirical press for "claim[ing] a man's freedom" and enjoying the pleasures of the modern city ("Female Bachelor" 582). Instead, she is a lonely, fatigued woman who has to tackle poverty and the grinding costs of coercive industrial speed. Such depictions of the stultifying effects of industrial mechanization are a common feature in an earlier literary form, the mid-century industrial novel, but that stultified body is predominantly a male worker. The *fin-de-siècle* narratives of the typewriter girl are valuable, because they prove to be among the few Victorian literary works that foreground the working female body and its regimentation by mechanized speed.

The Fastest Writing Machine

The typewriter, originally designed for the blind and deaf, has a long history of evolution dating back to the early eighteenth century (Jackson 5). After decades of innovation and more than 50 models made by 112 inventors, the first successfully mass-produced typewriter, the Remington No. 1, was developed in 1873 by Christopher Latham Sholes and Carlos Glidden (Wershler-Henry 65).[2] The model consisted of a type bar connected to a telegraph key (later changed to a piano key), which would swing up when pressed to hit a carbon-paper sandwich supported by a glass disc (66). The Remington No. 2 model, issued in 1878 at a price of $125, proved to be more popular by writing both capitals and lower-case letters and using a distinctive QWERTY keyboard. This keyboard arrangement, still

[1] Zimmeck writes that many of the early typists were well-educated New Women "honorary girls" from privileged backgrounds (80). This is quite different from America, where the tradition of female office workers runs longer and is traced back to the Civil War (Hoke 29). Most female typists in America were high school graduates from lower-middle-class, urban households (81). In Britain, the first batch of female clerks tended to be of higher social background. One example is Janet Hogarth, a first-class honors graduate in philosophy from Oxford and the first ever female clerk employed by the Bank of England. She wrote in detail in her autobiography about her monotonous duties that did not fit her intelligence ("The Arrival of Women in the Office").

[2] The concept of a typewriter dates back at least to 1714, when Englishman Henry Mill filed a vaguely worded patent for "an artificial machine or method for the impressing or transcribing of letters singly or progressively one after another" (Wershler-Henry 43). But the first typewriter proven to have worked was built by the Italian Pellegrino Turri in 1808, as a prosthetic writing device for his blind friend Countess Carolina Fantoni da Fivizzano. In 1870, the Danish pastor Rasmus Malling-Hansen invented the Hansen Writing Ball, which went into commercial production in 1870 and looked rather like a pincushion. Nietzsche bought one in 1882 to help with his failing sight, but gave up the attempt after "a couple of weeks" (Kittler, *Discourse Network* 193).

widely used today, was designed specifically to increase typing speed. To avoid the upwardly striking keys from jamming when typing in speed, the most often used letter-keys have to be placed far apart from each other. This arrangement also encourages alternation between the left and right hands, so that when one hand types a letter the other hand can prepare to type the next letter, making the process faster and more efficient while reducing errors and fatigue.

This key renovation was instrumental in propelling the Remington name onto the forefront of the new typewriter industry, and thereafter to a global stage. Initial sales, though, were very slow (Russo 20). Only 8 machines were put on the market in 1874. In 1881 Remington sold 1,200 machines, and in the following year 1,400 (Hoke 77). By 1885 the number climbed slowly to 5,000 (Russo 21). But after the mid-1880s sales took off, marking the commercial success of the typewriter almost ten years after its manufacture. Statistics vary, with one study claiming that in 1887 Remington sold 14,000 machines, and that by 1890 it sold more than 1.5 million typewriters (Hoke 77). Another claimed that by 1888 Remington was manufacturing more than 1,500 typewriters a month, and that the demand was still so great that foreign sales were temporarily ignored in favor of the domestic US market (Davies, "Women Clerical Workers" 38). Competing brands like the Caligraph, Crandall, Hammond, Underwood, Bar-Lock, and Corona became popular, too, but Remington remained the biggest manufacturer. Another study confirmed that more than 250,000 Remington machines were produced between 1896 and 1914 (Hutchison 148).

As early as 1874, Remington had already set up a London office at 100 Gracechurch Street to cater to the British market. But it was by the 1890s that sales began to grow, after Remington signed an extensive contract with the British Civil Service which entitled it to display the "By Royal Appointment" crest on its advertising. It supplied a number of UK Government departments, including the Post Office, and also provided typists when necessary (Zimmeck 77).

The typewriter is the latest invention in a long line of technological developments that seeks to speed up writing. Since 1810, the use of the rotary press and continuous form by the printing trade allowed typesetting machines to operate almost as quickly as one speaks. When Samuel Morse invented electric cable telegraph in 1840, textual messages could be transmitted at a much faster speed than manual communication. By the 1850s, two telegraph machines at either end of a telegraph cable would not only receive and print telegrams on to paper tape, but also provide a copy of the message at the sender's end. This turns the printing telegraph machine into a prototype typing machine. The imperative in those years was toward the invention of a writing machine that could operate almost as quickly as a man could speak. The Morse code allowed operators to understand code much faster than they could write it down, and stenographers couldn't transcribe as fast as they could take notations from a dictating person. A fast writing machine was direly needed.

An interesting note in this development is that the typewriter is, as Friedrich Kittler points out, a "by-product" of the American Civil War (*Gramophone, Film, Typewriter* 190). Remington was initially established in New York in 1816 as a firearm and rifle-making company, and transferred the standardization of component parts for the making of weapons to the making of civil writing instruments after the Civil War, when government weaponry orders petered out (Russo 18). The typewriter's fast speed, the upward striking of the keys at the push of the finger, and the continuous "click, click, click" noise of each strike underlines the affinity between these two types of machines. Kittler, quoting a German critic, compares typing to "a flying projectile" (190). The time between the stimulus and the pushing of the button, or between the reading eye and the hand muscles that operate the typewriter, is "about 250 milliseconds": "it only needs a starting signal," and then the typing is triggered and "goes all by itself" (190). The typewriter becomes a "discursive machine-gun," (191), a "rapid-fire weapon" (192), with "strikes and triggers proceed[ing] in automated and discrete steps" (191). Speed, in this sense, is the distinguishing trait of both the typewriter and the machine gun.[3]

The typewriter revolutionized writing speed. In 1867 *Scientific American* had predicted that an early John Pratt typewriter would make "the pen" "obsolete," and bring a "revolution" in writing because it could allow a man "to print his thoughts twice as fast as he can write them" ("Type Writing Machine" 3). The Remington model, which was inspired by Pratt, was even faster, and its trademark was advertised in eighty-four languages with the motto, "To Save Time Is to Lengthen Life" (qtd. in Russo 28). Russo quotes an 1888 article "The Typewriter: Its Growth and Uses," written by P. G. Hubert for the *North American Review*, which claims that "the chief reason" for the typewriter's "success and popularity ..., is, of course, the saving of time in business offices," a fact "so well known as to scarcely need argument" (qtd. in Russo 28). The article goes on to confirm that "based on a countless number of tests coupled with the experiences of nine out of ten of our active business houses, the typewriter, as compared to the pen, saves forty minutes an hour" (28). In 1898, Otto Burghagen enthuses over the typewriter's "significant savings of time" in the world's first monograph devoted to the typewriter:

> With its help one can complete office work in a third of the time it would take with the pen ... In the time it takes the pen to put a dot on the "I" or to make the "u" sign, the machine produces two complete letters. The striking of the keys follows in succession with great speed, especially when one writes with all finger; then, once can count five to ten keyboard hits per second! (qtd. in Kittler, *Gramophone, Film, Typewriter* 191)

---

[3] One type of machine gun was once nicknamed the "Chicago typewriter" (Wershler-Henry 247). Wershler-Henry writes that by the end of the First World War in 1919, a former Remington Chief Engineer John Taliaferro Thompson invented a hand-held machine gun, somewhere between a pistol and a rifle, which the criminals of the Prohibition era fondly called the "Chicago typewriter" (247).

In Britain, the very first mention of the typewriter in London's prestigious women's magazine *The Queen* in 1882 was of its speed, the "swiftness and exactness with which the work is done," which is "marvelous" (qtd. in Young 113). The new machine's reputation for speed was such that even a racehorse was named Typewriter, which the elite *Sporting Gazette* claimed was owned by Lord R. Churchill, very likely Winston's father Randolph ("Country Gentlemen" 710). An 1888 article in *The Girl's Own Paper* claims that while the average penman could sustain a speed of about fifteen or twenty words per minute, "a competent operator" of the typewriter "will for hours together work at the rate of forty words per minute" and "on an emergency" "sixty or seventy words per minute" ("The Type-Writer and Type-Writing" 745). By 1892, a new Hammond ad was claiming in the London journal *Pick-Me-Up* a fastest speed of 181 words per minute, "equal to 758 finger movements, or an average of $12^1/_2$ per second" ("New Model" 335). This promotional language by a manufacturer might be more hype than fact. A more official record was achieved by the seventeen-year-old American Rose Fritz at 82 words per minute at the first World Typewriting Championship in Chicago in 1906.

Reflecting a popular interest in new technological inventions and particularly in machines of speed in those *fin-de-siècle* years, which turned, for instance, bicycle races and motor races into huge public spectacles and cycling or motoring champions into record-breaking celebrities, the typing champion Fritz also became famous in both America and Britain. The Prince of Wales, later King George V, asked her to autograph a letter she typed for him. Fritz's record was formal, because previous such championships held in America using Remington and Caligraph typewriters were designed more to test the machines than the typists using them. Three years later, in 1909, Fritz improved her record in London, by "typing, under the strictest conditions, at a rate of 107 words a minute, consisting of an extract from a newspaper article, which she had not previously seen," at a publicized though unofficial test at the London *Daily Mail* office in 1909, which "entitled" her "to the world's typewriting championship" ("Typing Like the Lightening" 237). The London journal *Answers*, which reported the test, went on to ask Fritz to write a detailed article fielding questions from readers about how best to type.

A Woman's Machine in the Office

The typewriter did not start out as a woman's machine. Remington did not at first hit upon the idea of promoting the typewriter as an office machine, nor did it target women exclusively until later. Designed initially as a writing machine for male writers and authors at its launch in the 1870s, the typewriter was first promoted as a literary machine—indeed, "the literary piano"—for writers to compose literature in the same way musicians composed at the piano (Current, *Typewriter and the Men* 9). Mark Twain claimed in his autobiography to be the "first person in the world to apply the type-machine to literature" when he wrote *The Adventures of Tom Sawyer*, and Remington sought to maximize sales by printing his picture and testimonial in early ads (Twain, *Autobiography* 450).[4] Targeting novelists and poets, these ads promoted the typewriter as the best aid to "to save time and 'language'—the kind of language that soothes vexation" (qtd. in Russo 20). Yet even Twain's assurance that the Remington was "a great help to me" because it could "print faster than I can write" was not enough to lift sales (20). After a dismal beginning, in 1876 the company made another attempt at greater publicity by displaying the typewriter in the Centennial Exposition in Philadelphia. This, again, failed to succeed as the typewriter was overshadowed by another invention: Bell's telephone (21). It was obvious that amid a flurry of late-nineteenth-century technological inventions of speed, the typewriter in the early stages was not attracting sufficient attention or spotlight.

Other early ads suggest that the manufacturers were trying to appeal to anyone and everyone in a variety of use settings. Although the inventor Sholes used his daughter Lillian to demonstrate his machine as the "world's first typist" in early promotional exhibitions, after Remington acquired the patent an 1875 Remington ad published in the *Nation* celebrated the "type-writer" as "an ornament to an office, study, or sitting-room" and a "beautiful Christmas present for a boy or girl" (qtd. in Hoke 83). Even though another Remington ad in the same year targeted women by claiming: "No invention has opened for women so broad and easy an avenue to profitable and suitable employment as the 'Type-Writer,' and it merits the careful consideration of all thoughtful and charitable persons interested in the subject of work for women," the same ad also appealed to "Editors, authors, clergymen" and families, as well as business and government (83). It is clear that Remington's initial target included women, but also a wider public.

A similar story took place in Britain, where the typewriter took a little longer to get a foothold. Early reports mostly focused on introducing the new machine as an exotic American invention that was still far from well-known in England ("Typewriter and Type-writing" 745). When the typewriter actually started to catch on in Britain, it was initially received, much like the early bicycle and motorcar, as the latest toy or technological gadget for young, fashionable, forward-thinking men. The few early Remington ads that appeared were mostly in upscale men's sports magazines like *Horse and Hound*, which catered to upper-middle-class men. An ad for "the Hall Type-Writer," the "only portable and complete machine extant"

---

[4] It was actually *Life on the Mississippi*, not *Tom Sawyer*, that was typewritten. Twain did not type himself, but dictated to a typewriter girl. Twain is also known to be among the first people to have a home telephone. In *A Connecticut Yankee in King Arthur's Court* (1889), Twain records through the character of Hank Morgan an enthusiasm for new technologies of writing, information, and communication such as telegraphs, telephones, typewriters, and typesetting machines. Twain later bankrupted himself through investment in the Paige typesetting machine. See Seltzer, *Bodies and Machines*, pp. 7–12.

sold by Witherby & Co., appeared in the *Sporting Times* on January 24, 1885 (8). *Horse and Hound* ran a weekly ad for the Remington Standard Typewriter, celebrated as "most rapid and most durable," from March 3 (180), until July 28, 1888. Another ad for the "English Typewriter," available for twelve monthly payments of 1 pound and 10 s., appeared in the London journal *Golf* on Friday, February 20, 1891 (23). *Boys' Own Paper* reported on Remington, Hall, and Columbia typewriters in July 3, 1886 ("Correspondence" 639); three years later it reasserted the typewriter's image as a progressive machine for men when it reported that the scientist-cum-clergyman Rev. J. G. Wood, the "popularizer of natural history," had used the typewriter for his writer's cramp ("Death of the Rev. J. G. Wood" 494). The journal *Cycling* also writes in 1891 that because cycling, pursued in those early years by progressive men, has the "reputation of being as much up to date—or possibly rather more so—than any other," it is no surprise the cycling houses are among the first to "discard the old-fashioned" pen and take up typewriting instead ("The Cycle Trade and the Typewriter" 165). The typewriter is an elitist gadget for privileged people who are "well abreast of any new inventions or discoveries" ("Occasional Notes" 26). According to an 1890 report in *Le Follet*, entitled "Typewriting Has Become Quite a Fashionable Accomplishment," "the Prince of Wales is so pleased with a typewriter he has, that he has taken great interest in using it, and his secretaries are, by his direction, becoming quite adept in its manipulation" (170).

As a machine of speed, the typewriter's noisy click, fast speed and a heavy, "sufficiently ugly" look (Twain, "First Writing-Machine" 325) points to a rather masculinist technology. But within ten years of its first manufacture, the typewriter became closely associated with women and was seen predominantly as a woman's machine. In the case of Remington, following an initial period of dismal sales, by the mid-1880s it achieved great success after promoting the typewriter as an office machine especially suitable for women operators. As the trade journal *Penman's Art Journal* wrote in 1887, "Five years ago the typewriter was simply a mechanical curiosity. Today its monotonous click can be heard in almost every well regulated business establishment in the country" (qtd. in Davies, "Women Clerical Workers" 37).

Remington claimed all along that its deliberate tactic to feminize the typewriter single-handedly brought about the wide-scale entry of women into office employment. They promoted the typewriter as "obviously a blessing to mankind, and especially to womankind" (qtd. in Srole 87). Many historians and commentators also chimed in. A 1923 book on Sholes credits the typewriter for bringing about feminism, claiming that Sholes represents the best "choice of some historic figure to symbolize [the feminist] movement": "Economic emancipation was won and from this great triumph has resulted every other development of modern feminism. The suffrage, the winning of greater social freedom, the wider participation of women in every phase of public life, all these are children of the same parent"

(Herkimer County Historical Society 140). Even Kittler quipped in 1985 that "Apart from Freud, it was Remington who granted the female sex access to the office" (*Discourse Networks* 352).

Remington may want to take all the credit, but this development has to be contextualized not just in the evolution of speed technology, but also, as many historians have pointed out, in wider socioeconomic trends in the second half of the nineteenth century that contributed to the unprecedented expansion of the modern office (Davies, "Women Clerical Workers" 31; Hoke 78; Shiach, *Modernity, Labor and Selfhood* 63). In Britain, the second half of the nineteenth century saw an explosive increase in correspondence, record-keeping, book-keeping, and office work in general, as a result of rapid expansion of domestic and international markets. Businesses in the British banking, insurance, retailing, and transportation sectors surged in size and scope, and government agencies supervising and regulating these businesses also expanded (Davies, "Women Clerical Workers" 31; Hoke 78). Not only did clerical activities explode in volume, but their nature and function also changed as labor was increasingly divided into new organizational hierarchies. The traditional nineteenth-century office had been, for most of the time, a one-room or two-room setup staffed by a couple of clerks who followed rather informal social relations and unsystematic administrative procedures (Lowe 138). This changed as the paces of industrialization accelerated and a greater centralization took place. To stay ahead of fierce competition, businesses pursued lower costs, higher productivity, improved profit margins, and tighter control over internal and external affairs, seeking to inject efficiency into organizational life. A vast increase of routine clerical positions was created at the bottom of the organizational hierarchy, supervised by a small number of managers at the top. This rigid division heralds the later arrival of Taylorite Scientific Management by the turn of the century (Weber 973).

Another reason that contributes to the rise of the typewriter girl is a changing scene in women's employment. The need to fill in a new class of cheaper, low-skilled clerical workers in charge of highly specialized, routine, and often mechanized tasks finds a ready answer in middle-class women. In the last decades of the nineteenth century, demographic imbalance between men and women in Britain and the limited number of traditional jobs available to genteel women led to a situation when there was an "immense number of women who ... [were] in search of employment," as claims the *Englishwoman's Review* in 1873 ("Events of the Quarter" 160). Arlene Young writes that when London's metropolitan post-offices advertised for eleven "junior-counterwomen" in March 1873, over one thousand young women applied to the Civil Service Commissioners (103). The crowd of eager young women blocked the steps and courtyard of the offices, brought traffic on Cannon Row to a standstill, suspended business in the area, and caused such a scene of "extraordinary excitement" that the police were called in (103). The situation did not improve by the 1890s. Clara Collet, social investigator for the Board of Trade, wrote in 1892 that one out of six women in England and Wales, and one out of five in London, remained unmarried ("Prospects" 540, 545). This is confirmed by Gissing's 1893 novel *The Odd Women*, where the New Woman typist Rhoda famously claims that "there are half a million more women than men in this happy country of ours," and that there is "no making a pair with" so many "useless, lost, futile" odd women (37). It is clear that many of these women were in dire need of finding some sort of employment.

The newly expanded office work offered a new option of work for these women, and offices were willing to hire women clerks because they could pay less for equal, sometimes even better work. When the Inland Revenue applied in 1878 for permission to employ two typists to keep copies of indexes to probate records at Somerset House, it stated that the cost of three male copyists was 35s to 41s per week, amounting to £296 per year; if they were to buy two typewriters at £21 each and hire two women "Machinists" at 17s to 23s per week, the cost would only be £146 per year, saving £150 in the first year and increasing thereafter (Zimmeck 72). Employers also praised women's patience, loyalty, and good work. The UK Post Office, the first government agency to employ women clerks as a kind of experiment, reported the "very satisfactory results" of this "experiment" in the *Civil Serve Review* in 1876 (qtd. in Young 105). In 1882, *The Times* praised women clerks for doing more work than "many of the males who have been employed on the same duty" (105).[5]

Women clerks may be paid lower, but compared with other jobs available to women, typewriting still proves to be much more remunerative, a finding reported in an 1892 article in the women's journal *Hearth and Home*. Needlework, as it points out, does not pay well unless done very well, art or handicraft or special branches of education need special training and practice, and nursing requires tact, patience, and fair health. Typewriting, in its turn, could afford a capable lady "thirty or forty pounds a year" and is both "respectable" and "remunerative," as one article points out in 1892 ("What to Do with Our Daughters" 790). A study in London shows that while nurses average 24 to 40 pounds a year, women clerks' pay compares favorably to other occupations even though they earn much less than male clerks (Fleissner 66).

Writing in *Women's Penny Paper* in 1890 on "Employment for Women," J. D. Date berates the "flood[ing]" of the typing market by "a host of incompetent workers, who are content to accept starvation wages, and bring discredit on business women generally" (566). This flooding, however, is itself proof of the comparative attraction of typewriting for job-seeking women, for it could be "quickly

---

[5] Government agencies were so satisfied with women's work that by August 1890, one year after the Society of Typists was established in London at a June 1889 meeting of the Society for Promoting the Employment of Women, *Women's Penny Paper* reported that the permission given to public departments to employ women typists was now permanent ("Current News" 483).

and cheaply learnt," and is the "best opening for women to launch into commercial life" (566). "Still to an intelligent, methodical and striving young woman I cannot recommend a more promising career," she concedes eventually, and urges young women to seek proper training at a reputable typing school (566). One point worth noting is that these women did not altogether displace male clerks. As Elizabeth L. Banks writes in "New Paid Occupations for Women" in *Cassell's Family Magazine* (1893–94), typewriting for women encounters less resistance from male workers than other occupations like printing and law writing, which the Society for Promoting the Employment of Women also seeks to train women for, because many male clerks have moved to higher-paid, newly opened tasks with the expansion of office work and its increasing specialization (586).

It is thus clear that a whole cluster of factors has combined to facilitate the rise of the typewriter girl. Technological development is one reason, but wider socioeconomic changes in modern business culture and women's employment have also played a key role. In Britain, yet another contributing factor is that women had already been employed as telegraph operators for some time, and that the 1870 merger between Britain's telegraph system and the Post Office helped to make the idea of women clerks not unpalatable (Fleissner 67). As Meta Zimmeck points out, the role of new technology depends very much on the organization of office work, "the size, degree of centralization, extent of division of labor and type of supervision/control of offices" (88). The typewriter certainly is not the sole tool of female emancipation, but part of, albeit a significant part of, the Taylorization of office work designed for greater speed and efficiency, which made women office workers economically desirable. Rather than single-handedly bringing about women's entry into office work, Remington was tapping into wider changes already taking place in office work and women's employment.

Still, Remington's sales strategy to highlight the typewriter girl's sexual appeal does play a key role in shaping her popular representation. Starting in America in the mid-1880s, almost ten years after its first production, the Remington typewriter underwent a radical strategy shift in its ads (Figure 1.1). Men all but disappeared from its ads, replaced instead by young, pretty, fashionably dressed women in an office setting (Hoke 83). In Britain, Remington ads began to peter out from men's sporting journals, and appeared heavily in women's journals like *Women's Penny Paper* and *Myra's Journal of Dress and Fashion* after 1891. Young, attractive women featured predominantly in these ads (Figures 1.2 & 1.3). Remington also set up showrooms and employed young women dressed in the latest fashions and taught some basics of the Pitman's "touch" method to demonstrate the typewriter. For customers wanting a trial run, the typing machine often came with its female typist. Remington both tapped into the growing business need for female office workers, and also facilitated that need by promoting women typists as feminine,

Figure 1.1 Remington, *Case and Comment*, Aug. 1897, Vol. 4, Issue 3, p. 23. Indiana University Library.

pretty, and largely free from the discomforting threat of unwomanliness. From then on, the typewriter girl is perceived as young, pretty, and sexually desirable. This image soon "gained a life of its own," as it appeared not just in ads, but also journalistic and cultural discourses of the *fin-de-siécle* period (Keep, "Cultural Work" 416).

"Machine Woman": The Allure of the Mindless

In 1887, on a visit to America, Rudyard Kipling recorded some complex impressions of a typewriter girl he encountered in San Francisco, impressions marked both by fascination and unease:

Figure 1.2 Bar-Lock typewriter, *Hearth and Home*, May 24, 1900, p. 157. Gale Primary Sources.

The type-writer girl is an institution of which the comic papers make much capital, but she is vastly convenient. She and a companion rent a room in a business quarter, and copy manuscript at the rate of six annas a page. Only a woman can manage a type-writing machine, because she has served apprenticeship to the sewing-machine. She can earn as much as a hundred dollars a month, and professes to regard this form of bread-winning as her natural destiny. But oh how she hates it in her heart of hearts! When I had gone over the surprise of doing business and trying to give orders to a young woman of coldly clerkly aspect, entrenched behind gold-rimmed spectacles, I made inquiries concerning the pleasures of this independence. They liked it—indeed, they did. 'Twas the natural fate of almost all girls—the recognized custom in America—and I was a barbarian not to see it in that light. (*From Sea to Sea* 15–16)

Figure 1.3   Hammond typewriter, *Judy*, Dec. 20, 1899, p. 612. ProQuest LLC.

The "independence" of the typewriter girl, who regards earning her own bread as her "natural fate," marks her radical departure from the traditional feminine ideal of domesticity and dependence. This emboldened, confident new girl, with her "coldly clerkly" manners, seems to "surprise" and unsettle Kipling, but he finds comfort in portraying her as sexually desirable and lovable. At the end of the passage, Kipling writes "Now in the name of all the Gods at once, what is one to say to a young lady (who in England would be a Person) who earns her own bread … ? That one falls in love with her goes without saying; but that is not enough. A mission should be established" (16).

Kipling may attribute such disruptive female independence to a "recognized" American custom, but not long afterwards British newspapers were awash with reports of homegrown typewriter girls working for their own keep. Initial response in the popular masculine press, which Kipling rightly points out to have made "much capital of," was one of alarm and unease over the unconventionality. Echoing prevalent medical views on the female constitution and its unsuitability for heavy, fast work outside the private home, many reports were at first vociferously opposed to women's typewriting, arguing that it is harmful to the female body and reproductive system. One commentator insists that women are unable to keep up with the fast pace of work, as "not one woman in a hundred can stand the physical strain of the keen pace which competition has forced upon every line of business today" (qtd. in Davies "Woman's Place" 14). Another argues that "the female mind and constitution would be certain to break" under the "strain" and "physical danger of so arduous an undertaking" as typewriting (qtd. in Keep, "Cultural Work" 402). Yet another announces that a woman clerk "simply could not produce as much good work as a man," "because of unblinkable facts of nature: every four weeks she lost temporarily a fifty of her 'vital power'" (qtd. in Current, *Typewriter and the Men* 119).

The London journal *Atalanta* laments that while in the past women's only work was "to cook, to dust, to sew, or at the most to teach," they are now entering the business office, "until lately the sanctuary of man" ("Typewriting and the Typist" 52). It avows that typing will wear out women's nerves and feminine charm, and endanger their chance at matrimony and motherhood, because it will have "a Sally Brass-ifying effect, which Heaven forbid!" Sally, as the reader is reminded, is the obnoxious "dragon" sister and real authority in Charles Dickens's *Old Curiosity Shop*, who only wants to "warn" and "command" (52). The London satirical paper *Funny Folks* also berates the "latter-day girl" for refusing "feminine work" like washing, and threatening men's employment by taking up typewriting:

> Here is a thing to suggest
> To the delicate maids
> Who've begun to infest
> Man's professions and trades!
> ...
> She will cheerfully tap
> On the typewriter keys
> ...
> Nay, it may be the sex,
> As its leaders advance
> Man's domain to annex,
> A contemptuous glance
> On such matters will cast.
> Till the male for his pelf
> Will be driven at last
> To the wash-tub himself! ("Won't Wash" 406).

More comments deride women's perceived dumbness and mindless passivity, and their inability to meet typewriting's demands for speed and precision. When *Funny Folks* reports in 1889 on a protest by "[d]owntrodden typewriters" against the "tyranny of harsh employers and paltry wages," its flippant sarcasm is not directed at selfish employers but at what it sees as dumb typists, who "could not hopefully be able to record but also to put down" these "grievances" properly ("Multiple News Items" 342). Even a mermaid could be trained to be a typist, as the *Illustrated Chips* wisecracks in 1899, advising that in hot weather one should "sink clerks in diving clothes in sea and train a mermaid for typist" ("During the Hot Weather" 4–5). The irritation with the typewriter girl's perceived incompetence escalates into a sadistic desire to slap her childish face, as is seen in one 1892 *Fun* piece. It claims that a typist's voice, "mingled with the chop-chop of the type thing," is like "a child being slapped at a pork-butcher's while they are working the sausage machine" ("Our Typewriter" 168). The ignorant female typist is likened to a child in the butcher's, because both need to be severely punished for being in a place where they should not be. The article portrays the typing machine's speed as noisy and ruthless, crushing the girl's mind and reducing her to a whimpering simpleton. When she is unable to catch up with the machine's speed and makes mistakes in her typing, she "bursts into tears, and suggests she is a poor, lorn girl," while clumsily "upset[ting] the waste-basket with her skirts" (168). The writer mocks the typewriter girl's mindless passivity, and ends the article with the declaration that "there is nothing like female work in the labour market. Thank goodness there isn't!" (168).

When the typewriter girl does manage to catch up with the speed potential of her machine and reaches a marketable speed of at least fifty words per minute, the nature of typewriting work in the *fin-de-siècle* office seems to further aggravate her passivity. Apart from doing long hours of repetitive copying work, the typewriter girl is also trained to reproduce every word of the dictating boss almost as fast as he speaks. Although literacy and a certain level of education is necessary for the typist to understand the dictating boss or to read the copy, she is widely seen in those years as "at the service of the mind, the wits, of her employer," her training and efforts urged to be "centered upon the swiftest and most accurate voicing of his ideas, in whatever direction those ideas may run" (Bird 126). She must, as the guidebook *Careers for Girls* advises, learn to "efface herself, to consider herself as the receptacle of her employer's thoughts, words, etc" (qtd. in Keep, "Blinded by the Type" 159). In other words, the most successful typist with the greatest marketability and highest rates is she who has learnt to erase her mind and turn her disciplined body, shaking in synchronization with the machine she operates, a passive conduit for the boss's mind.

This perception of the mindless passivity of the typewriter girl runs in alignment with, not opposition to, to another argument that asserts that women are more suited than men for typewriting work. When the Post Office official Mr.

Scudamore defends his decision to hire women clerks, he claims that women, long accustomed to sedentary domesticity, "take more kindly than men or boys do to sedentary employment, and are more patient during long confinement to one place" (qtd. in Fleissner 67). Another office manager declares that women are more "temperamentally reconciled" to the repetitive work of typewriting than male clerks, where they are expected not to think but "simply to copy" (qtd. in Kessler-Harris 148). Docility and passivity are stressed as feminine traits and built into the female body, which equips women ideally for the increasing routinization and mindless repetition of office work. It thus seems that assertions both of female incompetence and of her suitability start from the same belief in her weaker, more passive nature.

Some business owners even go so far as to declare that speed, or the "keen pace" of "competition" which earlier commentators avow as alien to the female body, is a winning trait of women typists (qtd. in Davies, "Woman's Place" 14). Writing in the journal *Work and Leisure*, one employer of female clerks swears that women "work quicker than the men, and they stick to their work" and are more loyal (qtd. in Young 105). This interesting change of rhetoric again occurs when manufacturers like Remington promoted the typewriter as the woman's machine, and claimed that women type faster than men because of their nimble fingers and physical dexterity. But such an acknowledgment of women's faster speed does not mean that these commentators believe women to be more savvy in technology. Instead, typewriting reinforces and carries on traditional ideas of the female body, as the reference to female nimbleness points to some function built into the natural female body, rather than to the controlling intelligence behind the use of technology.

In some reports in the masculine press, the typewriter girl emerges as what Andreas Huyssen calls a "machine woman" (68), especially suited for and even conflated with the machine of speed. The interchangeability of the word "typewriter" to refer both to the machine and the girl operator, as is shown in the 1894 *Cycling* interchange between Mr. Whitwell and the three young ladies, demonstrates the pervasive masculine denigration of the mechanicality and "want of brains" of the typewriter girl ("Whitwell Roasted" 137). This machine woman image arises because, though women may long be associated with organic, cyclical nature, once their body is exposed to mechanized speed, their perceived innate passivity and lack of agentic mental capability makes them even more vulnerable to the danger of pollution (Huyssen 70). The typewriter girl proves to be a quicker operator than men, because her patience and passive submissiveness, qualities long associated with women and seemingly embedded in their body and psyche, allows her to bear more easily the brunt of mechanization and submit to the coercive regimentation of speed. In this way, the preindustrial woman-as-nature slides easily into the machine woman.

This new image of the machine woman reflects an effort by men to "displace" and "project" "the destructive potential of modern technology" onto the more vulnerable female body (Huyssen 81). Victorian voices have long railed against the mechanizing impact of industrial modernity on the human body, but this fear of mechanization is now displaced onto women when they enter modern speed culture. The rise of the image of the typewriter girl as machine woman in the 1890s reflects conservative anxieties over the unprecedented en masse entrance of middle-class women into work and commerce, at a time when accelerated industrialization triggered increased body–machine tensions. This projection serves to ultimately preserve the male body as in control of and uncontaminated by the threat of the machine.

A further point of interest is that this machine woman image is also constructed as erotically appealing. Much of the *fin-de-siècle* popular press, especially that which caters to the male reader, plays up the typewriter girl's pretty looks and seductive power over her male boss or colleagues. The visible and eroticized body of the typewriter girl, as Victoria Olwell argues, "spectacularized gender in the workplace' (49). This sexualization is contributable to her disruption of the gender norms of separate spheres and her public visibility in work and business, which *fin-de-siècle* discourses often warn would lead to a troubling "sexual anarchy" (Showalter, *Sexual Anarchy* 21). Yet while all women leaving domesticity for work in the urban public space—for instance, the shop-girl—are subject to the sexualization of their body, it is the typewriter girl, with her deeper exposure to technology of speed, who is more often both mechanized and sexualized.[6] The typewriter girl, as Lena Wånggren points out, is both "machine and woman" (45). The typewriter girl's membership in a new breed of mobile, independent women in big cities gives her a certain "fastness" and sexual availability, endowing her with greater intrigue than her stay-at-home sisters. She is also more desirable because the discipline of mechanized speed makes her even more tame, subservient, and passive, and thus more suited for wifely roles. Both reasons, though conflicting, derive from the impact of her access to mechanized speed.

Thoroughly disciplined and tamed by speed, the typewriter girl is no longer the unfeminine, emasculating "Sally Brass" in early representations. Typing and working in offices actually prepares women better for taking on the role of wife and mother. *Sporting Times* jests in 1890 that the passive, docile typewriter girl makes an ideal wife, so much so that a husband wishes "if I ever marry again, I shall try and hitch with a typewriter, for it would be such a treat once in a way to get a woman who is used to being dictated to" ("Sporting Notes" 1). Another comic

---

[6] As Fleissner has pointed out, worries over the mechanization of the female body are also directed toward working-class women laboring in the nineteenth-century factories (78). However, this discourse is countered by a different one in which the middle-class philanthropists emphasize the virtue of work and discipline to battle the sloth of the poor. See Rabinbach's citation of nineteenth-century studies on French female factory workers, p. 33.

line in *Judy* in 1899 runs like this: "Why do you marry a typewriter girl? Because you can dictate to her" ("Just So" 598). Even the modern office where the typewriter girl works, previously seen as the opposite to sanctified domesticity and a disruptive space for feminine decorum, is now reconstructed as an extension of the comfortable home. One business owner claims in the *Ladies Home Journal* that the office is a "pleasant, peaceful, and homelike place" (qtd. in Hoke 81–82), because typewriting's disciplinary speed trains the typewriter girl to better fit, rather than challenge, her traditional gender roles.

Once bereft of her disruptive potential, the tamed typewriter girl appears to be enhance her sexual allure. In a 1894 *Funny Folks* poem entitled "In Chancery," the male speaker waxes romantic over a "Trim little typist of Chancer-lane," who "come[s] tripping, in sunshine or rain" "every morning at ten" down London's famed lane for law firms (13). The speaker professes to have a heart "leap" every morning "you flutter in view" (13), and subjects her to an eroticizing gaze by taking down every detail of her body. "Habited neatly in dark navy blue,/ Big picture hat—at the side there's a Wren—/ Dainty *bottines* that are just No. 2/And *gants de Suede* of a Quakerish hue" (13), the typewriter girl is fashionably dressed, from her big picture hat down to her dainty boots. But while following the latest trends she also takes care to keep up her respectable appearance, picking a dark "Quakerish hue." She is both highly visible, displaying herself daily to the voyeuristic male gaze, and also tries hard not to be mistaken for the dubious "public" woman of the street. This blurred boundary seems to be the very source of her attraction, her edge over the traditional stay-at-home girl. Calling her a "Lady Primness," the speaker confesses that it matters little if she comes from common backgrounds or has "commonplace" names like Sue or "even commoner" names like Jane. Once she joins the army of typewriter girls, the new face of fashionable, out-and-about, "fast" womanhood, she is instantly elevated in glamor and attraction. "Yet what does it matter, my dear? You are *you*,/ Trim little typist of Chancery-lane!"

The typewriter girl's access to fast speed seems to be a cause of titillation as well as threat to the male speaker, for he hastens to propose to return her back to married seclusion. "Do you have a lover?" the speaker asks, vowing to be a "Lancelot true" to her maiden in distress, because the girl is under the tyranny of her boss "the stern Mr. Screw," who is "Dictating, with voice like the boom of Big Ben, /folios, folios, all the day through." Here the tyrannical tolls of her typewriting work, in making her all passive and tame, actually increases her erotic appeal and stimulates the speaker into heroic jealousy. The poem ends with the speaker calling on the typewriter girl to not waste "the spring-time" but "make rose of my hue," and type him a "billet doux" love letter in answer (13).

Other satirical pieces make crasser jokes on the typewriter girl's sexual availability. Playing deliberately on the double meaning of the word typewriter, one article claims that it "pays" to "always have such a pretty typewriter" ("A Great Advantage" 14). A 1890 piece in *Pick-Me-Up* jokes that "your typewriter blushed when you buttoned its glove the other evening," referring both to covering up the machine and buttoning up the glove of the typewriter girl ("Things Not to Dwell On" 136). *Boys of England* pretends to be dismayed by the "abominable ... careless way" in which typist (the girl) and typewriter (the machine) are used interchangeably, but goes on to advise, scarcely suppressing a laugh, that the best way to tell which one the man is referring to is to "watch his face" ("Miscellaneous Jokes Section" 128). Another joke claims that this interchangeability is "remarkably lucky" for the male boss, especially those "in the habit of talking in their sleep," because the wife on his side would not get suspicious ("'Fun's' Philosophy" 60).

Eroticizing the typewriter girl also serves to better control the male workforce. *The Dart: A Journal of Sense and Satire* quips in a series of typewriter jokes in 1897 that the boss always "select[s] her for her beauty" because the male clerks, who used to "stay away on the least provocation," never do so now as they have "fallen dead in love with her," and would not let others "get ahead of him" (14). The typewriter girl boosts office morale and productivity, and male clerks fight over one another to "sharpen her lead-pencil for her" and curry her favor ("Degrees of Genius" 15). Once she leaves, though, everyone in the office "looks as blue as indigo" even if the business is still thriving, prompting the boss to reflect that she is indeed a valuable asset ("Gloom" 15).

Commenting on the use of female sexual appeal for better control of the male workforce in the modern factory, Huyssen points out that this idea of the machine woman as both mechanized and sexually alluring achieves two purposes; it allows men to equate female sexuality with "technology-out-of-control" (77), and also recasts male fears of the machine in terms of the male fear of female sexuality (81).[7] The emphasis on the typewriter girl as both passive and also alluring helps to displace and allay such fears over the machine, and promises the reassuring confirmation of existing sexual hierarchies.[8]

In this existing sexual hierarchy, it is the male boss who wields the ultimate power over the typewriter girl, as the latter is both tamed as a passive receptacle and sexualized as a love interest. Even the many jokes over the girl's image as a home-wrecker points not to her active power but to her sexual availability to an exploitative boss. A boss in a *Pick-Me-Up* piece, for instance, admonishes his male clerk for taking the pretty typewriter girl out "without a chaperone"—a "most abominable thing"—and threatens to discharge him if he ever speaks to her again; but the next minute he himself proposes to take the girl out to dinner and theater that very night, so as to show her that "for a girl to go out with a penniless clerk is

---

[7] Andreas Huyssen's example of the machine woman invented by modern imagination is the classic 1926 movie *Metropolis* by Fritz Lang, where the male factory owner seeks to manipulate his rebellious workers through the machine woman's sexual allure. In the late nineteenth-century context, the typewriter girl in many popular discourses already embodies that machine woman image.

[8] Mary Ann Doane (25–31) points out that this machine woman complex is still a preoccupying concern in twentieth-century cyber-literature, including works like *Alien* (1979) and its sequel *Aliens* (1986), and *Blade Runner* (1982), which carries on the double threat of the machine woman image.

ruination for her" ("Love and Lucre" 30). The young, pretty typewriter girl is often set up as a home-wrecker, embroiled in a war of jealousy with the boss's older, nagging wife. *Pick-Me-Up* jests in 1894 that hiring a typewriter is costly, because apart from paying for her salary, dinner, flowers, and theater, the boss has to buy extra chocolates, sealskin, and clothes for the wife to placate the latter ("What a Typewriter Costs" 38). When a man hugging his young typewriter in a foggy night is run into by his wife, he stammers out a lame excuse that he is only giving her final instructions for the morning's work ("Found in the Fog" 14; Figure 1.4). Sometimes the wife is taken in, as when one wife believes that "Little Peach" is the make of a typing machine, because her husband has told her it is his favorite typewriter ("Whyte" 4). Other times she retaliates by firing the typist or threatening to visit

Found in the fog.

Mrs. Fastleigh (suddenly meeting her husband): "Why—John——"
Fastleigh: "Oh—ah—er, quite so—my dear. Just giving my typewriter final instructions for the morning in case I'm late!"

Figure 1.4 "Found in the Fog," *Pick-Me-Up*, Dec. 1 1900. Gale Primary Sources.

the office during business hours ("Ah!" 8). The typewriter girl is so fatally attractive that a "smitten" boss "inveigle[s]" the girl into the office telephone box and professes love, only to be startled by a "a buzz at the telephone" with his wife's voice coming through to thank him for his love. The shock is enough to kill him, and both the wife and the little typewriter girl know that the cause is more than the doctor's verdict of heart failure ("Not Revealed by the Inquest" 220).

Even in cases where the grueling reality of typewriting work is touched on, the pieces trivialize the serious socioeconomic implications by focusing on the sexual escapade. *Judy, or the London Serio-Comic Journal* in 1900 offers a rare glimpse into the merits of women clerks when an embarrassed husband tries to defend hiring a pretty typewriter girl to his angry wife. The "straight-forward, practical, and business-like" consideration of doing business is to "buy in the cheapest market," he proclaims loudly, and goes on to explain:

> [A] lady typewriter is cheaper than a male, quite as efficient, and more desirable for many other reasons; doesn't drink, doesn't want to go out for half an hour at lunch, lunches off a bun and a cup of tea, and doesn't go to sleep after it, hasn't been making a night of it on the previous evening, and doesn't turn up in the morning late to start with, half asleep, and with a head that is incapable of mastering the simplest directions. ("Tiffs and Tales" 40)

Even the dire situation of the typewriter girl is mentioned when the boss claims that "beggars mustn't be choosers," and that, however cheaply she is paid, she must be grateful for such "a good chance offered her to earn her own living" (40). These realistic touches reveal that the lady clerk is a hardworking professional and a serious force to contend with, with better efficiency, discipline, and work ethic than the average male clerk. But this image is soon forgotten when the scene descends into a comic bickering between a philandering husband and a jealous wife. The wife angrily asserts that three or four long, straw-colored hairs are found on the husband's coat sleeves, the same color as the typewriter's hair, and the husband, muttering that he must have brushed up against her accidently when she was bending over her keys, agrees with extreme reluctance to "send her off tomorrow." He ends the piece, though, with a disingenuous warning that they might have to face the prospect of the workhouse if he can no longer hire the cheaper typewriter girl (40).

Eroticizing the girl and subsuming her under the existing sexual hierarchy tames the typewriter girl and recasts her access to speed as manageable. In early 1890s stories featuring the typewriter girl, a similar focus on the girl's sexual desirability portrays her unconventionality as just a temporary phase, before she is finally recuperated back into married domesticity. One of the earliest literary portrayals of the typewriter girl appears in an 1893 story "The Type-written Letter" (1893), penned by the Scottish–Canadian writer Robert Barr for *The Idler*, the literary monthly he founded. This, along with "A Type-Writer's Romance" (1894) appearing one year later, carries on the satirical tone of the popular masculine press and many of the latter's recurring tropes about the typewriter girl. In Barr's story, narrated from a male point of view, the main protagonist Denham is a middle-aged business owner who has "battled poverty all his life"; now that he is rich, he realizes that he is lonely and he longs for the warmth of family life (597). The "only woman in the world with whom he was on speaking terms" is his typewriter girl, Miss Gale, and he knows her "merely because her light and nimble fingers played the business sonata of one note on his office typewriter" (599). The story emphasizes Miss Gale's difference from traditional women; she is "a modern girl," with a "somewhat independent air," "very different indeed" to the boss's childhood sweetheart who later "married the baker" (599). The story hints at some family misfortune Miss Gale has suffered that forces her to "come down in the world" and take up typewriting, but she still keeps up the air of a lady and "kept the clerks at a distance" (599).

The story does not probe deeper into the socioeconomic pressures that have forced Miss Gale to "come down in the world," but simply presents her typewriting as affording more chances for male sexual interest. Miss Gale may be a modern girl, but her paramount quality is still her looks. She is "pretty of course,—all typewriter girls are" (599). It is significant that Miss Gale leaves an impression on her busy boss, who has no time for leisure or female company, because of two things: her pretty looks and her "light and nimble fingers" playing the "business sonata of one note" on the typewriter. Speed and sexual allure come together to make Miss Gale highly desirable even to the drab Denham, who is called "the old man" behind his back by his clerks (598). These two attractions are enough to persuade the boss to propose marriage to her, despite knowing very little of her. The humor of the story is that the boss, clumsy in all matters outside the counting room, makes his proposal in the form of a business letter seeking a business partner, sent to Miss Gale's home twice, before she realizes it is not a mistake. Her happy acceptance is also, appropriately, in the form of a typewritten business letter, where she states solemnly that she is resigning her typing post to accept "a better situation" as "partner in the house of Richard Denham," playing on the double meaning of house as both home and business house (605).

Like the masculine press, this story nods to the machine woman motif by presenting typewriting as the conduit for greater female desirability and marriageability. Miss Gale used to play the piano beautifully, but being "a sensible girl who realized that the typewriter paid better than the piano," she "accordingly turned the expertness of her white fingers to the former instrument" (599). These "light and nimble" fingers fly over the typewriter and, despite the clicking sound being a monotonous "business sonata of one note," Miss Gale's access to speed adds to her erotic appeal for two reasons. One is that her typewriting in the modern office, much like her previous piano-playing in the society drawing-room, enhances her feminine bodily display to the male gaze. Second, her typewriting makes her even more desirable because it is constructed as a passive and mindless use of speed. Mr. Denham dictates to Miss Gale and the girl meekly and swiftly copies every line. Miss Gale's role as the passive, subservient typist obeying every order of the dictating boss recommends her as great wifely material. Indeed, when Denham insists on dressing his marriage proposal in the guise of a typed business letter, it is not merely because of his social awkwardness, or his inability to speak the "unknown tongue" of eloquent emotion required in a romantic situation (598). Rather, it is because he wishes to replicate and extend this office power relationship into their marriage.

Mr. Denham in the story is a boring, miserly, aging man with "grizzly" gray hair (597). Coming from poverty, and fighting all his life to rise up in the world of commerce, he works nonstop for many years like "the running dog, with its nose to the ground" and seeing "nothing of the scenery" (597). He denies himself any pleasure except the accumulation of wealth, has no friends nor any social skills, and would be lost in any regular "drawing room" (598). But in the counting room he is the boss and rules the roost, obeyed by the subservient typewriter girl who submits to him at the peril of immediate dismissal. Though the story portrays Mr. Denham as very shy about his marriage proposal and protesting time and again that "I don't wish this arrangement to be carried out on a monetary basis—not altogether," Miss Gale certainly understands it perfectly, framing her boss's proposed marriage as "a better situation" than her typewriting job (605). Miss Gale may be "modern," and her typewriting work unconventional, but these only serve to enhance her sexual availability and subservience, and ultimately aid her return to traditional domesticity. The monetary and transactional nature of the marriage proposal underlines the seamless translation between the role of the typewriter girl and that of the obedient wife.

A Professional and a Feminist Activist

The popular masculine press seeks to tame women's access to speed by both mocking her mindless submission and eroticizing her faster body. Women's press hotly retaliates against this trivialization, and especially bristles at male constructions of the typewriter girl as a seductive love interest, dismissing this as a mentality of "the Dark Ages" ("Wanted Common Sense" 606). Instead, the typewriter girl portrayed in women's press is first and foremost a serious professional, who is an adroit user of typewriting speed and an overall symbol of women's emancipation through active work.

Women's press has long been a leading voice on the hotly debated Woman Question, forcing public attention on issues of women's education, women's nature and rightful place in society, as well as women's work. A recurring column in women's press in the last decades of the nineteenth century was "What to Do with Our Daughters," which highlighted the dire situation of women who had to find a self-supporting livelihood. In an 1874 article "What Shall We Do with Our Daughters," the anonymous author compares the drastically different prospects for sons and daughters. "We middle-class parents," writes the author, give "our sons" a good education so they can "honorably support" themselves, but with our daughters after their education "there the matter stops"; the sudden death of their father "forces them to earn their own living at a terrible disadvantage," if they do not want to "throw themselves most unfairly on the resources of their brothers" (2). From the late 1880s until December 21, 1894, the column appeared every week in *Hearth and Home*; it then moved to *Myra's Journal of Dress and Fashion*, where the discussion of the problem took on an even more urgent tone. Not just the editors and columnists, but also ordinary women made their voices heard, sending in letters, comments, or accounts of their own experiences. The focus is always on possible employments for women, but while most suggested jobs are traditional feminine ones like Christmas card painting, wood engraving, gardening, or teaching, typewriting stands out as the most profitable new form of employment and the most enthusiastically recommended. As Arlene Young points out, typewriting and nursing offered women two of the biggest channels of employment by the end of the century, but typewriting's links with technology, speed, and a traditionally masculine business culture give it a special cachet (7).

Women's press is among the first in the British press to report on typewriting and recognize its emancipating potential for women. In 1884, when the first typing agency in Britain—the Ladies Type-writing and General Copying Office in London—was established by the Society for Promoting the Employment of Women (SPEW) under the management of Marian Marshall, the event was enthusiastically reported in the *Englishwoman's Review* ("Type Writing" 480). *Work and Leisure* further expresses their "rejoice to chronicle this new and very promising department of work for women" ("The Ladies Type-Writing and General Copying Office" 421). Women's press is also keen to point out the serious, intellectual nature of typewriting work; typewriting affords women "a means of earning a livelihood," but more importantly it "also tends to educate, as every manuscript must be thoroughly studied before being copied" ("Type Writing" 480). Access to typewriting speed is therefore enabling and liberating, a source of positive energy and knowledge.

In 1885, Marian Marshall, manager of the London office, predicts optimistically that although "[t]he number of ladies at present actually employed in type-writing is very small," "there is every reason to hope that in future a large number of educated women will be able to make a living by this occupation" (qtd. in Keep, "Cultural Work" 407). In 1888, *Girl's Own Paper* published one of the first detailed introductions of typewriting "to clear up much misapprehension," claiming that "type-writing is doing much, and will do more, towards solving the problem of finding suitable employment for ladies, it being an occupation peculiarly fitted for their nimble fingers" ("The Type-writer and Type-writing" 745). The article also praises the typewriter for its "speed," "legibility and neatness," and, interestingly, better "health" than the pen, because the typist "sits upright," allowing her "chest and lungs [to] have free play," so that "the stoop about the shoulders, so noticeable in many clerks, is conspicuous for its absence" (745). By 1893, Marian Marshall enthusiastically claims in an article in *Shafts* that typewriting is an occupation "ennobling and improving in many ways," and that typists "of intelligence and capacity" have many opportunities for "instruction and higher development" (260).

Women's press also reports a very friendly relationship with Remington and other manufacturers, who shifted the bulk of their typewriter advertising to the women's journals and worked closely with SPEW to set up typing schools, agencies, and the Society of Typists ("Meeting of Society of Typists" 4). This Society was set up in 1889, so as to "fix a minimum rate for typewriting work," "promote better understanding between typewriting offices," "grant certificates of efficiency to operators," and "form an employment bureau for the use of those to whom certificates have been granted" ("Society of Typists 1889" 2).

By regularly reporting the work of female-headed typing agencies and typists' union, women's press seeks to stress that, instead of being passive and silly, women are actively involved in and contribute to the development and proliferation of typewriting skills. This empowered use of speed, and the inherent association of typewriting with energetic work and female emancipation finds a strong echo in some early literary representations as well, where the typewriter girl often appears as a radical feminist activist. A good example is "A Woman of Seasons," written by Beatrice Kipling (Alice Fleming), sister of Rudyard Kipling and a prolific writer in her own right. Published in the *Pall Mall Magazine* in 1895, the story depicts a narcissistic, affected London society lady who seeks to relieve her ennui by pursuing typewriting and feminist charity work. Though her enthusiasm is short lived and the woman soon wearies of such work, the story equates the noisy, fast-clicking typewriter, operated in her home by a tireless feminist friend bent on social change, with purpose, fast action, and robust energy which is diametrically opposed to her usual passive idleness. Access to speed does not make women passive, as is claimed in the popular masculine press, but instead helps women to break free from passivity.

A female wannabe aesthete, the lady in the story pursues sensual pleasure to the last detail and affects a most languid pose of world weariness. Everything about her dress, food, and home decor speaks for exquisite beauty and limitless expenses, yet all these "gestures and glances of beauty" are artificial, and only "costumed for the part" (402, 397). She does not live a real life but spends her days talking and seeking an audience for her self-absorbed confessions, showing off "up-to-date phrases" and "little flashes of wit" (398). Even her tortured agitation in love is acting out a part, duly copied from the jilted and lovelorn heroines of yellow-backed French literature. Desperate for new things to titillate a jaded palate, the heroine turns to the narrator as her confidante—a thinly veiled Beatrice—who is a fresh-faced Anglo-Indian just returned to England. Months later, however, the narrator returns from a stay in the country to find a completely changed woman in her friend.

"She entered with a rush—never had I seen her move in such an unstudied manner—and gave me an unwonted firm grasp of the hand" (403). Suddenly energized and sped up, the lady professes herself to be extremely busy. She has no time to sit in her beautiful sitting room, which she now pronounces as "silly" (404). Instead, she leads the speaker to another room where "a sharp, decisive tapping sound came through the open door, an unexpected sound—the voice of the typewriter," over which a famed feminist is working diligently at a huge writing-table running over with papers (404). "There are five more ready for you to sign," the feminist calls out to her host without looking up from her typewriter, which rattles on producing leaflet after leaflet without stopping (404).

The fashionable society lady is now an enthusiastic activist and philanthropist, partnering up with the feminist to give free boots to poor children and save the souls of the poor. All her old pleasures and idle languor are abandoned to give way to purposeful action and serious work. The lady does not type herself, but her proximity to the austere, simple, and efficient typewriter seems to affect both her own appearance and the décor of her home. Her rooms now look "bleak and flowerless"; the guitar, zither, and mandolin are tucked away, and the easel unceremoniously covered with a coarse flannel (403). The lady has abandoned her fashionable, dainty dresses for a severe black serge dress, smooths her curls into a plain hair knot, wears no jewelry whatsoever, and eats only "nondescript" meals of jam and buns. All her "little graces and affectations" are erased, and a "vehement, awkward woman" is standing in front of the narrator, busily enumerating various tasks in swift earnestness, "the clicking snap of the typewriter form[ing] a fitting accompaniment to her altered speech" (405).

In this scene, the "clicking" and "snapp[ing]" typewriter merges with the lady's eager, high-pitched voice to form a symphony of swift action and absorbing work. Kipling's story, with this side swipe at the languid passivity of aesthetic life, echoes some of her brother's scathing critique of the London aesthetic circles in his poems and letters of the late 1880s. The "long-haired" young men "[i]n velvet collar-rolls," who "talk about the Aims of Art" and "moo and coo with womenfolk/About their blessed souls" ("In Partibus"), are to Rudyard Kipling symptomatic of the national degeneration plaguing England. In his machine eulogies like "McAndrew's Hymn," Kipling has long advocated a machine-exacted efficiency and discipline to remedy the decadence of comfort and indolence.[9] In Beatrice's story, typewriting's

---

[9] Kipling has always advocated the cultivation of raw masculine courage at the borders of Empire to counteract British national degeneration (McBratney 23). He is also fascinated by machines and engines and their demand of discipline and efficiency from the human operator, which he believes will jolt up and toughen the debilitated English national character. See Kipling, *Letters 3*, p. 151.

mechanized speed adds a similar injection of discipline, efficiency, and fast action into the lady's indolent life. Here, speed's disciplinary power, in hammering the same austerity and toughness into the lady's body, clothing, and home décor and depriving them of any suggestion of frivolous indulgence, is not crushingly negative but a source of positive energy and a much-needed chastening-up.

The aesthete lady, however, eventually fails to pass the test of speed. Soon she tires of charity work and gets rid of the feminist friend and her typewriter, before moving on to the next fashion. Feminist activism is just one of her many fads. When the narrator comes back from a visit to the country weeks later, she finds the lady and her house back to its pre-typewriting glory and indulgence. When she tries to explain herself, the lady blames the typewriter and its loud, ceaseless, noisy "snap" (405), "such a wearying sound" (406). This high-pitched, jarring sound, so different from the soothing elegance of her usual mandolin, is the sound of mechanized speed and a pumped-up, busier pace of life, constantly urging her to shake off her sloth.

Compared with this would-be New Woman, the New Woman typist in George Gissing's novel *The Odd Women*, published two years earlier, proves to be made of tougher material and decidedly embraces this energizing speed. This is one of the five "Women's Problem" novels Gissing wrote in the 1890s (Harman 373), together with *In the Year of Jubilee* (1894), *Eve's Ransom* (1895), *The Whirlpool* (1897), and *New Grub Street* (1891) where such a theme constitutes a partial plotline.[10] Gissing's interest in the Woman Question and his readings of feminist writings is well recorded. He is, for instance, known to have read up all the literature on women's movement in the British Museum before writing *The Odd Women* (1893); he also attended suffragette meetings, and even went to hear the famous French feminist Louise Michel during one of her lectures in 1888 (Walters 4). In his letter to his brother Algernoon on March 1, 1894, one year after the publication of *The Odd Women* wherein he describes a feminist typing school, Gissing claimed that he was unaware of such schools in real life during the novel's composition in 1892, and that he believed at the time that his fictional school was "an original idea" (*Collected Letters Vol. 5*, 210). But Gissing was very likely aware of the women's typewriting offices that had opened under the auspices of the Society for Promoting the Employment of Women since 1884; many of his novel's descriptions of the typing school in Great Portland Street, with its Remington machines on the ground floor and books and lectures on the upper floor, bear similarities to the Society (Liggins, *George Gissing* 112).

Gissing is deeply influenced by feminist valorization of typewriting work, and in this novel he focuses more on the radical politics of the feminist movement,

---

[10] Some reviews find *The Odd Women* rather harsh on its women characters, including an 1897 review in *Saturday Review*, which accuses Gissing of despising women and calls his fiction "a sustained snarl at the sex." Fifty years later, George Orwell complained that Gissing saw all women as natural inferiors and even the best of them as having a miserably limited outlook (qtd. in Walters ii).

and the educational and character-building benefits of typewriting as a means of female emancipation. The novel does not go into details on the exact nature of typewriting as labor or technology, nor does it offer insights into the day-to-day life of the typewriter girl after she joins the workforce as a member of a "significant laboring group" (Chase 233). Instead, the narrative centers on typewriting as an ideal and a means of cultivating a new, active, sped-up, hardened femininity. To Rhoda and Mary, the novel's two feminist operators of the typing school, women should no longer passively wait for marriage but should choose practical, intelligent work like typewriting. They reject traditional feminine jobs, such as teaching or nursing, and celebrate typewriting as the key to "the greatest movement of our time—that of emancipating her sex" (245), because it not only offers financial autonomy, but, more importantly, fosters "rationality," "active responsibility," and a worth ethic, "something new," something using "intelligence" and "moral strength," "those which have been thought appropriate only in men" (54). In "[s]tartling women into healthy activity" (54), typewriting speed will activate women, "free" them "from the reproach of womanliness" (136), and propel them as "hard-hearted" "invaders" into the traditional male world (135).

In this sense, the novel, following the tone of the women's press, constructs typewriting's disciplinary speed as a source of positive rejuvenation rather than as repression or coercive control. But this is arrived at not because of a radical interpretation of the traditional opposition between the organic and the mechanical, but rather because of an urge to instill the moral importance of swift action and agentic work. Typewriting will speed women up, remedy traditional female passivity, and "set an example to the sleepy of our sex" (136), so declares the New Woman Rhoda: "There must be a new type of woman, active in every sphere of life" (87). Rhoda more than once refers to "Satan and idle hands" (82) when discussing the harmful effects of idleness, particularly middle-class women's enforced passivity in domesticity: "pottering about the house, because they have nothing better to do" (99).

Idleness is certainly a sin to Gissing's feminists, but not all forms of work meet their approval, either—and certainly not work traditionally deemed as feminine. Gissing's sympathy toward those "lost, futile" odd women is tinged with criticism of the ineptitude of traditional genteel upbringing, which has reduced women to "childish" uselessness (51). In an 1893 letter written soon after the publication of *The Odd Women*, Gissing blames the lack of rational, practical education for the "ignorance and childishness of women," and urges for "female 'equality'" because "there will be no social peace until women are intellectually trained very much as men are" (*Collected Letters Vol. 5*, 113). Typewriting in this novel is held up as the right remedy because it inculcates rationality and speedy, almost masculine action. Here, typewriting's discipline does not seem to mechanize women or erase their mind, a claim often piped in the popular masculine press, but rather empowers women and imbues them with intelligence. Again, Gissing's message does not address the actual impact of mechanized speed on the organic body, but rather focuses on typewriting's symbolic associations. Typewriting is exemplary, because it brings women into what used to be a men's world of business and public affairs, and demands a certain level of education, knowledge, and understanding of technology; "[W]hatever man could do, woman could do equally well" (54).

In this sense, this work ethic championed by the two feminists has a particular gender dimension. Work as moral rejuvenation is a long-standing theme in Victorian literature, which often celebrates productive work as character building, a substitute religion, and even a way of making sense of an incomprehensible universe (Travers 3). Christian teachings have also emphasized the morally ennobling value of work as opposed to the sin of idleness, and by the early nineteenth century middle-class moralists were eager to impose the value of work, reinterpreted as a bourgeois virtue, upon the idle poor (Rabinbach 25–26). This working body, however, is always intrinsically masculine, as work outside the home is deemed corrupting or unsuitable for women and clashes with the ideal of Victorian femininity (Young 126). Feminist activists, in their campaign for women's employment, protest against this entrenched belief and argue vociferously for the cultivation of work ethics among women. In Emily Pfeiffer's 1888 report on *Women and Work*, which Gissing is known to have read soon after its publication, Pfeiffer rejects medical objections to women's overtaxing of their bodies in the workplace, and insists that female education should help prepare girls for the "variety of callings" now available to women (qtd. in Liggins *George Gissing* 69). The feminist valorization of work continues in Olive Schreiner's 1911 work *Woman and Labour*, where Schreiner urges women to "demand to have the doors leading to professional, political and highly skilled labour thrown open to them" or face "the danger of enervation through non-employment" (Liggins *George Gissing* 69–70).[11] In 1913, Rebecca West described working women as "the women who were alive," and Clementina Black wrote in 1915 of "that wave of desire for a personal working life which forms so marked an element in the general development of modern women" (Marcus 41; Black "Introduction" 4).

Gissing's feminists likewise celebrate the morally uplifting function of active work. But, in *The Odd Women*, neither Monica nor her sisters could be accused of idleness. The five Manning girls all work hard to support themselves after the sudden death of their doctor father. One becomes a nursery governess, one a board school teacher, one a companion to an old lady, and the other two shop-girls. By the time the narrative begins, two have already died from overwork and work-related disease, and two elder sisters are physically sickened and prematurely old because of the harshness of their work. Monica, working as a shop-girl, has already

---

[11] In an 1889 letter, Gissing finds Olive Schreiner's decision to live alone and pursue "the intellectual kind of life" quite "remarkable." See "Letter to Margaret," 29 September 1889. *Collected Letters, Vol. 4*, p. 117.

suffered one nervous breakdown due to fatigue and stress (35, 106). Yet to Gissing's feminists, only typewriting is held up as serious work and amounts to a "calling in life" (98), while other forms of female employment, such as shop-work, governessing, or nursing, which demand no less grueling labor, are dismissed as trivial and wasting. Here, obviously, concerns other than the work ethic motivate the feminist valorization of typewriting.

To Rhoda and Mary, the elder Madden sisters are a pathetic sight not just because they suffer from ill health due to overwork, but also because their genteel accomplishments and work experiences confine them to feminine domesticity, rendering them passive, timid, and "useful for nothing" (51) in the outside world. Many of Gissing's educated heroines are, as Liggins points out, unprepared, either by their traditional education or their own expectations, for the difficulties of finding new forms of employment; nor do they have friends or contacts of professional networks from which to seek advice (68). When the Madden sisters lose their old jobs as governess and lady's companion, they instinctively follow Monica to London. But, once there, they fail to adapt to and make use of the fast-paced life in the big city, and still cling desperately to a traditional indoors life in a rented room, passively praying for more such traditional posts to land in their lap.

Even at the center of the great metropolis, the Madden sisters remain stuck in domesticity. Every day they sit in their tiny room, cook meager meals on an oil stove, and read or talk listlessly while weighed down by ill health, hunger, and despair. Even a surprise letter from Rhoda, their childhood friend, costs them five minutes of fearful debate before they open it with tremulous hands. The sisters are frightened by the bustling, crowded London streets, and only under the influence of alcohol does Virginia summon the courage to briefly venture forward: "She walked into Trafalgar Square and viewed it like a person who stands there for the first time, smiling, interested." The street and "its clamorous life" give her a "delightful animation," "rarest of boons," and "new strength," and she feels "calm," "contented," and "unconsciously hopeful" (18). Emphasizing this moment's sharp contrast with the sisters' usual sedentary passivity, the novel hints that their inability to catch up with the speed of modern urban life inevitably dooms these ill-equipped women.

By contrast, Rhoda the feminist typist presents a completely different picture. Like the Madden sisters, Rhoda started out as a small-town girl and tried various jobs, such as teaching, which "most girls" would choose "as a dreary matter of course" (22). Yet Rhoda has managed to prosper because she has embraced typewriting and cultivated efficiency, discipline, and determination, qualities essential for a new breed of independent women: "I was vastly improved in health, and felt myself worth something in the world" (22). Strong, healthy, almost "masculine," Rhoda boasts of a "vigorous frame" and "a brisk movement," and radiates "self-confidence," "intellectual keenness," a "bright humor," and "frank courage" (20). Her "countenance seemed masculine, its expression somewhat aggressive—eyes shrewdly observant and lips consciously impregnable" (20). Access to mechanized speed leads to discipline, but also invigoration and energetic action. Rhoda's work in the business world has equipped her with the right knowledge to advise the sisters on how best to invest their money, or to warn and help Monica when her marriage irrevocably breaks down. The sisters have been pondering opening a school for a long time, but are unable to make a decision for fear of losing their last remaining funds; Rhoda steps in, props them up with sound advice and encouragement, and finally injects real action into the sisters by pushing them to open the school.

Rhoda regards traditional feminine work as trivial and "harmful" to women's efforts to expand their horizon, because it calls on innate feminine traits such as nurture and emotional support (136). This explains why teaching is also discouraged by these feminists. Rhoda specifically points out that it is not teaching itself that is trivial, but rather the way women approach this profession and become teachers almost instinctively, as if it is "as simple as washing up dishes" (98). "We can't earn money in any other way, but we can teach children!" (98), mocks Rhoda. These feminine traits, located in feminine instincts and the naturalized female body, are the opposite of rational, intelligent work like typewriting, which needs disciplined cultivation. Such "womanliness" must be abandoned so that women, as Mary urges in her speech to her students, could be "militant" and "defiant" (136), and meet the challenge of a "time of warfare" (13).

In this sense, a shift of focus has occurred away from the traditionally moral dimension of work to one that involves a more gendered dichotomy between masculine work and feminine labor. Not all work is morally uplifting to Gissing's feminists. To them, labor that is active, intelligent, and assisted by technology is truly uplifting, while labor inculcating innate feminine qualities remains at the level of nature and is of little redemptive value. Rhoda and Mary welcome typewriting's utopian potential and the "new order" it would usher in (135), because access to mechanized speed trains women to be disciplined, fast, tough, and intelligent, just like men. This picture scares some men, of course. Mary, for instance, receives a letter from an angry male clerk who complains loudly that by training women to be typists the feminists "unsex" or masculinize women and literally feminize men by undercutting salaries and taking jobs away from male clerks (134). But Rhoda and Mary dismiss such male resistance as irrelevant, claiming that this is now women's chance after such long exclusion from "the men's sphere" (135). Typewriting and mechanized speed is to be wrestled from men's hands and used as a weapon, for women to effect an "armed movement" and an "active warfare" (135, 136).

This belief in the inherent passivity of the female body and its alienation from mechanized speed aligns Gissing's feminists uncomfortably with the masculinist conservatives they try so hard to fight against. Another place where they find themselves in similar agreement with the conservatives is when they claim that typewriting is comparable to piano-playing and especially suited to nimble female fingers. When Monica first goes to see Rhoda, Rhoda asks her if she learned piano-playing as a child, assuring her that typewriting is especially congenial to women because of their "light and supple and quick" fingers (36). This may have started from a desire to ease public acceptance of women's typewriting, a desire that also motivated many reports in the *fin-de-siècle* women's press that likewise highlighted women typists' bodily dexterity. The *Girl's Own Paper*, in one of its earliest reports on typewriting in 1888, claims that typewriting is great for women's employment because it is "an occupation peculiarly fitted for their nimble fingers" ("The Type-writer and Type-writing" 745). The novelist, socialist, and women's advocate Margaret Harkness also averred in 1881 that women are temperamentally, physically, and emotionally suited for office work (375). But for Gissing's feminists, this argument is especially problematic, because by suggesting that typewriting is feminine and suited to qualities embedded in the female body, it runs counter to their otherwise insistence on typewriting as masculine, intelligent, and opposed to the (feminized) body.

In other places in Gissing's novel, this conflicting approach to the exact nature of typewriting work again shows itself in Rhoda's rejection of female sexual desire. Rhoda's admirer Everard finds that, beneath her almost masculine appearance, there actually lurks in her a "possibility of subtle feminine forces that might be released by circumstance" (21), or by the right man. Yet Rhoda rejects his proposal for free union because she views sexual love as detrimental to her rational work. Women must have a "widespread revolt against sexual instinct," "for women's emancipation must also have its ascetics" (84). In the end, this ideal typewriter girl is no longer a complete woman, nor her body a real one. The sped-up, disciplined typist is held up as positive and emancipated, but only at the cost of "negation of the sexual" (Shiach, *Modernism, Labor and Selfhood* 70) and negation of the body, itself gendered as feminine. Women's potential for action, intelligent work, and positive energization is embraced almost in spite of their gendered body.

In this insistence on a desexualized and defeminized typing body, Gissing's feminists prove even more radical than most of the women's press. Many women's rights activists may agree with Gissing in viewing typewriting as "serious work," superior to the "frivolous," "domestic" traditional female occupations of nursing and governessing (Banks 586; Bulley and Whitley 41). They may also urge women typists to refrain from the common perils of frivolous femininity, such as "giggling, [being] tearful, or unpunctual," or any "silly self-consciousness or foolish desire to attract notice," and admonish them to be "prompt," "diligent," "thorough," "impersonal," and adopt the disciplined professionalism of the masculine business culture (Lady Jane 117). But they still make a point of emphasizing women typists' abundance of ladylike "charm" and "womanly qualities," and their possession of a decorous femininity little different from that of their stay-at-home sisters (117). In their eagerness to seek greater public acceptance of the typewriter girl, women's press insists that this agentic use of speed does not detract from her femininity. Lady Jane celebrates the progress in women's employment when "our girls in great numbers have become wage-earners," "work as many hours," and are "of just as much account in the business world as are their fathers and brothers" (117). But she hastens to appeal to traditional paradigms of decorous femininity, and insists that the "girl in business" has the same "charm" and "womanly qualities" as the stay-at-home maiden, and that she brings into the office the same feminine qualities that "have distinguished homemaking and housekeeping women in what seems women's natural sphere" (117). This is designed, of course, to appease conservative anxiety, but Gissing's novel goes one step further by constructing typewriting as almost alienated from conventional femininity. His feminist typist is not just a serious professional, but also seemingly masculine and "free from the reproach of womanliness" (*The Odd Women* 136).

Alone in the City: The Struggling Bachelor Girl

Gissing's novel was published in 1893, when the typing school of Mary and Rhoda was still, according to him, "an original idea" (*Collected Letters Vol. 5*, 210). After the mid-decade, when businesses began to adopt typewriting more widely, the typewriter girl became a more familiar figure. In 1895, the *Girl's Own Paper* wrote that typewriters were now to be found "in every town in England," and that "typewriting is rapidly becoming a power in the land" (228). By the last years of the 1890s typewriting as a woman's job was increasingly occupied by girls from humbler backgrounds. In 1898, the feminist magazine *Women's Penny Paper* expressed concern over the increasingly declassed nature of typewriting by insisting that typewriting is suited for the "New Woman," a "modern channel where the New Woman's superfluous energies have been profitably directed" ("Lady Shorthand Typist"). In other words, the New Woman takes up typewriting to spend her "superfluous energies," not as a desperately needed livelihood. This New Woman is emancipated but also privileged. The article names good education, foreign language skills, "tact, energy, affability, unlimited perseverance and some capital" as the necessary skills for ultimate success, thus ruling out less well-educated and less wealthy women with no claims to "capital" ("Lady Shorthand Typist").

This reference to the class status of the New Woman typist partly explains some of the disgruntled impatience exhibited in other reports over the glut of half-educated typists, who seem to imperil the respectable status of typewriting work. Already in 1893, an occasional report like "To the Girl Typewriter" would lament that the "enthusiasm" for livelihood among "raw youths" from the "ranks of wage-earners" has gone "beyond the lawful goal," and that as a result "we have the typewriter who cannot spell" (608). The article strongly urges those typists to go back to "the intermediate grade of a public school," or simply "take up some branch of work that does not imperatively demand a considerable degree of mental culture" (608). "It is better," the article concludes rather condescendingly, "to be a first-class seamstress than a fifth-class typewriter" (608). Typewriting, as the *Englishwoman's Review* asserts, "is distinctly a profession and not a trade," which "require[es] education, energy, and the other characteristics which make it essentially work for educated women" ("Is Type-Writing a Successful Occupation?" 82). By the last years of the decade, more and more reports expressed alarm over the flooding of the market by lower-class female typists. While this exposes the class exclusivity of the touted emancipation attributed to typewriting, it also shows that typewriting is no longer the feminist quality work celebrated by the women's press in the early years. Instead, it is increasingly an ordinary urban job open to "the lower ranks of 'skilled' labour" who have to endure long hours of monotonous work for dismal pay (qtd. in Young 122).

By the end of the century, typewriter girls were frequently equated with "restaurant-girls" or waitresses. *Chambers's Journal* goes so far as to question in 1899 "whether the restaurant-girl or typewriter is really better off than the servant in a reasonably good place" (Cuming 17). *Myra's Journal of Dress and Fashion* complains in 1900 that "the whirligig of time" has "brought about its revenges," and that "Mary Ann now works the noisy typewriter and serves as a 'young lady' behind the counter," while "her erstwhile mistress busies herself with the pots and pans" at home ("Employment for Ladies" 15). In 1902, the social investigator Clara Collet wrote that typewriting and office work is a profession on a par with domestic service, chosen only by the "average girl" (*Educated Working Women* 139). In 1903, the UK Treasury attempted to bring into typing posts "young workers of the same class as factory workers, dressmakers and domestic servants," and to pay them only 15 shillings a week (Zimmeck 80). The plan was thwarted by the opposition of Clara Collet, but it went ahead anyway in the Post Office instead, where working-class girls of seventeen years of age were hired (81).

With the rapid expansion of the typewriting profession and its increasingly declassed status, literary works published after the mid-1890s start to move away from the idealism and feminist activism of early representations, and focus instead on the daily reality and harsh life of the typewriter girl as an urban worker. Gissing's novel exposes the punitive workload of the modern shop-girl and offers typewriting as an uplifting alternative, but soon, in later literary works, the typewriter girl's life is portrayed in dismal terms not quite dissimilar to the shop-girl. The heroines are restless with the confinement of domesticity and long for greater freedom in living their own lives, but often they find the costs painfully harsh. In these later works, mostly penned by women writers and written from the typewriter girl's point of view, the symbolic, idealized body of Gissing's feminist typist gives way to a suffering, fatigued, and seemingly mechanized female body. Typewriting speed's inculcation of "prompt," "diligent," "thorough," and "impersonal" qualities in women (*The Odd Women* 54), comes with a heavy toll on the typewriter girl's material body as she struggles to stay afloat in the alienating modern city. The heroines in these stories certainly have an abundance of the "honest effort" and hardworking responsibility championed by Gissing's Rhoda (136), but typewriting as an "invasion" into men's province does not seem to be sufficient, by itself, to bring about "a new order for women" (22). Even typewriting's acclaimed masculine nature, its freedom from the "reproach of womanliness" is much compromised here, as typewriting now becomes firmly a woman's job and a lowly position in the modern office hierarchy (136).

Writing about *fin-de-siècle* responses toward the New Woman, Ann Ardis argues that these could be grouped into the following questions:

> First, what happens to the New Woman herself as she ventures out into the public world? Second, what happens to the nuclear family when women choose careers other than marriage and motherhood? And finally, what happens to the social system as a whole when women enter the workplace in significant numbers for the first time? (21)

In answering these questions, Gissing valorizes the revolutionary impact typewriting brings to women, family and society as women now eschew marriage and dependent femininity for independence and active work. Later literary works seem to be more preoccupied with the first question, and with what immediate costs the New Woman has to pay after she ventures into the public world. Typewriting's disciplinary speed, its radical shake up of the female body and psyche, and its entailment of a self-sustaining life in the whirlpool of the big city away from traditional domesticity become sources of new opportunities but also painful burdens in these later works.

Ardis argues that *fin-de-siècle* narratives describing women's foray into professions like journalism, written by female writers such as Sara Jeanette Duncan and Mrs. Andrew Dean, tend to "delegitimize women's ambitions" because they often end with female suicide or capitulation to marriage and motherhood (152). Typewriter girl stories similarly position work as temporary and transitional, "a stop-gap before marriage" (Liggins, *George Gissing* xvi). But some stories begin to view marriage as unrealistic and focus instead on the girl's lonely struggle as an urban worker. Even when stories do end in a happy marriage, when the typewriter girl abandons her work with relief, the abrupt manner of the happy ending and its apparent inability to reconcile with the better part of the narrative throws into further relief the problems that refuses to go away. The typewriter girl chooses marriage not because she values traditional domesticity, but because life as a working woman is simply too precarious and harsh, threatening to throw her over the edge at any minute. In this sense, the stories ultimately redeem themselves by an unrelenting realism in revealing the ambition, agony, and pains of the lonely typewriter girl.

Some stories describe the typewriter girl finding solace and camaraderie in a male fellow struggler, who could be the "pallid" clerk working in the "dark, unventilated" half-underground room of a small bank ("A Typewriting Episode"), a junior clerk who risks his own place in order to help her ("A New Leaf"), or a young assistant doctor who saves a penniless typewriter girl from suicide ("The Skylight Room"). But marriage for these two is impossible as both struggle to stay afloat in the big city. In other stories the typewriter girl faces the need to exchange love for money, as is in the case of Geraldine in "Uncle Bob" (1897). Working as a typist but still unable to pay for her invalid sister's keep, Geraldine bows to the "mercenary spirit of the age" by agreeing to marry a much older, vulgar-mannered colonial from Australia (591). Fortunately, she is spared her agony and sacrifice when, by an arbitrary stroke of the author's pen, the suitor, "old enough to be her father," turns out to be her long-lost Uncle Bob (591). A painful confrontation with brutal reality turns into an occasion for humor when the Uncle, all his disgusting roughness as suitor now seen as funny in an uncle, could still offer the same monetary protection without having to exact the price of sex.

An occasional story features a strong typewriter girl who helps other girls and finds strength in solidarity. In "The Powder Mutiny," a young boss seeks to restore a "straight-laced, whale-boned, old-fashioned" commercial house to its old "rectitude and integrity" by banning cosmetics, rouge, or powder on the typewriter girls (80). When Margot defies the order and is given one week's notice, all the girls show their support by staging a mass strike, forcing the boss to give in. The story might celebrate the girls' collective power, but in revealing the real reason for Margot's defiance it also underlines the pathetic fate of the typewriter girl once she gets old. Margot later tells the boss that she wears her powder in order to help shield Miss Brown, the senior head lady clerk in the office. Cosmetics, it turns out, are less for female vanity and more a necessary tool of survival for the typewriter girl. "[W]ithout her teeth, her front, her rouge and her tight dress" Miss Brown, the head lady clerk, would look really old and not be able to find a job, because "nobody wants old people" (80). She "has toiled in London offices" for "forty years," and "was sacked at place after place until she began to make up" and hide her gray hair (80). Whatever her professional expertise, typewriting offers no long-term job stability for the typewriter girl. In work, just as in marriage, she is still ultimately valued for her sexualized body display, and would be denied both if she loses her youth and allure.

In displaying a longing for the security and comfort of marriage and romance, some of these typewriting stories share a similar "boomerang" plot which Ardis identifies in other narratives about the female professional, a plot that ultimately returns the New Woman back to domesticity and "brings the narratives back into alliance with ... the Victorian code of womanliness" (154). But in their concomitant recognition of the need to toil on in poverty and pain, and in their naturalistic detailing of the harsh tolls of repetitive, mechanized work, these stories also harken back to the mid-Victorian industrial novel. This is seen in "The Exception" (1896, Figure 1.5), written for the *Windsor Magazine* by Mayne Lindsay (the pseudonym of Miss Rosina M. Hopkins), a story that, according to a review in *Windsor* six months later, "revealed the pathetic conditions under which typewriters in London work" ("Rising Stars" 383). Like the typewriter girls in her story, the author came from a genteel family that had gone down in the world after the early death of her British-Consul father. Lindsay tried all kinds of work, including housekeeping for her brother in India, helping in a sheep station in Western Victoria, Australia, and typewriting and shorthand writing in London after coming

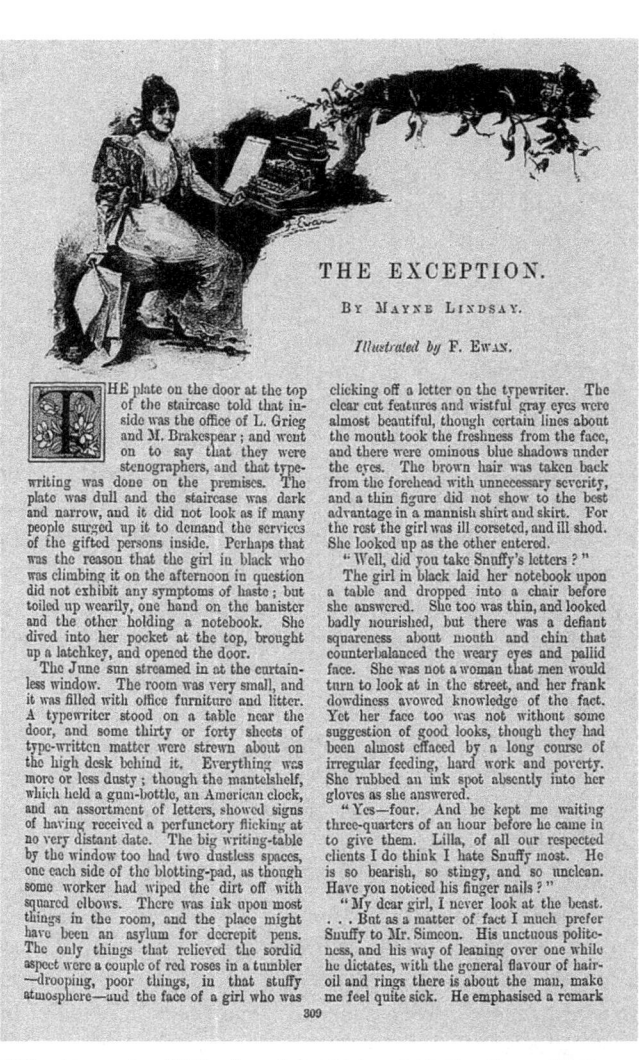

Figure 1.5   "The Exception," *Windsor*, Jul. 1896, p. 309. ProQuest LLC.

back to England. The review commends Lindsay profusely for her "directness of style" and "quickness" "of perceptions," and reveals that within twelve months of returning to England she has had five stories, of "much originality," accepted by *Windsor* (383).

Lindsay had, as the reviewer claims, a "very brief experience of City life" (383) as a typist and shorthand writer, which allows her to inject into her story a raw authenticity and some very precious first-hand knowledge of the daily ordeal of the typewriter girl. *The Exception* opens with a "dark and narrow" staircase that leads to a small, dismal typewriting office at the top of a building, suggesting both the physical and symbolic hardship of climbing to a self-sustaining life as a typewriter girl. Two single ladies use this office, and everything in the curtainless room is dusty and ink-stained, with "some thirty or forty sheets of typewritten matter ... strewn about on the high desk" behind the typewriter (309). Like the two "droopy, poor" roses on the mantelpiece, "the only things that relieved the sordid aspect" of the stuffy room, Miss Lilla, the young girl typing a letter on the typewriter, is still beautiful, "though certain lines about the mouth took the freshness from the face, and there were ominous blue shadows under the eyes" (309). The story reveals that typewriting is far from what feminists call the working women's "El Dorado" (Bulley and Whitley 41), but instead exerts a debilitating toll on the health of these women, who are badly nourished and weary from long hours of repetitive work. The other girl—Miss Mildred—is older, and shows further signs of the exhaustion brought by "a long course of irregular feeding, hard work and poverty" ("The Exception" 309).

Typewriting brings women into the man's world of business, but the increased heterosexual interaction does not, as is claimed in earlier male-penned stories, bring about romance and marriage; instead, it leads to greater exploitation and sexual harassment. Mildred reveals that a male client, nicknamed Snuffy, has kept her waiting for three-quarters of an hour before giving her four letters to type. He is the most hated of all her clients, because he is "bearish," "stingy," and has "unclean" finger nails. Lilla, however, reminds her that most men are even worse, like Mr. Simeon, who "makes me sick" with his "unctuous politeness, and his way of leaning over one when he dictates, with the general flavor of hair-oil and rings about the man" (309). That leech-like Mr. Simeon "emphasized a remark yesterday by laying that fat, bejeweled fore-finger caressingly on my hand" (310). And when Lilla whips it away he just "rolled his eyes in a languishing manner and smiled a nine-inch smile" (310). The horror of lascivious men taking advantage of vulnerable typewriter girls has to be put up with as "part of the discipline of life," because "one must make a living" (311).

In scenes reminiscent of Gissing's traditional, poverty-stricken Madden sisters, the two girls skip lunch, pretending not to be hungry, and sit down to a meager tea made over a small oil lamp. In *The Odd Woman*, Gissing sees typewriting as far more remunerative and less toilsome, which allows Rhoda to be vigorous, strong, and nourished by a healthy diet that obviously includes meat, because she kindly offers some to the starving Virginia Madden when the latter comes for help (20). But here the two typewriter girls do not fare much better than Gissing's helpless, pathetic, traditional women. They are as hardworking, disciplined, and intelligent as Rhoda, but they still end up as "a pair of superfluous women" ("The Exception" 310). Often exhausted and at the end of their means, the two girls contemplate suicide to end their struggle, through the help of "a little charcoal and some brown paper pasted over the chimney" (310).

In terms that resonate with Victorian concerns with mechanistic theories of fatigue and energy dissipation and with the alienation of the laboring body from the natural order of things, Lindsay's story stresses the harsh toll of typewriting on a woman's vulnerable body.[12] Lilla, for instance, complains constantly of "the ache that never leaves me"; after "two long years of hopelessness" and ceaseless typing, she is gnawed by an aching sense of alienation and a "sick longing for sight and touch" (310). Lilla is newer to typewriting work, but already the ravaging tolls of relentless work are showing in the hard lines around her mouth and "ominous blue shadows" under her eyes (309). Typewriting may be white-collar office work and operated by the genteel girl, but with her eyes and muscles constantly strained by repetitive work, ears dinned by the ceaseless clicking, and nerves worried by the attempt to keep up the speed and not lose focus, the typewriter girl is exposed to a human–machine encounter that parallels in many ways the working class on the factory floor.

In the industrial novels of Dickens and Gaskell and their criticism of the suffering of the poor and the maiming effects of machinery, machines are described as grinding "like tortured creatures, clanking their iron chains, shrieking in their rapid whirl from time to time as though in torment unendurable, and making the ground tremble with their agonies (*Hard Times* 44). Little Nell, wandering with her grandfather in "a great manufacturing town," finds the whole place "reeking with lean misery and hungry wretchedness" (445). Historical records confirm permanent bodily deformities such as stoops, suffered by the worker due to prolonged crouching over textile machinery (Sussman 101). Typewriting work may be less dangerous and gruesome, but like the factory workers who are often reduced to "Hands," a dehumanizing name used by Victorian factory owners to refer to their workers (Stiltner 194), the typewriter girl is valued only for her nimble hands, an "animated segment" generating speedy work and fast service in the Taylorite office (194). That segment, like the factory "Hands," is liable to deformation from prolonged strain. A *Pick-Me-Up* piece reports on March 26, 1892, that "Typewriters' Stub Finger" is a "new affliction" among typists, and that this "deformity" comes

---

[12] Anson Rabinbach writes that the discovery of the laws of thermodynamics in the second half of the nineteenth century led to a new understanding of the material world and the human body, grounded in the concept of "energy" and "work." The human body is seen as the "human motor," a thermodynamic engine that has limits of efficiency and needs rest to combat the fatigue of overwork (2).

from long hours of typing, which "has transformed their fingers into thumbs" (418).

What makes Lindsay's typewriter girl special is that this laboring body is a distinctly female one, a rare occurrence in Victorian literature. The female factory worker rarely makes an appearance in the mid-Victorian industrial novel, even though in reality their numbers were significant. The 1851 Census finds, for instance, that 140,000 women over the age of 20 were employed in domestic service, 125,000 in clothing and shoemaking, 11,000 in teaching, 9,000 in the silk industry, and the remainder in other branches of manufacture (qtd. in Colby 4). Catherine Barnes Stevenson also confirms that in the textile town of Preston in the 1850s, 55.8 percent of the factory labor force consisted of females over the age of 13 ("The Working-Class Woman in *North and South*"). But even when Elizabeth Gaskell makes women the central characters in her industrial novels, these are either middle-class lady philanthropists such as Margaret Hale in *North and South*, or seamstresses like Mary Barton, who avoids factory work because of her father's insistence that this is not a woman's "proper" job. The only female factory worker in *North and South* is Bessy Higgins, but she has already left work and is resting at home because of lung disease contracted in the carding room. In the rare instances where women's work outside the home and in the factory does get represented, as is the case in Charlotte Elizabeth Tonna's 1843 story "The Forsaken Home," the story blames the mother's work as a machine operative for the neglect of her children and the ultimate breakdown of her family. Female work's disruption of gender norms, rather than the female laboring body itself, forms the center of attention.

In this sense, *fin-de-siècle* literary works featuring the typewriter girl link her to a long-standing Victorian literary tradition, but also enrich this tradition by foregrounding the hitherto neglected female laboring body. With the increasing number of middle-class women leaving domesticity and entering new professions opened up by modern commodity culture, that laboring body and its trials and tribulations inevitably engage attention. In Lindsay's story, Lilla looks at her increasingly emaciated body and is painfully reminded of younger days in the countryside before the death of her father, when she was "plump and placid" (311). Her thoughts run briefly to a childhood lover now believed to be dead from shipwreck. But she is also clear-eyed that the only kind of romance available to typewriter girls is either with "a pasty-faced youth behind a counter," or as a kept woman living with richer men, "one of Mr. Simeon's kind" (311). Love would not be possible without money, and it would be hard to imagine that there are "nobler passions in the world than hunger and jealousy and hate" (311). When Lilla suddenly receives a letter informing her of the miraculous return of her shipwrecked lover and of the imminent end of her slavery through marriage, the other girl, Mildred, is briefly moved into declaring that true love is "worth waiting for years, or a lifetime" (311). She is soon, however, awakened by the noise of the London streets below their window. Concluding that love "is not the rule of life for the superfluous woman" (311), Mildred tells Lilla that life "has not altered and will not alter," and that "in the state of life unto which we've been called," "you are The Exception" (311).

Lindsay's story navigates an uncertain path between a yearning for traditional romance wherein a long-lost lover returns to rescue a maiden in distress, and a sober-eyed realization that this is only a fairytale. In its very title, and in its ending, the story comes back to bleak realism, exposing Lilla's story as not just "an exception" but also logically improbable, little more than a jarring concession to the conventions of the romance story. The reader is left with the nagging belief that Lilla in real life is more likely to follow the path of the older Mildred, who is the more realistic representation of the vast majority of typewriter girls who could have "so little chance of the real [love]" and are actually "better without what is foisted upon her for the article" (311).

In this group of female-penned narratives detailing the opportunities as well as the dangers of being a typewriter girl in the big city, a most representative example of gritty realism is Geraldine Edith Mitton's novel *A Bachelor Girl in London* (1898). The typewriter heroine Judith Danville is a typical New Woman who is frustrated with static domesticity, but also finds that the costs and burdens of life in the fast lane far outweigh the initial promise of freedom. Mitton's novel gives more space to a critique of the crippling passivity of traditional domesticity and a celebration of the broadened horizon brought by typewriting work, but it also remains sober-eyed regarding the high costs of that independence. In its foregrounding of the pains, fatigue, and restlessness, as well as the thrills, of the typewriter girl's body as it interacts with modern speed culture, the novel achieves such "exemplary care," "such pains," and "such effectiveness" that a reviewer for *Hearth and Home* finds it highly commendable ("Books and Authors" [1898] 1060). The novel's "tragicomic scenes" of Judith's "daily round in London" obviously touch a chord with the reviewer, who admits to being a bachelor girl in London herself, for she writes that Judith's experience brings "a peculiar pleasure" to those working women who "have been there before," "met the same interviewer in real life," "clung to the racing omnibus," "dined in dubious restaurants," and generally recognize their own arduous struggle (1060).

The titular bachelor girl, Judith, is one of "so many girls out of the country with souls full of a certain melancholy ambition," who are "swept" "into that great whirlpool" of London (9). One of four daughters born to a country doctor, whose death leaves the girls ill-provided for, Judith refuses to follow the lot of her sisters who rely on matrimony or handouts from relatives because they "had no equipment with which to fight their own battles" (13). Judith is a New Woman, who "leapt somewhat higher," (43) and "wanted to be, to do, not to stagnate" (8), rejecting the "soul-sickness of uselessness" (170). Like Gissing's Rhoda, she is drawn to the magnetic appeal of London, "the hot blood in her crav[ing] excitement and adventure" (21), and sees shorthand and typewriting as a powerful weapon to aid her launch into London's fast-swirling life.

Whilst at home, Judith already loves the thrill of speed and adventure. Her stepmother, Mrs. Danville, "was passionately fond of driving" and "imbued" Judith "with her own love for it" (8). Judith relishes her rides with her stepmother, and "together they flew about the country in a high dogcart" (8). These riding trips, a highlight in Judith's otherwise stagnant life, gives her the "jolt" she needs to "lift" her "out of her rut" (8). When she finally gets permission to come to London and become a typewriter girl, she is initially excited by the swirling energy of a fast-paced cosmopolitan life. "Everything [i]s new to her," as she navigates the "main arteries of the great body of London," and she is fascinated by the ceaseless crowd "who passed for ever in and out" (16). Like Gissing's Virginia Madden when she steps out from her homebound life into London's busy streets, Juliet is swept up in "a strange, dreamlike excitement" which "possessed her" (167), and even the low-class loafers on the street, who "filled the byways and eddies of the crowd" like "the shrimps of the great London shore," captivate her with their raw energy and care-free nonchalance (19): "Like flies they were carried about on every chance current, but if they missed their regular acquaintances, others were easy to find" (20). "They needed no credentials," "had also no responsibility," and they inspire Judith with an urge to "fling off that weary loaf of care" and just live for the moment (20). Gissing's Virginia needs the aid of alcohol to give her courage, but Judith seems braver. Exhilarated by this energetic flow, Judith, too, "walk[s] fearlessly and straight on her path" as "the working woman, the bachelor girl of the period" (64).

Many such typewriting heroines in these female-penned stories start with similar high hopes, enthusiastic over the liberating potential of women's participation in modern speed culture. But once she has "flung herself" into this whirlpool, Judith soon finds that her life in London can be "mean" and "sordid" (167), "turbulent and black" (9), covering her with "smuts" and forcing her to "lose hope and heart" (167, 168). London's pushy crowds, feverish turmoil, rushing traffic, and fast shifting demarcations often prove to be disorientating, whereby "she was only one person of no particular importance among crowds of others" (12). She is "overwhelmed by discovering what herds of poverty-stricken, unattached women there were in the world," all striving and scraping in order to survive (9): "Some had grown old and wizened in the struggle, others went sullenly on day by day, doing work which was toilsome, uncongenial, and poorly paid, hating their lives, but seeing no hope, and uncomplaining from mere want of any surplus vitality" (9). Typewriting and self-reliant work may enable these bachelor girls to "fight their own battle" (13), but this battle is harsh and never-ending, as they face the daily threat of being wiped out by London's indiscriminate, devouring torrents.

Like all these typewriter girls, Judith struggles to find work. For three weeks she goes for interviews, climbs many a long flight of stairs, and gets nothing but rejection. "We have difficulty in finding employment for our permanent staff as it is," one assistant apologetically but firmly tells her (10). Even a pathetic attempt to work as a servant ends in rejection, and Judith faces the dismal prospect of having to pawn her clothes just to hang on. Right on the verge of despair, she finally lands a typewriting job at a silk agent's office through the help of a rich society lady. Mr. Dasent, the silk agent who offers her the job, declares that he has had scores of girls applying already, signaling the tight competition in the market. Judith does not get the job because of her experience, which she admits to have had none, but because Mr. Dasent has romantic inclinations for the rich society lady who recommended her, again proving that a girl without connections could barely survive in the big city.

The novel touches on the dehumanizing impact of typewriting as onerous labor. Judith may be extremely grateful to land the job, but she is immediately exposed to the coercive discipline of mechanized speed: "The afternoon went on leaden feet, there were none of the breaks which had helped the morning," and "the work was one eternal typing" (67). For a fresh-out-of-home girl who has never experienced heavy work before, the tolls of typewriting are sudden and overwhelming. "The clock moved by minutes," and Judith "tried not to dawdle" (68). But "her back ached," and "as she grew more tired she began to fumble at the notes and strike them wrongly, and once or twice she had to retype a page" (68). Even later after she gets more used to typing and "custom had strengthened the requisite muscles" (90), the work still leaves her exhausted and "fit for nothing else" after returning home. Judith started with high hopes, but she ends up realizing that "I am a machine," "a cog in the world's machinery" (75, 170).

Gissing's feminists celebrate typewriting for its elevation of intellect, mind, and technological knowledge and its distance from the naturalized feminine body. In Mitton's novel, the typewriter girl's body is very much a real, physical one that is heavily taxed by "soul-crushing" (309) work and in daily need of food and protection for survival. The novel's opening setting is the large, noisy, smelly, bustling restaurant on the first floor of a women's boarding house where Judith rents a small room on the fourth floor. Far from the serene elegance of the typical Victorian drawing-room setting of traditional literary heroines, this public, indiscriminate congregation, where "two great incandescent gas burners beat and glowed on the heads of half a hundred men and women," is filled with the "penetrating din of chatter," the "clatter of knives and forks," and the "mingled odours of various forms of cooked meat and vegetables" which "rose with the heated air in one vast unappetizing smell toward the ceiling" (1). Eating is no dainty, leisurely ritual but noisy and hasty, with food gulped down by strangers oblivious to each other and ready to hurry on to the next stop in their daily round. The vulgar commotion of this opening scene sets the tone for what is to come of Judith's days in London, as her life in the fast lane is far from the elevating adventure she had hoped for.

This public restaurant may be alienating, but a vast army of single women call this their home. Many of the small tables fit for two persons are only occupied by one woman who sits there alone, with an "indifference of attitude" which suggests that they are long accustomed to eating out alone. These unattached women, like Judith, lodge at the rooms above the restaurant, in what represents the many real-life women's boarding houses which sprang up in the last decades of the nineteenth century, offering "the freedom of rooms, and the comforts of a club" to single working women (2). Judith could come and go at will, has no need for a chaperone, sees gentlemen and lady friends upstairs in her own room, and generally enjoys a freedom that her sisters in her country home could never dream of. Compared with the private, cheap lodgings of Gissing's odd women, these women's mansions are safer and more comfortable, and their higher rates denote more status. Such women-only accommodation started out as feminist clubs such as the female Writers' Club and the Women's University Club, founded in the 1890s in the male club-land of West End's Paul Mall, which held lectures and seminars, and offered resting, dining, and accommodation facilities for women from outside of London (Rappaport 166). As more women took up professional work and needed to navigate the city as single women, these establishments increasingly became an acceptable space to cater to the accommodation and networking needs of working women.

However, these institutions do not come cheap and often prove beyond the means of most working women. An 1891 report in *Girl's Own Paper* on a Residential Club for Ladies in Sloane Gardens House reveals, for instance, that the 130 ladies who live in it, including "authoress, governess, artist, typist," have to pay between 7 and 13 shillings a week for shared facilities and an unfurnished room ("Sloane Gardens House" 526). *The Young Woman* also reports that the "bachelor girl in the big city" often lives in cubicles and has to scrimp on food (qtd. in Liggins, "Life" 225). Mitton's novel confirms these real-life reports, offering a depressingly naturalistic portrait of the life of the typewriter girl when every penny counts. Judith has to pay eight-and-six for her small fourth-floor room, sixpence for the maid, at least a shilling for coupons for oil and coal, one-and-eight for meals, and one-and-six for washing (63). This leaves almost nothing from her weekly thirty-shilling wage. As Judith lies on her bed planning her weekly expenses, she realizes that she has to give up breakfast at the restaurant and only eat porridge in her own room in order to live within her income.

Feminists such as Amy Levy may celebrate these women's boarding houses as going a long way in helping to combat the "practical disadvantages" and "isolated position" of the professional woman (qtd. in Liggins, "Life" 227), but Mitton's novel offers a bleaker picture by revealing that this new living arrangement leads to more loneliness, which "began to creep into [Judith's] bones" (59). For days on end Judith speaks to no one, and in a desperate desire to speak and to "hear the voice of some one who recognized her personality," she makes an excuse one evening and goes downstairs to see Miss Wilton, "the only woman who had spoken to her since her arrival in the house" (60). When she cries hopelessly like a child in her small, unlit room, she realizes that she could indulge in this pastime until the morning without anyone coming to disturb her. The "futility of looking for any chance of external comfort" shakes her to the core, as she looks out of her fourth-floor room into the street below, desperately seeking comfort by watching the street boys play their games (11). The typewriter girl, now that she has stepped out into the real world, has no one to look up to if the "solid ground is cut away from under her own feet," and her "ramshackle raft" turns into a "piteous shipwreck" (13).

Judith seeks comfort and solace in the raw energy of London's bustling streets, but even these often prove treacherous. The public streets of big cities, traditionally a most immediate spatial indicator of gender segregation demarcating respectable domesticity from morally dangerous public space, was, by the last years of the nineteenth century, increasingly turning into a shop-lined commodity spectacle and business center appealing to a heterosocial public. This in turn allowed a form of pleasurable rambling and public spatial exploration for women that started to stretch, move, and rewrite gender boundaries. Young women of "good style and repute" would now walk the streets of London without a chaperone, loving "liberty more than safety," wrote *The Queen* in 1882 (qtd. in Rappaport 138). In Mitton's novel, Judith, as a bachelor girl, seeks to be similarly emboldened and energized by her immersion in the rhythms of the huge London crowds, as she yearns to cultivate a new street talent in her urban navigation. But the lingering danger of traditional street gender politics still places powerful constraints on her *flânerie*.

One night, when she is swept too far by her enthusiasm for exploring London and ends up in an unfamiliar and disreputable part of the city, she is mistaken by a policeman for a prostitute. "How dare you speak to me so? I am a lady," Judith cries with mortification, citing her ladylike clothes and refined accent as proof, but she is immediately dismissed as a liar when the policeman, "condemnation in his glance" (23), finds that she could not even afford the bus fare, let alone a hansom. A hansom would cost three shillings, "half a week's dinners—good hot dinners such as she had denied herself" (27). Crestfallen and humiliated, Judith walks for hours and only reaches home after tearfully begging a hansom driver for a free lift. Judith may believe, just like Monica in Gissing's *The Odd Women*, that women "ought to go about just as freely as a man" and be "every bit as free" (164), but in this particular instance it is still by resorting to the traditional gender role of the weak, helpless woman in need of protection that she manages to extricate herself from danger.

When Judith first arrives in London and walks the streets of London's business center trying to find work, she is accosted by an elderly female beggar hoping to sell her some lavender. Judith declines by saying that she herself is a "fellow-creature in distress," but the old woman leers at her in disbelief, claiming that "[w]hen you're young and good-looking, my dear, you need never know want" (*A Bachelor Girl* 59). To the old woman, the modern, independent, working woman, often vilified in the popular press for their sexual promiscuity and avail-ability, is equally suspected of bartering her body for money just like the prostitute.

Indeed, as a typewriter girl in the big city, Judith occupies a position of extreme "precarity" (Young 141). The novel was published in 1898, when typewriting was already very much "a trade" and not the "profession" insisted upon by earlier fem-inists ("Is Type-Writing a Successful Occupation?" 82). The typewriter girl was increasingly declassed and closer to the "cheap typewriters and shopgirls" derided in the masculine press ("The Stranger" 128). In Mitton's novel, Judith claims to be a lady from a good family, but while this is enough to get her credit in shops in the countryside, in London she finds herself "not of a different order from those who had wrecked themselves, and been sucked down into the green slime" (*A Bachelor Girl* 22). Even when she is working she lives paycheck to paycheck, and is hardly better off than the low-class loafers on the street, "the clothes they wore" being "all they had" (20).

The ultimate proof that Judith's lady status offers no defense from the tolls of poverty occurs when she finds that honesty and loyalty, qualities she asserts to come naturally to a lady "as a matter of course," could be easily bartered for money (64). In her first day in the office, her boss, Dasent, asks Judith not to hold herself a lady or bring over the manners of the posh drawing-room, because "we don't have any ladies here, we are all working men and women" (62). This remark may be less than sincere, for Dasent is certainly an extremely wealthy "working" man. But as a fast-rising Jew he is referring to new boundaries in an accelerating commodity culture where money increasingly trumps hereditary class. Judith is eager to prove that she, too, is not short of diligence and talent, but, deep down, in her heart she still clings on to another quality seen as essential to a lady. When Dasent tells her that loyalty and honesty are valuable business qualities required in her work as a typewriter girl, Judith is slightly amused that he should ask that of a lady. "[S]he was a lady, and had been so brought up"; "it was no merit to her, and her new employer should never regret having taken her on so slight a recommendation" (64).

Yet Judith's almost arrogant belief in her ingrained honesty is seriously jeop-ardized when she is later forced to accept bribery and betray her employer. As a typewriter girl Judith is in daily contact with the dealings of her boss and is cognizant of his business secrets. This unique access to the heart of business, cel-ebrated by many feminists as a sign of women's increasing inroads into business culture, also places the typewriter girl in a position of danger as she is now vulner-able to the machinations of business enemies and spies. When a highborn brother of the society lady who gets Judith the job, a blackguard masquerading as an ele-gant gentleman, cheats Judith into accepting a ten-pound bet in exchange for key business information, the temptation of the money is simply too strong: "What a haven of rest that ten pounds represented! An easing of the sore burden of life for many a week"; "she might put it in the bank as a refuge in case she broke down;

or she could buy new boots or gloves, and those dozen exceteras which she was painfully conscious of needing" (216).

The needs of her body to rest from taxing typing, and to be nourished by warm food and clothing, trump her adherence to symbolic principles of honesty, as Judith ultimately accepts the bribe. She has found out, at a great cost, that she is not above selling her loyalty for a price. "She had been bribed and betrayed her trust," and the fear of losing her livelihood later prevents her from confessing to her boss even when his business is hurt by the betrayal (292). When Dasent eventually finds out and she is dismissed in disgrace, "a wretched, worthless creature" who would never ever find more typewriting work, Judith realizes in great distress not just her financial but also her moral bankruptcy. She is just "as frail and unreliable as the weakest," her starving and fatigued body linking her irretrievably with the "sinning, suffering mass whom before she had looked down upon from an immeasurable distance" (23, 64).

Judith finds it hard to fully reconcile herself with a new urban hierarchy of shifting demarcations, in which as a typewriter girl she is just an anonymous member of a vast army of toiling urban workers. This is further seen in her complicated relationship with another urban worker: the omnibus driver, Ireland, whom Judith befriends in her occasional rides to and from work. Unlike her "trivial" and affected high society acquaintances (20), Ireland is solidly honest and the only source of human warmth and generosity for Judith in London. A bastion of moral integrity and ungrudging chivalry, he is also "an exceptionally fine strong man, with crisp hair," "a healthy face," and "the most cheery and imperturbable good humour" (103, 102). Judith finds sympathy and "recognition" in their conversation (118), practical help and support in his advice as a seasoned Londoner, and "a whirl of irresistible admiration" for his bravery and skills as a driver (154). Despite her initial condescending interest in studying him as a specimen of a "life so different from her own" (15), no doubt as part of her urban *flânerie* from a position of self-satisfied superiority, Judith finds herself admitting "a sudden, wild desire" to be with Ireland. "[I]t would be like a fresh sea breeze after the inanities of the Bachelors' Club," the haunt frequented by her rich society friends (122). Compared with Pitt, the cynical high-class sophisticate with a reputation as a "lady killer, a gay man about town," who at the end of the novel proposes to Judith and saves her from her misery and trouble (328), Ireland comes off as a real gentleman, of "absolute honesty," "moral worth," and "great manhood" (187).

Every time Judith is with Ireland, her body experiences one of the few active thrills and excitements Judith still finds in her life in London. This is not just because of her unacknowledged attraction to his good looks, manly body, and honorable conduct, but also because of the many bus rides she takes with him, chatting with him and enjoying the new urban pleasure of bus riding. Ireland stands for the exhilarating thrill of active speed and sexual attraction, in stark contrast to the secure but staid domesticity offered by the languid Pitt: "These drives were a never-ending delight to her, for the types of faces flowing over the pavement, the great flood of working humanity seemed to sweep over and obliterate the narrowness and dinginess in her own life" (102). When Judith sits beside Ireland as he maneuvers his bus with great skill and bravado, viscerally feeling the thrill of speed and agentic control of movement, Judith's bus-riding offers an experience of active speed that could ideally rejuvenate her and compensate for the passive, coercive speed she toils under in typewriting labor. When feeling "depressed and worried" about her life, Judith would look out for Ireland's omnibus, and "a great brightness opened up to her," "as refreshing as a tonic" (149). In one of her rides with Ireland in a thunderstorm, Judith is at first terrified of being in the middle of "a chaos, a hubbub of water and fire," which "seemed to catch the vehicle and carry it along detached from any earthly support" (152). But she soon finds strength and "comfort" in the "steady solidity" of Ireland's "broad back," and gets a taste of excitement in racing along with Ireland as he skillfully steers the bus on its good pace without an accident (152).

In another scene, Judith is no longer satisfied with being a spectator but wants an active part in the thrill of speed, goading Ireland to "go on, go on" at a faster speed (276). Judith has been suffering under the weight of "the most oppressive time" and the "strain and stress of life" (265, 267), and for relief and a bit of a rejuvenation she joins Ireland in one of his races with a fellow omnibus driver to see who gets to Westminster Bridge first. "They flew along on the wide way with the fresh keen air blowing in their faces," and "even Judith was satisfied at the pace they went" (271). When Ireland warns her to get off the bus because the bus would be driving with one wheel on the pavement of the narrow road and might go over any minute, Judith cries "no, no" "in a fever heat of excitement," insisting that "I'll see it through now" and urging Ireland to "go on, go on" (276). "With a bound and a bump the off-wheels sprang on to the curb," and "then began a royal race" "at a tremendous rate," "which would have frightened Judith if excitement has not swamped fear" (275, 277). This excitement sees Judith to the very end, as she partners up with Ireland and basks in the shared glory of his ultimate win, to the loud clapping of a large crowd of admiring spectators (278).

In the end, though, such thrilling rides with Ireland are not enough to keep her surfing on the urban sea of humanity. Despite her initial desire to plunge into the whirlpool of London and float with the tides, Judith is ultimately not prepared for the reality of life in the fast lane nor its high costs. When Ireland proposes to Judith after she is sacked from her job, Judith is greatly horrified and blurts out "How could I marry a man of your class?" (285) Judith is now a penniless and unemployed typewriter girl, while Ireland has £300 saved up and plans to invest in his own bus and set up a small business. Both are what Judith's boss calls "working men and women" (62), and, as an experienced bus driver, Ireland is in many ways better off than a typewriter girl like Judith. He is self-disciplined, discrete, knows better than Judith on how to tell a gentleman from a blackguard, and is poised to become a successful self-made man in the future. As Ireland's pal later tells Judith, "you are not ... anything so grand yourself" (294). Yet Judith, unable to reconcile herself to the declassed status of the typewriter girl, insists that the yawning gap between herself and the average urban worker is so wide that "it's just impossible" (286). Clinging on to her lady status, Judith would never bring herself so low as "to his level," as "our ways of thought, out habits, everything is so different" (285, 286).

It comes as no wonder that, ultimately, Judith's failure to adapt to the fast life of the modern city leaves her with little choice but to bow out. The novel starts with Judith's eager impatience to stake a claim for herself in modern speed culture, however "hurt and bruised by contact with the rougher edge" of London (334). But it ends with the bachelor girl quitting London, giving up her typewriting and retiring into slow-paced, sheltered domesticity. When Pitt, the high society lady's man, suddenly yearns to wash away the "sloughs of old sins" by "a good woman's love" (338), Judith gratefully accepts his offer of marriage. "[H]er greatest gift," Judith realizes, is not her determination to prove her own worth by self-reliant work, but the "sanctified...power of raising and ennobling man" (339), the traditional wifely, angel-in-the-house virtue she has spent all her life avoiding.

2

"The Literary Piano"

Typewriting, Automation, and Creativity

In *A Bachelor Girl in London*, Judith's complaint about her profession is not just directed against typewriting as onerous labor, but also against what is perceived to be the mechanizing impact of its techno-aided speed. Typewriting fatigues and tames her body, and it also stultifies her mental life, destroying any remnant of spontaneous creativity. When Judith first comes to London, typewriting is not her ultimate goal. Instead, she "had secret literary aspirations—at once the hope and despair of every girl whose mind is wider than her environment" (8). At the same time that she looks for typewriting and clerkship vacancies, she also knocks at the doors of the editorial offices of journals and leaves her manuscripts for consideration. Like many real-life New Woman typewriter girls of the 1890s, Judith starts out with literary and journalistic ambitions, and treats typewriting as a more secure and available day job to tide her over.

This high hope often flounders, as the periodicals market is so flooded that any event that happens would immediately be described by "armies of special reporters in the papers" (10). But Judith soon finds to her dismay that her typewriting work poses a much graver obstacle to her literary dreams. The mechanical nature of rhythmic, repetitive typing to meet the speed of the machine threatens to turn Judith into an automaton, wherein "every vital thought is dried up" (67). "All the sensations," "all her vivid grip of life," "her eyes that saw," and "her ears that heard," are "wasted and atrophied" (172). It is only after she leaves London and goes back to her country home for a short holiday that the "journalistic instinct, which had been covered by the necessity for hard, mechanical work, leapt to the surface and flowed over all other feeling" (171). Judith has earlier linked country life with suffocation and stasis and London life with speed and excitement, but after months of harsh labor in the fast-paced city, she now longs for the countryside and equates that with organic creativity. Though she soon tires of country life and again longs to go back to London, Judith still finds it very difficult to become a writer if carrying on the typewriting job, for, as her boss describes her job, "a little more of a machine would suit me better" (205).

In these scenes, as in many other *fin-de-siècle* writings about the typewriter, typewriting seems to fuel a polar opposition between automation and creative agency, as it is perceived to erase the unique trace and organic agency of the human

The New Woman and Technologies of Speed in Fin-de-Siècle *Literature*. Eva Chen, Oxford University Press.
© Eva Chen (2024). DOI: 10.1093/9780198922285.003.0003

subject. The typewriter does extend the speed of writing and transmission of documents, but it also threatens to turn the human operator into an automaton and empties out her mind and original emotion. In the chase for fastest speed, the organic human body completely internalizes the exigencies of the typing machine. In this sense, typewriting speed does not just tame and discipline women by turning them into docile labor for capitalist exploitation, it also threatens to empty their mind and subjugate the human subject to the will and dictates of the machine.

The typewriter, as Friedrich Kittler argues, drives a mechanical "wedge" between text and hand, and interrupts the natural flow of organic intelligence transmitted from handwriting to paper (*Discourse Networks* 195). In both its operating process and the typescript produced, which is a uniformly standard and mechanically reproducible form of machine writing, the typewriter stands for the polar opposite of agency and creativity. Since the typewriter is operated predominantly by the typewriter girl and the perceived standardization and depersonalization of its typescript is projected upon her, she is portrayed in those years as the antithesis of the manuscript-writing creative writer. Often set up as a contrastive pair, their irreconcilable difference becomes a site around which all the complexities of the modern body–machine complex coalesce.

This chapter argues that automation and creativity, or the mechanical and the organic, do not necessarily work in stark polarization but allow room for mutual accommodation. The human subject is indeed coerced by industrial speed, but, in learning to adapt to speed and perpetually reorient herself, the typewriter girl could still lay claim to what Daly calls a "retooled" subjectivity that harbors agentive potential (42). This chapter will first examine the operating process of typewriting as a technology of speed, particularly its unique "blind" side that seems to aggravate its mechanizing impact. It will then seek to collapse the body–machine polarization by engaging the example of piano-playing, a nineteenth-century machine of sound often compared with the typewriter, for a contrastive study on whether creative emotion and mechanical energy could be assembled in a way that does not lead to stark opposition. The third section further considers the issue of automation and creativity by reading literary works which take a more nuanced approach to typewriting's mechanizing impact. Most of the typewriting stories published after the mid-1890s focus on the dehumanizing impact of disciplinary speed, but some occasional pieces take a more positive view and set up the typewriter girl as adapting to and actively using this machine of speed. In some *fin-de-siècle* literary representations, such as Allen's *The Type-Writer Girl*, the New Woman typist further cherishes a literary ambition of her own, and succeeds in her aspiration to become a writer. This dual role of typist and writer allows her to embody typewriting's perceived threat to human interiority, while also forcing more discussions on the meaning of organic agency, or what it means to be a creative writer in the *fin-de-siècle* cultural scene.

Typing Like a Machine?

When the typewriter first became widely adopted in offices and businesses in the 1890s, journalistic writings often hailed its fast speed as a symbol of efficiency and modern progress, but anxieties over its threat to the emotive and the organic were also rife. In his 1897 essay "The Writing of Essays," a satirical criticism of the state of essay writing in contemporary periodicals, H. G. Wells makes the somewhat flippant statement that the right kind of pen, paper, or ink, not the controlling genius behind the writing, makes or breaks an essay. "For every pen writes its own sort of essay," and the quality of the pen decides the quality of the writing (*Certain Personal Matters* 120): "Wed any man to his proper pen, and the delights of composition and the birth of an essay are assured" (120). While this suggests that tools of mediation like pens, papers, and ink already override the organic body and cast his agency into doubt, Wells's subsequent ranking of different types of pens, papers, and ink still follows the pastoral, antimachine tradition by judging how much each bears the trace of the agentic subject and his embodied exertion. Only a quill, so it seems, should be used for literature, because the "quirky, idle noises" of the quill and its uneven imprint gives it the "subtle informality" and "delightful easiness" most suitable to activate the literary faculties of the writer (120). The cheap steel pen—uniform, precise, and much easier to use—stands for the "beginning of the inferior essay" because it only produces a "bald, clear, scientific style" (120). The typewriter comes at the very bottom of the hierarchy of writing, because "you could no more get an essay out of a typewriter than you could play a sonata upon its keys" (121). Even a hard steel pen shows more of the embodied imprint of the controlling intelligence wielding that pen. But a typewriter, "[i]f mechanical clitter-clatter did not render composition impossible," "would still be beneath the honour of a literary man" (121).

Years later, Wells would proudly declare himself a skillful user of the typewriter in his testimonial for the portable Corona typewriter. In this testimonial, published in a 1921 ad, Wells claims "I have needed a typewriter for years" and states that he finds "complete satisfaction" with the portable Corona, which is "light and small," "hardy, willing and easy," "exactly the typewriter for an author like me" (Cane). The ad continues to claim that "[w]ith Corona's help, H. G. Wells has written the story of the human race—'The Outline of History'—and achieved a literary masterpiece. You, too, can hasten your success with this wonderful, modern writing machine" (Cane). These might be hyperbolic words by the advertisers, but Wells certainly lent his endorsement, denoting a significant change of heart. Still, his earlier reservations are noteworthy because they touch on a unique dimension entailed by typewriting: its perceived severing of the organic body from the fruits of his creative mind. Many other machines of speed, while offering a prosthetic extension of human faculties, also lead to what Mark Seltzer calls "the double logic of technology as prosthesis," in which "self-extension" is accompanied by "self-cancelling," a certain disembodiment of the agentic self ("Serial Killers" 99).[1] But typewriting as a prosthetic extension of the hand in writing speed seems to threaten a greater degree of "self-cancelling," largely because of the distinct spatial setup of the typewriter in order to ensure maximum speed.

The typewriter's arrangement of keys does not follow alphabetical order but the QWERTY system, which positions the most often used letters far apart from each other. This is designed so that the upward-striking type-bars would not clash together when typing at speed. But this arrangement, serving foremost the mechanical needs of the typewriter rather than the expediency of the human operator, means that the fingers would have to cover maximum distance in the typing of most English words. The un-alphabetical positions of the keys, with their corresponding letters, must be memorized before words can be impressed on the paper. The need for memorizing the special positions of the keys leads to a "blind" dimension whereby fastest speed in typing is achieved by not looking at the typed work nor at the machine at all, but by working "blindfolded" from memory, whereby the appropriate nerves and muscles are automatically triggered. This also explains why before the introduction of the "view typewriter" in 1898, all models wrote invisible lines, which became visible only several lines down. As is stated by Angelo Beyerlen, the engineer and founder of the first German typewriter business:

> In writing by hand, the eye must constantly watch the written line and only that. It must … guide the hand through each movement. … By contrast, after one presses down briefly on a key, the typewriter creates in the proper position on the paper a complete letter, which not only is untouched by the writer's hand but is also located in a place entirely apart from where the hands work. Why should the writer look at the paper when everything there occurs dependably and well as long as the keys on the fingerboard are used correctly? (qtd. in Kittler, *Discourse Networks* 195)

The typewriting scholar Hisao Yamada claims that in typewriting the fingers are not directed by the intentional will of the typist, but by the "subconscious cortical reflex of the cerebrum in response to visual stimuli from the manuscript" (qtd. in Wershler-Henry 233). The process of typing has been so internalized that the typist's minimal unit of motion is sequences of letters, rather than individual letters, and at least 400 hours of repetitive, disciplined practice is needed to develop enough cortical reflect patterns in order to attain fast speed. This, as Wershler-Henry points out, means that professional typists type reflexively, "as

---

[1] This opposition between human agency and prosthetic technology is questioned by Bernard Stiegler. Stiegler argues that, from the anthropological point of view, human evolution is always a history of technical evolution wherein human bodily alterations are never simply biological but technical, incorporating the use of new technics and tools. In this sense, human essence is predicated on technicity, and the body's interiority and exteriority "compose with each other" rather than oppose each other. The prosthesis is not just exterior to the body to be used by an interior agency but the "very constitution of this body *qua* 'human'" (152–53).

part of an assemblage that processes strings of letters based on the criteria established by the human/machine interface that have little to do with syntax, meaning, or alphabetical order" (233). This seems to encourage an image of the passive typist working automatically to the absence of mind.

In *Discourse Networks*, Kittler sees the unique spatial keyboard arrangement of the typewriter and its "blind" dimension as leading to the domination of the human by the machine. This late-nineteenth-century technological invention requires repetitive, rhythmic working of the human muscles and nerves, the touching of fingers, and, in many cases where dictating is involved, the stretching of keen ears. The tactile, machine-tackling body is, to Kittler, dangerously free from the working of the controlling human intellect, as it severs, disrupts, mediates, and impersonalizes the mind. Typewriting, according to Kittler, drives a mechanical wedge between subjectivity and writing, a wedge that "unlinks hand, eye, and letters" (195). Staging typewriting as the archetypal modernist technology, Kittler claims that writing is now not only mediated through the machine but is also fragmented, because the artificial spacing of keys and the dislocation of where the hands work, where the letters strike, and where the eyes look, if at all, breaks the illusion of handwriting as a "continuous transition from nature to culture" (194). Whereas handwriting reflects the individual hand as guided by the mind, and allows for the immediate translation from mind to hand and from the spiritual to the physical, typewriting abstracts the body from writing and impersonalizes and fragments writing. "Spatially designated and discrete signs—that, rather than increase in speed, was the real innovation of the typewriter" (Kittler 193)—this, to him, is crucial in impacting on the symbolic system of representation, and particularly on modernist literature where fragmentation and impersonality and the taking apart of language and its defamiliarization are the reigning qualities.

The late nineteenth-century typewriter girl, typing to the dictation of the male boss, particularly seems to embody the fragmentary and "blind" dimension of typewriting. *Pitman's Typewriter Manual* advises students that in order to reach fastest speed and thus most profitable marketability, the typist must completely denounce the "bad habit" of looking at her work or checking for errors, a desire viewed as the narcissistic trace of her own self and intentional mind (157–58). Only when the use of eyes is given up and herself erased will the least errors be committed. This would allow the body's muscles and nerves to take over so that the words could move unread and unobstructed from the dictating male mind to the paper, through the transparent medium of the typist. This "blind" nature of typewriting work—which seeks to train primarily the tactile body, not to elevate the mind but to seemingly erase it—further reinforces the image of the typewriter girl as one of obedience and passive service. What is more significant is that the typewriter girl is not just subject to the dictates of the male boss, but also to those of the typing machine in order to pursue fastest speed.

The typewriter does extend the hand in writing speed, but it is also obvious that during that process the limits of the human subject are impacted upon in a substantial way, so that the human operator seems to be adapting to and chasing after and imitating the fast machine. Not only is the human mind seemingly inhibited or suspended because reading for meaning or comprehension hinders high-speed performance, but the human body is increasingly traversed by mechanized speed, to the extent that the body is perceived as an inefficient obstacle, to be overcome in order to attain maximum speed. The only obstacle seems to be the human body, which should be disciplined to adapt to the infinite speed potential of the machine. In a 1909 article "Typing like Lightening," the world-record-holder Miss Rose Fritz urges "repetitive practice" so that readers could aspire to emulate her "lightening" speed of 107 words per minute (237). Proclaiming herself to be "a firm believer" in this repetitive practice, Fritz praises the merits of "constant typing and re-typing of particular phrases till they can be run off in perfect form at top speed" (237). The typing body should be made faster, and also rid of any whims and unruly disobedience. Fritz particularly stresses the need to rein in the body by warning against any tendency toward being slipshod, or letting down the body's guard in the hope of later correction: "Little faults and failings neglected in this way quickly become habits; and habits—especially bad ones—are tenacious things, difficult to eradicate" when "they have become *too much of oneself* to be remedied" (237; emphasis added). Though this admission points to the stubborn presence of the erring and individually trace-leaving human body, which has a natural tendency to slacken and delay and often fails to conform, the article stresses that the "pure" state without any need for remedy is indeed the machine-like precision and consistency of the typewriter, a state which the human operator must emulate. Any signs that speak to the presence of whims or disobedience, signs traditionally valorized as human agentic willpower, are to be emptied out.

It seems, then, that what is in need of erasure is really the typing human in all her constitutive elements, so that she becomes a pure instrument of speed, and the conduit through which the machine impresses and words flow. This pure state is the state of the machine, and any sign of obstruction or resistance is a sign of defect and malady. This explains what Christopher Keep calls the "quasi-medical" discourse of the typing manuals of the 1890s, represented best of all in *Pitman's Typewriter Manual* ("Blinded by the Type" 157). "It is with the object of radically curing defects noticeable in average typewriting that we enter upon the first portion of this Manual," declares the book's opening statement (2). One such "cure" is, of course, persistent "practice," which will "do much to bring the muscles into perfect condition" (22). But the manual is further dissatisfied with the typing body's irregular reflexes, pulsations, and spasms, and urges the typist to reform her posture, muscle, and nerves to match the exigencies of the machine, so that consistent performance could be ensured and instinctive muscle and nerve reactions automatically triggered. The unruly and defect-ridden human body must be tamed and treated to match its mechanical counterpart, and care and discipline of the typist body must be maintained even to the exclusion of certain exhaustive leisure activities or harmful eating or sleeping patterns. The ultimate purpose is, as one chapter in another manual is titled, "Making Your Body an Efficient Machine" (qtd. in Olwell, "Body Types" 52).

"This little piano-like machine": The Typewriter and the "Musical Steam Engine"

The imperative on the human typist to empty out her agentic self and become a transparent medium for the machine aggravates anxieties over the threat to the organic body, and triggers even greater insistence on the irreconcilable opposition between the human and the mechanical. But one interesting example for further analysis is the piano, a modern machine of sound often compared with the type-writer during the early years of typewriting. In "The Solitary Cyclist," Sherlock Holmes may conclude that a pianist has "a spirituality about the face" which "the typewriter does not generate," but at the first sight of the piano teacher, Miss Violet Smith, even the sharp-eyed Holmes "nearly fell into the error" of supposing that she is a typist (Doyle, "Solitary Cyclist" 3). "[C]ommon to both professions," as Holmes points out to Watson, is "the spatulate finger-end," a slight flattening to the finger tips as a result of prolonged hitting of the keys (3). Pitman's 1888 typing manual also compares typing to piano-playing, claiming that women's skills at piano-playing make them ideal candidates for typewriting—"The type-writer is especially adapted to feminine fingers. They seem to be made for type-writing. The type-writing involves no hard labor, and no more skill than playing the piano" (qtd. in Keep, "Cultural Work" 405).

Piano music is strongly linked with organic emotion, expressing the musical passions and creative imagination of the pianist while inducing strong sensations in the audience. Yet the piano in the mid-nineteenth century was also viewed as a "musical steam engine," a technological invention producing similar industrial rhythms and energies as factory machinery (Ketabgian 147). This is because, long after Bartolomeo Cristofori invented the modern piano in 1700 by using wooden hammers to strike its strings, the piano was greatly improved in the nineteenth century by technologies developed in the Industrial Revolution. The 1822 pianoforte produced by the English firm Broadwood, for instance, contained a skeleton of iron bars and plates. Like the steam engine, which harnessed contrasting forces of hydraulic expansion and compression, the piano used heavier hammers; thicker, tighter, high-quality piano wires for strings; and precision casting for massive iron frames, which produced higher levels of tension, dynamic contrast, and powerful emotional expression (151). Whereas the typewriter extends the human hand in writing, the piano as a machine of music mimics and amplifies the organic sound in emotive expression. This interesting combination of mechanical power and emotive energy allows a more accommodating approach to the human–machine encounter which may also illuminate a study of the typewriter.

In many ways, the piano anticipates the later arrival of the typewriter, partly because it is also played by using a keyboard: a row of eighty-eight black and white keys standing for different music notes that the performer presses down with the fingers and thumbs of both hands. Many early writing machines resembled the piano, and the first prototype typewriter patented by Christopher Sholes and Samuel Soule in 1868 used eleven piano keys, both black and white, laid out in two rows. Scholes was earlier inspired by an article he had read in the *Scientific American*, which reported on the Pratt writing machine and described it as a "literary piano" (qtd. in Current, "The Original Typewriter" 392). One source suggests that Sholes's first mental image of the typewriter was informed by the operation of a piano, when a short type bar would swing up at the pressing of a certain key, like the way "a pianoforte's hammer" would strike from below against the strings (Beeching 3).

When the typewriter later came into common usage, many commentators remarked on the affinity between the two machines. An 1892 article "Our Pepper Box" in *Pick-Me-Up* describes the typewriter as "this little piano-like machine" (418), and one 1897 French advertisement for the Hurtu typewriter portrays a young, fashionably dressed woman raising her fingers high in the air above a typewriter, much in the fashion of a pianist ready to strike the keys of a piano (qtd. in Gray 495). An 1893 piece in *Women's Penny Paper* further compares the two instruments in a section titled "Typewriters v. Pianos." Though it ends up calling for "More typewriters and fewer pianos!" and urges women hoping to be journalists to learn the "invaluable" skill of typewriting and ditch the impractical piano-playing, it also implies that, for most of its readers, the two skills are quite similar and the switch to typewriting is not likely to be difficult (423). Women's press often referred to women's suitability for typewriting because of their piano-playing. *Girl's Own Paper*, for instance, declares in 1888 that typewriting is "an occupation peculiarly fitted for [women's] nimble fingers" ("The Type-writer and Type-writing" 745). Even Gissing's New Woman typist Rhoda in *The Odd Women*, when encouraging the youngest Madden sister Monica to learn typewriting, asks if she has taken piano lessons, for a pianist's "light, supple and quick" fingers are ideally suited for typewriting (36).

Pianists, of course, decry this equating of piano-playing with typewriting and insist on the higher creative merit of the former; one pianist, advising a disappointed mother in an 1895 joke in *Boys of England*, quips that "Your daughter will not become a pianist, but after practice with her fingers she can become a typist" ("Letting Her Down Easy" 208). This mockery of typewriting as an inferior and corrupt form of piano-playing, however, still shows a belief in the two's interchangeability, particularly where young girls are concerned.

Indeed, in terms of techniques there are many similarities in the operation of the two instruments. One of the early methods of piano-playing is the five-finger practice, as is detailed in *Musical Standard* in 1895 ("Methods of Practice" 216). This involves the use of all fingers in striking different keys, a method also advocated later in typewriting—the "All Finger Method"—for maximum speed (Wershler-Henry 234). A nimble-fingered lady pianist finds it much easier to learn typewriting, but typewriting also proves to be beneficial for musicians. *The Musical Standard* writes in 1896 that the five-finger method of typewriting makes the muscles and fingers "equally exercised and evenly developed," "which must be of service to the pianist"; furthermore, because the touch of good typewriting is "very light, firm and staccato," learning to typewrite can greatly "improve" a "heavy touch on the piano" and offers better training in "velocity" and "accuracy" ("Typewriting and Touch" 327).

Even the "blind" dimension in typewriting is also evident in piano-playing, where the pianist using the scales practice is urged to memorize a sequence of keys for the corresponding notes and aim for the "automatic training of the hand" to select the "proper combination of black and white keys" without looking at the keyboard ("Methods of Practice" 216). As the champion typist Miss Rose Fritz declares in 1909, good typewriting is just like good piano-playing, and typists should follow the example of the pianists and only direct their attention to the copy: "no good pianist looks at the keys of the instrument; he looks at the music from which he is playing" ("Typing like the Lightening" 237); "The position of the notes must, of course, be learnt in the first instance; but that once accomplished, the keyboard is glanced at as seldom as possible" (237). Remington ads of the time also referred to this "blind" affinity to advertise their typewriters: "It should be no more necessary for a typist to see the typing than it is for a pianist to see the keyboard" (Adler 176). Another similarity is that, like typewriting, piano-playing is also spatially discrete, involving the dislocation of where the hands work, where the keys strike (producing the sound), and where the eyes look, which breaks the illusion of a continuous process of organic sound production.

Apart from techniques and mechanical arrangement, the piano and the typewriter further claim a shared gender dimension, since both were operated predominantly by nimble-fingered women. As one of the most important luxuries for middle-class families in the nineteenth century, the piano was an important means of status display, and piano-playing was an essential feminine accomplishment for middle-class women. The harpsichord had been the musical instrument of choice for most families in the eighteenth century, but by the nineteenth century the piano's adoption of heavier hammers, increased stress, and more dramatic gradations of volume turned it into an extremely versatile instrument not just for concert settings but for domestic use as well (Burgan 53). By the second decade of the century, even families with modest incomes could afford a piano (Pflueger 469), and in 1847, 20,000 pianos were produced in England alone (Wainwright 60).

In 1883, the *Music Opinion and Music Trade Journal* notes that the piano is the "finest instrument" in the world and "complete in itself" because of its "orchestral effects"; for women in particular, "the pianoforte came to be regarded not merely as the only instrument for a lady to cultivate, but also as one which every lady was bound to learn" ("Emancipation of Women" 181).The piano became popular not just because it is a key emblem for middle-class progress and a particularly bourgeois instrument for status display and social climbing, but also because it is crucial in maintaining the gendered domestic ideology of the middle class. Closely associated with the idealized feminine image of the "angel in the house," the piano-playing woman crystallizes all the virtues of beauty, leisure, harmony, purity, and refinement attributed to the private bourgeois home. In Thackeray's *Vanity Fair* (1847–48), nothing is more telltale or heart-wrenching about the ruin and loss of status of the Sedleys than Amelia's forced forfeiture of her beautiful white piano, and the very first thing Dobbin does to help the Sedleys' and particularly Amelia's sullied image is to buy back her piano.

Music is the most sensual of the creative arts and appeals directly to the tactile body. Literary works abound in the portrayal of the penetrating, mesmeric impact of music, linking it, as is the case in Thomas Hardy's "The Fiddler of the Reels" (1893), with Dionysian abandon and devilish passion. Piano-playing for concert use since the eighteenth century is often associated with virtuosos such as Mozart and Liszt, who embody the Romantic ideal of the artist as genius, capable of spontaneous, sublime creations that produces trance-like fervors in the audience. For most ordinary middle-class women players in the domestic sphere, such experiences of the sublime are not to be expected, but aesthetic pleasure and emotional refinement are still crucial targets encouraged in piano-playing as an integral part of middle-class women's education. Nineteen-century education for middle-class males did not encourage piano-playing for amateur performance. The music historian David Wainwright cites a Victorian commentator who observed that "gentlemen also sang and duets were in high favour, but play the piano gentlemen did not, that being considered a task only fit for ladies and professional musicians" (147). The piano is closely linked with middle-class women, partly because its sensual and emotional capacities are seen as congenial to women, in harmony with women's perceived embodiment of organic nature and sympathetic sensibility.

But the piano is also a machine of sound, producing mechanical sounds without natural cadences. It mimics but also intensifies the natural voice with mechanical energy and technical precision. Working powerfully on the sensations of the listener, the piano embodies the increased reach of the machine and its potency over the human. By surpassing the organic sound and harboring new, more intensified expressive vigor, it offers a prosthetic extension of the human subject through harnessing both organic and mechanical energies. This prominence of mechanical power is seen even in the case of Romantic prodigies like Liszt, famous for creating "Liszt-mania" in his audience. An 1876 caricature of Liszt, entitled "The Bayreuth

Musical Steam Engine," celebrates the great virtuoso's musical power by evoking a factory scene, with the piano-playing master portrayed as a controller of an assemblage of industrial devices of dial, bell, and steam whistle, while his agent fires the piano's furnace and a French horn serves as a smokestack (qtd. in Ketabgian 148). Music geniuses such as Liszt incarnate the Romantic ideal of sublime creativity, but to the nineteenth-century public their inimitable magical power is also greatly intensified and extended by the machine of music. Such power is at least partly attributable to geniuses' ability to unleash the piano's mechanical energies. Liszt and Beethoven are famous for projecting a powerful sense of their unique self through, for instance, Liszt's use of the single-instrument piano recital as a "musical soliloquy" or Beethoven's musical "speaking" style of "flowing melodies" (150, 151). But this highly individualized, speaking-voice type of organic emotive expression is mediated through the piano and accelerated by its mechanical prowess.

Another example of such human–machine melding is that, for the pianist to play the piano well and achieve maximum levels of sublimity and emotive affect, he has to endure long, punitive hours of repetitive practice and disciplined training that seeks to mimic the mechanical perfection of the piano. The virtuoso is therefore a combination of opposing forces. He is both the Romantic genius artist and also the repetitively training automaton; both the source of creative imagination and also the incarnation of industrial rhythms.

This automation of the human body comes, of course, with a price—a price that, like the typewriting training that came decades later, involves harsh regimentation of the unruly body, to an extent where the body has to be tamed and cured of its defects to match the exigencies of the machine. As one noted Victorian pianist tells an admiring audience in an 1895 article in *Musical Standard*, the human hand is flawed and an extremely "dissatisfying" "contrivance quite curiously unadapted to the purpose" of playing the piano ("Piano Playing without Practicing" 350). "Not naturally fitted" for the piano, the fingers are uneven and of varying lengths and strengths, and the "tendons of three fingers are all tied together in a manner most provoking from a pianist's point of view" (350). Only through "incessant exercising of the rebellious muscles" can one tame and cure this flawed body (350). "The spirit is willing but the flesh is weak"; the unruly body should be "persuaded" to do the pianist's bidding and no longer stand in the way of the piano's mechanical perfection (351). However, this does not mean a decimation of the organic. Using quasi-medical terms, the article claims that the new method of corrective practice, based on "sound anatomical principles," involves contracting the muscles so that the "waste materials" of "stale, used-up blood" are expelled and "fresh, sound blood" is injected from the arteries. New flows of revitalizing blood, in this case, are not entirely traced to the human heart, but generated by the "unnatural," mechanical practice of piano-playing. This mechanical, repetitive practice bends the body's natural instincts to the will of the machine, and gives the piano a sort of reproductive power whereby a machine-twisted body, with new fresh blood, comes into being.

This automation of the organic body does not just produce new sources of vital blood, but is also capable of expressive powers. In the case of the virtuoso, his role as mere automaton does not seem to curtail his concomitant performance as the passionate artist, but serves instead to help fuel and magnify his genius-like singularity. Playing this highly complicated machine of sound demands near-automatic technical skills, attained through strict discipline and repeated practice, but it also paradoxically facilitates a powerful expression of artistic creativity and individual passion.

If the genius artist could synchronize the mechanical and the emotive in such accommodating ways, the same potential for constructive improvement is not completely absent in ordinary middle-class women's piano-playing. Maria Edgeworth, in her essay on "Female Accomplishments, Masters, and Governesses" in *Practical Education* (1798), may complain of the forced labor behind middle-class girls' piano-playing, and urges mothers not to turn their daughters into an "automaton for eight hours in every day for fifteen years" at the piano (qtd. in Burgan 60). But piano-playing still expands powerfully the expression of emotion even where genius is lacking and mediocrity reigns. For these ordinary women, although their playing is often encouraged more for the moral inculcation of industry, discipline, the habit of application, and adherence to rules than for the sublime expression of aesthetic passion (Pflueger 471), the expressive capacities of the piano, and especially its percussive aspects, makes dramatic "salon" music possible, allowing a channel for emotive assertion. As the piano historian Cyril Ehrlich points out, simple chords and arpeggios could be made to sound as impressive as contrapuntal patterns, and young Victorian women often played for effect by pounding on the keys, a popular practice for the amateur (12). In performing a popular battle piece composition, one young lady used a special "swell" pedal to amplify the effect and simulate the sound of a cannon explosion, which may be technically crude but is still emotionally strong in effect (Burgan 57). As a complex assembly uniting human emotion with mechanical precision, the piano thus offers an illuminating lesson in how the human–machine encounter may work to their mutual facilitation, and not necessarily at the cost of the human.

The "Remingtonese": Creative Literature and Mechanical Typescript

If the emotive power mediated through and intensified by the piano's mechanical rhythms is celebrated as sublime, then what about the typewriter? Typewriting's pressing of keys produces letters and texts, which works on the eye and mind of the reader, as well as sounds, which aligns it with the piano. But this sound is noisy, monotonous, and repetitive, devoid of the emotional nuances or variations of the piano and jarring on the ears of the listener. In many ways it acts as a forceful reminder of the industrial rhythms of the factory floor. This adds to the impersonality and dehumanization which the typewritten text—uniform, reproducible, and lacking the embodied imprint of the human subject in handwriting—already suffers from. An 1894 piece entitled "Some Literary Typewriters" may seem to praise the typewriter over the piano, but by claiming that the piano is more liable to abuse by bad players whereas the typewriter's sound is "much more soothing to the ear" because it is much more uniform even when used by inexperienced operators, it again reinforces the perception of typewriting as more mechanical and monotonous and less accommodating to human interference (321).

Yet even this most obviously mechanical side of typewriting is not totally devoid of a regenerative potential. Henry James, an artist of great aura and creativity, provides a case in point. James suffered from a severe bout of rheumatism and fatigue in January 1897, and decided to use a typewriter and a secretary for dictation. He did learn to use the typewriter himself later on and typed his own private letters, but for his creative writings he preferred to dictate to his secretary who typed on a Remington Standard. The "admirable and expensive" typewriter's clicking sound, as James wrote in one letter to a friend, both constrains him, weaving "an embroidered veil of sound" over his efforts at unfettered communication, but also enables him by "bridging our silences" and embedding the machine's clatter somewhat in the very fabric and soundscape of his writing (qtd. in Hutchison 157).

It is when James dictates to the typewriting secretary to compose his literary works that his own musical voice blends seamlessly with the clicking sound of the Remington Standard, creating an enriching interplay between the human voice, the creative imagination, and the clicking machine. Hazel Hutchison argues that James's mature writings have an "expansive" and "leisurely" pace and are meant to be read aloud, a distinct quality impacted by his resorting to dictation after buying his typewriter (148). The dictation highlights James's speaking voice, which has a strong musical quality, lending an allusive pattern of echoes and resonance to the style of his later works. But in this highly distinctive soundscape, the mechanical, continuous clatter of his Remington typewriter also plays a part. His secretary, Mary Weld, wrote in her diary that James "had a melodious voice," and that "typewriting for him was exactly like accompanying a singer on the piano" (qtd. in Hutchison 149). Theodora Bosanquet, who later replaced Weld in 1907, wrote that:

He had reached a stage at which the click of a Remington machine acted as a positive spur. He found it more difficult to compose to the music of any other make. During the fortnight when the Remington was out of order he dictated to an Oliver typewriter with evident discomfort, and he found it almost impossibly disconcerting to speak to something that made no responsive sound at all. (150)

Two interesting points stand out from this passage. One is that the Remington typewriter makes a different sound from the Oliver—a sound that reassures and appeases James, almost like a living, speaking, and responding being. This being is distinct and individual, and seems to defy the familiar notion of typewriters as uniform, standard, and indistinguishable machines. The second is that instead of making a monotonous, mechanical clatter that threatens to annihilate the well-spring of creative imagination, the typewriter actually serves like an accompanying piano to echo, supplement, and amplify the human voice and its emotional, creative expression. In the case of James, it even proves to be an active spur and prompter, without which the poetic inspiration is gagged and suspended.

The Remington is not just a useful tool to relieve James's writers' cramp; it also actively impacts on his literary style and output, with friends and later critics claiming to know at what point of James' works he began to dictate to the typewriter. James himself would later call his own dictated work "Remingtonese" (qtd. in Hutchison 148), crediting the typewriter for an indispensable role in creating a new, medley language of both mechanical and organic rhythms. This language is indisputably literary and creative, but it is also contributed to and enabled by a constructive cooperation between the genius novelist and the typewriting machine.

James's case offers a good example of the invigorating assemblage of human agency and prosthetic technology. In ways not far removed from those of the piano, whose mechanical sounds work to facilitate the genius and self-projection of the virtuoso, the clicking typewriter could also work with and not necessarily obstruct organic forces, thus blurring the boundaries between the two. In a few late 1890s and early 1900 stories on the typewriter girl, the plotline hints at this more positive vision of the human–machine encounter, reinterpreted as co-adaptation. More than anything else, this more nuanced approach demonstrates itself in the stories' portrayal of the relationship between the typewriter girl and the creative writer.

The bulk of these typewriting stories still highlight the unbridgeable gap between the typewriter girl and the creative writer. Even when they portray the creative writer as a young, struggling man hoping to make it in the big city together with the typewriter girl, the sense of camaraderie and mutual sympathy between the two is not sufficient to override the fundamental difference in their situation. The stories may sympathize with the plight of the typewriter girl and the tolls of her harsh labor, but in depicting her passive resignation they tend to attribute this to her closeness to the machine and her corruptibility by its mechanizing power. The most the typewriter girl could do, as is shown in "Dunbar's First Lesson" (1899), is to act as the subordinate helpmate to the aspiring male writer, who, despite his adversity, would never compromise his principles even amid a world of mechanization.

One story, "Phoebe Strange" (1897, Figure 2.1), however, stands out in this group by giving a more agentic role to the typewriter girl and debunking the myth of the auratic writer. The story's protagonist is Phoebe Strange, who is a London typewriter girl helping to type the manuscript of a young, struggling writer, Raymond. Both are portrayed in terms of hardship, with the young man, "pallid" and poorly dressed, presenting to Phoebe a manuscript that looks dog-eared and dirty, as if from multiple rejections (126). Poverty and struggle, however, does not prevent the young man from remembering his manners when he apologizes for making Phoebe work late into the night. Phoebe, "unaccustomed to any kind of sympathy," answers with raised eyes and a smile. A budding friendship ensues,

Figure 2.1 "Phoebe Strange," *The English Illustrated Magazine*, May 1897, p. 125. ProQuest LLC.

motivated by shared loneliness in an impersonal, alienating modern city, where Phoebe has "come into contact with very few men" (126).

This scene aligns the story with the gritty realism of other tales where London is presented as a "mean" and "sordid" whirlpool (*A Bachelor Girl in London* 167), full of "the used up feeling of the air, and the close, sickly smell" of dust ("A Type-writing Episode" 348). The love and company of a fellow striver is the only thing that makes the "great, never-ceasing hum of London" "worthwhile" ("Dunbar's First Lesson" 72). This love relationship is also highly unconventional, as young men and women meet in chance encounters without introduction and often ignorant of family backgrounds. In this story, a chance meeting in the street in the rain gives a boost to the two young people's acquaintance, when Phoebe offers to lend an umbrella to Raymond. "She felt no more hesitation about asking him to enter her lodging than she would have done to invite him to come into her father's house a few years ago," before her father died and left her all alone (127). This casual spontaneity in their friendship extends a ray of comfort to both young people, after years of "forlorn" struggle where "you seem to work from the time you get up till you go to bed" and have "pretty much ceased to care for anything" (128). With Phoebe's friendship and encouragement, Raymond eventually finishes a great book and becomes famous. Just when happiness seems within reach, Raymond reveals to her a pre-existing engagement at home with a waiting country maiden whom he no longer loves. Phoebe quietly tells him to honor his promise, waves goodbye, and stoically carries on her struggle.

In its romance plot and in the portrayal of the relationship between the typewriter girl and the aspiring male writer, this story replicates many of the familiar themes of other stories. Phoebe is the muse and inspiration to the struggling writer, a ready helper and nurturer who plays the traditional feminine role of moral encouragement and quiet support. Despite their camaraderie, they eventually embark on completely different paths, as the creative writer attains success and recognition while the typewriter girl still toils in her menial labor. Yet the story also abounds in details that underline the agency and resourcefulness of the typewriter girl and her greater power of adapting to the fast-paced modern city than the disillusioned male writer. Phoebe is more than the passive woman who could at best serve as the medium for male success, with little agency of her own. Her vast typewriting experience, which includes typing "a dozen" literary manuscripts "more or less like" Raymond's first story (126), gives her a critical eye for quality and promise. This comes in handy when she later judges Raymond's work to be "ever so much better" than before and encourages him to carry on (128). Phoebe is not at all the passive, obedient copywriter mechanically taking down every note dictated by the writer, but rather the active party who comes up with the idea that Raymond should write a long novel instead of short stories. Both in the idea of the novel and in the execution of that idea, the typewriter girl plays the active role, pushing and propelling a hesitant Raymond.

When Raymond shies away, Phoebe makes him "a rather unconventional suggestion," proposing that he should write by installments and dictate to her right on the spot so as to speed up the writing. She even declines his offer of a dinner date until he finishes his daily installment. As he then dictates to her for hours in her room, Raymond's creative rhythm works in tandem with that of her clicking typewriter. "For a long time there was no sound beside the click, click of the machine," echoing and responding to Raymond, bringing out the best of his creative potential and injecting "a new lease of life" to his writing (128). Raymond's work before their cooperation has languished in mediocrity, but it reaches a much higher creative level afterwards, an elevation certainly unleashed and sped up by the combined energies of his literary efforts and Phoebe's typewriting. As he rightly says to her in gratitude, "it is half yours," "as much yours as mine" (130). Phoebe is not just the love interest and "inspiration" to Raymond; their new chorus would not soar high without her clicking typewriter and its urgent rhythms (130).

In this sense, the typewriter girl is far from just "my fairy" or "my Mascotte," as Raymond tenderly calls Phoebe in gratitude (130). Phoebe's deep immersion in machine culture does not deprive her of all sense of agency, but actually enables the construction of a new type of fast-paced, efficient, organized, and machine-savvy women capable of adapting to and making use of modern speed culture. The typewriter's time-compressing speed here becomes a source of regeneration, even extending its power to Raymond's creative writing and pushing him toward higher levels of emotive expression. Through the typewriter girl's participation in this speed culture, the creative writer is in his turn invigorated and expanded.

When Raymond can no longer face the humiliation after several rejections, Phoebe proves to be made of tougher material by taking up the full responsibility of marketing the book: "I'll be your agent and you shall hear no more of it till it is sold" (130). Phoebe "carefully cleaned some of the pages with bread," "smoothed the dog's-eared corners" with a hot iron, then re-typewrites the first page and the last. Though the cleaning, ironing, and typewriting speaks to traditional feminine tasks, she demonstrates a keen business sense of how presentation and style works to one's advantage. Her decision to send the book to a very good publisher—"too good for my stuff," as Raymond protests (130)—shows a shrewd instinct for the literary market that is eventually proved right. The book quickly sells out, and when Raymond reappears he is able to sport a brand new "black cut-away coat and a tall hat, the first time within Phoebe's experience" (132). The struggling male writer's success story, from rags to riches, is very much enabled by the active input, intelligence, knowledge, and dogged determination of the typewriter girl.

Even at the end of the story, when the narrative returns Phoebe to the self-sacrificial role reserved for ideal Victorian femininity, she is portrayed in an image of quiet strength. After Raymond marries the country girl and comes back to see her one last time, he couldn't stumble out one word of love even at farewell. Phoebe takes the initiative: "She drew closer, raising her chin. He stooped to kiss her. But as his lips touched Phoebe's she turned and passed through the small garden" (133). Just as she has led all the way in their joint book "venture," Phoebe is leading now in their love-making and in deciding how their love is to end. The narrative ends as Raymond the creative writer bows out of the modern city and retires to the country, while Phoebe the typewriter girl trudges on in London, stoically but doggedly.

This story further blurs the opposition between the typewriter girl and the creative writer by dethroning the latter from his height of unsullied originality. It suggests that much of the literature of the *fin-de-siècle* period, or the "bread and butter," run-of-the-mill stories Raymond publishes in magazines, is already informed by industrial rhythms and manufactured emotions, and no more original or creative than the typewriter's copy work. Raymond confesses to being "in a rut," "beaten to the average," and "kneaded into a plodding journeyman" years after coming to London hoping to make a success of himself (128). As he tells Phoebe, his stories are formulaic, repetitive, always "harping on one eternal string," and endowed with "as much originality ... as your typewriter" (128). Even his great book marks its so-called greatness by its market popularity and the five print-runs it goes into soon after publication. Its acclaimed realism is, after all, itself based on what S. Brooke Cameron, discussing Victorian realist fiction's affinity to photography, calls "a technique of duplication" which copies voices and images of reality (133). Like typewriting, which copies and repeats and charges by price-per-word, the literary manuscript is similarly embroiled in a shared cultural scene of commodities and industrial rhythms, with sell-by dates and cost–profit calculations. As sales now become the key barometer of success in a market increasingly dominated by mass readers, it is little wonder that the bulk of *fin-de-siècle* literature is what Grant Allen calls "unpretentious" stories that "slip down easily," guaranteed to appease the mass public before new, lookalike stories pop up further along the literary assembly line (qtd. in Morton 113).

The *fin-de-siècle* writer, as Gissing writes in *New Grub Street* (1891), his quintessential novel about late Victorian authorship and its corruption by the market, is increasingly turning into what Marian Yule calls a "Literary Machine," which turns out books and articles at great speed for the highest bidder (80). Writers and authors are increasingly the tradesmen, touting and selling their ware in a fiercely competitive market flooded by freelance authors. The ranks of "authors, editors, journalists, reporters" swelled exponentially in those years, reaching 8,000 in a 1891 census and 11,000 by 1901 (Morton 61). Though books and periodicals had expanded exponentially at the same time, the supply of writers far outstripped demand. Morton writes that some editors had around 3,000 unsolicited manuscripts a year to choose from, and a surprising number of periodicals never paid their contributors anything at all (68). As Arnold Bennett bitterly complains, "the freelance is a tramp touting for odd jobs, a pedlar crying stuff which is bought usually in default of better" (qtd. in Morton 69). Only people who have failed at all other trades would enter literature as a last resort—"When a man who knows how to put an English sentence grammatically together has no other resource left in life he sells himself, body and soul, in the last resort to the public press, and produces the fabric they call literature" (Allen "Trade of Author" 267).

With writers increasingly becoming literary peddlers and much of literature, as Raymond sees it, no less repetitive and unoriginal as "your typewriter" ("Phoebe Strange" 128), the lines between automation and original creation are increasingly blurred. This is given a further twist of irony in another story, "The Strange Tale of a Type-Writer" (1890), wherein the narrator pokes fun at the state of literature by claiming that a typewriter could compose creative literature just as well as a human writer. In a light-hearted tone, the story gives a fantastical account of how the type-writer machine, after being so long in the service of the narrator and receiving so much "stimulation" and "currents of thought passing through it," is actually "learn-ing to think." It "seemed to meet or even to anticipate my action," "outrunning the pressure of my fingers," and "recording ... of its own motion, the next following letter" (679). This next letter may not always be the author's designed one, but it is never, following the preceding ones, a wrongly spelled word.

The consummate evidence that the typewriter is catching up with and even upstaging the human subject is its ability to write creative literature by itself. Upon returning home one day after a few days' absence, the narrator hears a clicking noise in her work-room, and finds, to her shock and eerie bewilderment, that the typewriter is working by itself. Before her trip the narrator had used an invention of her own that would obviate the need of stopping to change the sheets of the paper at the end of the page. This invention has now allowed the clicking type-writer to keep reeling off sheets of finished papers and spreading them all over the floor. When the narrator picks up the papers, she finds that the typewriter has car-ried on after the first line "Once upon a time," which she herself had written before leaving. It has now completed a fantasy story entitled "A Type-Writer Fantasy" that has "nothing mechanical about it," but boasts of "invention, constructive power, and delicate satire, with an airy audacity entirely charming" (679).

Because the narrator has always made a habit of mocking the level of corruption in American society, and once claimed that she would surely become a member of the US Senate if she could make a large profit from her little invention, the typewriter also picks up this tone and pokes fun at all the venerable institutions of New York in its story (679). Featuring an old woman living on the edge of a thick wood who desires to read Balzac's novels, the story jeers at the state of public schools because the woman claims that her five weeks at school during youth is enough to give her all the education she would ever need. The corruption of the New York police also gets a mocking mention, as they can be hired by any private citizen and are revealed to be on the payroll of gangsters. The old woman does not wish to look ignorant before her bragging cousin, who claims to have read Balzac but could not tell whether it is written in French or German. Fired by an eager "desire for knowledge, persistence, and indomitable courage," she decides to go to Europe to find out about Balzac. However, because she could not be sure whether she should go to France or to Germany, she buys tickets for two vessels, setting out at the same time for France and Germany, and lies in a solid steel hammock suspended between the two, to a great fanfare of excited reporters and spectators who have come to see her off. As the vessels approach the English Channel where they have to part ways, they are greeted with the wonderful news that France and Germany, arch rivals in history, have decided to merge and become the Franco-German Republic. This relieves the old woman of her dilemma, since it no longer matters whether Balzac wrote in French or German. She decides to return home, whereupon she becomes a successful author of a "large octavo volume" in her own right, despite her mere five weeks of education (680).

The story's biggest object of satire is creative literature itself. If the machine of copy could rival the creative mind by producing "delicate satire" and audacious "original composition" (679), this speaks to the lackluster state of much contemporary literature. The narrator is so impressed by the typewriter's first attempt that she looks "with keen expectation" for another such effort, and even imagines one day that a "masterpiece of literature" will be forthcoming. The only qualm she has is where and how to obtain copyright, as the author in question is not a human being (679). This story plays down its seriousness by posing as a humorous fantasy, but the suggestion that a typewriter can imitate, overtake, and eventually upstage the human subject by excelling at creative power destabilizes the familiar opposition between typescript and literature, challenges human assumptions of superiority over the machine, and makes the two increasingly indistinguishable.

Her Literary Odyssey: The Typewriter Girl as Creative Writer

Phoebe the typewriter girl demonstrates resilience and an agentive appropriation of the benefits and skills brought by her typewriting work, but in Grant Allen's *The Type-Writer Girl*, published in 1897 under the pseudonym of Olive Pratt Rayner, the New Woman typist Juliet Appleton becomes herself an aspiring writer, embodying both mechanical precision and auratic creativity and further blurring the lines between the two.

Unlike Judith in *A Bachelor Girl in London*, where her nonstop, mechanizing typing work drains her of any energy or creativity to pursue her journalistic dream, in Allen's novel Juliet eventually achieves success by having her first stories accepted by a literary magazine. Allen's novel may be light-hearted and sometimes even flippant in tone, causing contemporary critics to pronounce the book "delightful," "amus[ing]," even "smart," but not good enough to be "call[ed]" "literature" ("Review," *Hearth and Home* 843). Later commentators were not more positive, finding the heroine Juliet a "typical New Woman heroine of commercial fiction," whose youth and sexual attractions are coupled with "the supposed folly of her desire for independence" in order to "defuse the threat of the New Woman" (Willis, "Heaven Defend" 53). But in portraying Juliet's struggles and hopes, and in presenting typewriting as both drudgery and also a means toward the attainment of new skills, the novel serves up a more nuanced commentary on the typewriter girl's interaction with mechanized speed. Juliet is made up of tougher material than Mitton's Judith, for while Judith finally bows out of the modern city and withdraws to sheltered domesticity, Allen's Juliet rejects a marriage proposal and chooses to carry on her immersion in modern speed culture. She also learns, in contrast to Judith's brief attempts at bus-riding as positive speed, to balance her typing work with the rejuvenation of bicycle riding, proving herself as a more rounded, capable user of speed.

Compared with his contemporaries, Grant Allen is ideally situated to write about the typewriter girl, as he has commented profusely on the woman question and learnt to typewrite himself five years before writing this novel.[2] His views on the woman question can be seen in his novels of the 1880s and early 1890s, where he portrays several New Women types, including female secretaries and female sleuths.[3] His first New Woman novel, *The Woman Who Did* (1895), famously rails, through the mouth of the New Woman character Herminia Barton, against the hypocrisies of Victorian notions of marriage, describing the institution as "vile slavery" (43). The novel also advocates for women's sexual liberation and freedom of choice in selecting partners and mating conditions. At the same time, Allen voices highly conservative views on gender roles and eugenics, often expressed through an evolutionary lens. His radically controversial views on free love and early mating are based on the need to answer "the voice of Nature within us" ("The Girl of the Future" 55). And his emphasis on a woman's role as a mother derives from his belief that "the race that lets its women fall in their maternal functions will sink to the nethermost abyss of limbo" (52). In "Plain Words on the Woman Question," published in 1889, Allen claims that feminists have endangered the ability of the "English-speaking race" to increase its population, because they encourage middle-class women to work and receive the same education as men, thus harming women's reserve energies for sexual reproduction (457). This complicated stand finds its voice again in *The Type-Writer Girl*, his second New Woman novel, where he is satirical about the New Woman character Juliet's naïve optimism in female independence, but also retains great sympathy for her later frustration and hardship as a self-supporting typewriter girl. In his portrayal of Juliet's ambition to

---

[2] Recent criticism on Allen has pointed out the need to discuss his literary output alongside his wide interest in other disciplines including economics, biology, evolutionary science, and feminism. See Heather Atchison, S. Brooke Carmeron, Sabine Ernst, and William Greenslade and Terence Rodgers.

[3] For more, see Foxwell xi, Greenslade and Rodgers 7, Kestner 134, Willis "Detective's Doppelganger" 144.

be a creative writer, Allen also touches on the familiar dichotomy between the typewriter girl and the creative writer.

Allen is one of the earliest writers to learn typewriting, and thus understands first-hand the intricacies of operating this machine of speed. Gissing wrote about his New Woman typists in *The Odd Women* in 1893, but he is not known to have learnt typewriting by then. Allen's novel came five years after he was reported to have picked up the skill. Unlike the similarly scientifically bent Wells, Allen never professed any distaste for the typewriter as being beneath the honor of a literary writer, but quickly took to typewriting as an indispensable aid to writers. In March 1892, *Novel Review* was still claiming that Mr. Grant Allen did not use a typewriter and "disbelieves in this refuge of the overworked author," even though he had been suffering from writers' cramp for six months and could barely write at all ("Gossip about Novels and Novelists" 357). But in June that same year, another piece in the same journal reveals that the reason Allen objected initially to the typewriter is because he could not see what he was writing. Now that this "blind" function is eliminated with the new visible typewriters, Allen is "getting on swimmingly" with typewriting, and no longer needs to dictate to Mrs. Allen ("Mr. Grant Allen and His Work" 261). An article printed on June 4th in *The Phonetic Journal*, a trade journal owned by Isaac Pitman, reports that Allen is so happy with his Bar-Lock typewriter that he has written a testimonial to the Typewriter Company Ltd.:

> I am very much pleased with the Bar-Lock. I greatly prefer it to any other machine I have seen. The alignment is perfect, the working easy, and the inestimable advantage of being able to see what you are writing and what you have already written, makes it the best instrument for a literary man. Though I have only learnt for one week, I find I can already write quite as much in a day as I used to do with my own right hand before it was disabled by writers' cramp. ("Typewriting Notes" 354)

At this early date in 1892, opposition to the typewriter, especially in literary circles, was still rampant. Opinions like the 1895 piece in *The Idler* are definitely in the minority, which claims that the "baldness" of typewriting could better transmit true creative worth and rid contemporary literature of "half its idiocy" because a typescript would not hide, much as the handwritten manuscript sometimes would, "intrinsic worthlessness" under illegibility ("No Title" 428, 427). Most take the position of *The Literary World*, which reveals in 1892 that although "Mrs. Grant Allen has taken to a Bar-Lock, and Mr. R. Louis Stevenson, even in far-away Samoa, typewrites his 'copy,'" the fight against the writing machine is still kept up by writers such as Thomas Hardy, who "has not yet succumbed to this destroyer of authors' MS" ("Table Talk" 13). Hardy "writes his novels with his own hand, in copying ink so that he is enabled to take a copy" (13). The article, however, takes a bleak view of the future of the handwritten manuscript: "But as the typewriter affords special facilities in taking one or more copies in facsimile without any extra trouble, Mr. Hardy also will, no doubt, be soon lost to the autograph MS. hunter" (13). *The Bookman* further blames Allen for the demise of letter-writing as an art: "Grant Allen was one of the first of the new generation of authors who by the use of the typewriter bid fair to kill letter-writing altogether as an art" ("Mr. Edward Clodd and Grant Allen" 152). It concedes that Allen had a legitimate reason for taking up typewriting because of his writers' cramp, and that Allen is not incapable of writing "interesting" letters, but insists that "most people flatly refuse to keep any letters that come to them in so hatefully mechanical form" (152). This article views typewriting as antithetical to the creative individuality of handwritten letters, and seems to blame Allen for spearheading a self-destructive trend that, through an embrace of technology and expediency, promises to destroy the organic value of handwriting, and also the creative profession itself.

Allen does not seem to entertain a similarly dystopian view of the impact of typewriting, but in his *The Typewriter Girl* he does explore this human–machine complex, especially as this is further complicated by the rise of the typewriter girl as a new type of working women. Allen's tone in this novel is not as serious as that in Gissing's *The Odd Women*, but the story reveals greater details of the hard life of the lonely typewriter girl as she ventures into the real world. As a scientific naturalist and disciple of Herbert Spencer, the "greatest philosopher that ever drew breath" ("Personal Reminiscences" 610), Allen frames the struggles of Juliet Appleton, the titular typewriter girl, in evolutionary terms of natural selection and "survival of the fittest" (*The Typewriter Girl* 8). Juliet is dismayed to find that "every girl in London can write shorthand, and typewriting as an accomplishment is as diffused as the piano" (6); so, to stay afloat in this "struggle of life" she has to "adapt myself to my environment" (6). Juliet's tools of survival are her New Woman qualities of intelligence, "energy," "promptitude," and "rapid resolution" (8), as well as her ladylike appearance and manners. Eventually she succeeds in landing a job, first at a lawyer's office and then at a publisher's, "prov[ing] myself fittest by the mere fact of survival" (8). In a moment of euphoria, Juliet congratulates herself on her success and compares her struggle to the Homeric "Odyssey" (247). The Homeric hero triumphs in his adventures because of his courage, intrepidity, and some auspicious aid from the gods, but in Juliet's case it is the belief in science, "the whole gospel of Darwinism," and the ability to adapt to new technology that has allowed her to navigate the "phantom-haunted channel of the Strand" (6). As Juliet gloats over her new independence while sailing down London's Charing Cross Road, she fancies herself a female "Ulysses," her typewriter a weapon of speed battling the "vast sea of London" (8, 2).

Allen views Juliet's struggles as cruel but necessary, justified on the grounds that every form of life needs to adapt in order to survive; even "the bacilli of typhoid fever" have the "common right to struggle of existence" (10). The survival of the fittest, with the power of competition allowing the strongest to flourish while eliminating the weakest, is seen in the Spencerian light as a part of nature's plan, which benefits society as a whole. The anarchist farm, which Juliet later joins to escape her typing job, may reject capitalist market competition and allow its members to work and rest at will, but it is destined to fail because, as S. Brooke Cameron points out, it is incompetent, inefficient, and not suited to "purposive adaptation" (232).

But Allen's position is also more complicated than this simple subscription to Spencerian evolution. As the novel progresses, the text sets up an opposition between "self" and "environment" (10), and between "soul" and "the struggle for life" (66), seemingly reserving more sympathy for the claims of the former two. Juliet may acknowledge, after the loss of her first typing job and the failure of her anarchist project, that she has "failed to accommodate herself to the environment," and has to "regard myself as one of the unfittest, who do not survive, and whom no man pities" (34). But the "rebel in my blood" could not stand the mechanization of the first job and the exploitation of the second (10). Rather, she makes a bolt for "freedom" (10) against the dictation of environment. The text presents Juliet's choice as impractical, but also seems to commend it for its refusal of meek acceptance. When Juliet later comes across the second typewriter girl in the novel—the pale, weak, under-educated Elsie, whom she has beaten to her second typing job—Juliet pities this specimen of the unfit and goes out of her way to help Elsie. "The struggle for life has not quite choked out my soul" (66). Ruthless competition gives way to soul and sympathy. In the many heart-felt portrayals of Juliet's frustrations, her determination to stay afloat in the survival of the fittest, and her brave attempts to confront poverty with a spirit of *sang froid*, the reader is reminded of Allen's own "ten years' hard struggle for bread" to provide for his family ("Physiological Aesthetics" 52).

Both Juliet and Elsie look on typewriting as offering a means of survival, but their hopes are often dashed by a tough competitive world wherein jobs are scarce and family support nonexistent. Juliet, as the ex-Girton girl, at first entertains a romanticized view of typewriting and the utopian prospects it entails. She throws all her remaining funds into the training of her typewriting skills, and, in words reminiscent of Gissing's Rhoda and Mary, compares her future to a voyage of great discovery. Invoking that great champion of women's rights—"John Stuart Mill, stand by me!"—she "mean[s] to sail away on my Odyssey, unabashed, touching at such shores as may chance to beckon, yet hopeful of reaching at last the lands of Alcinous" (17, 247, 255). Yet reality is far bleaker, and Juliet at one time has to pawn her typewriter just to get by.

The under-educated, lower-middle-class Elsie fares worse, and finds that even the "modest starvation" (8) afforded by typewriting work is often beyond her reach. In this portrayal of Elsie—the poor, ordinary typewriter girl who gets repeatedly rejected in job interviews and is driven to near starvation—the novel stays most true to reality, prompting critics such as Leah Price to argue that

Ellie is the real titular character, not the aristocratic New Woman Juliet (130). Considering that the novel was published in 1898, Juliet is closer to the privileged "honor girl" typist of the earlier years, while Elsie represents the wider army of lower-middle-class women who were flooding the typewriting market by the later years of the decade. Juliet first meets Elsie when seeking her second job at a publisher's, where Elsie, not versed in Greek and unable to spell difficult literary terms, is found to be incompetent and is rejected. The second time Juliet sees her is in Soho, where the starving Elsie is staring at a confectioner's window. Poorly dressed, pale, but still clinging on to the look of a lady, Elsie has not had a job for quite a while. She could type fairly well, but has no typewriting machine of her own and no money to buy one. Like a "cheap edition in paper covers," Elsie is one of thousands of ordinary, lower-middle-class typewriter girls barely able to stay afloat in the struggle for life (66).

Typing jobs are hard to come by and, when they do, they also subject the vulnerable female body to the mechanizing impact of the typewriter. Through repetitive, ceaseless practice Elsie has achieved a mechanical efficiency, and is able to type quite well and with sufficient speed. This access to speed is, however, accompanied by a complete lack of intelligence because, with only rudimentary education, Elsie could not understand more difficult words and works quite "unintelligently, like a well-trained Chinaman" (66). The later reference to even the sub-human squirrel that "turns the unceasing treadmill of his cage" underlines Elsie's total lack of agency and her status as a machine (66). As long as she is given a copy without the slightest call for intelligence, she could work on "like a machine" and "reproduce each word with mechanical fidelity" (66).

Even Juliet, the well-educated Girton girl, is suffocated by her mechanizing work; at the first lawyer's office she is required to passively take dictation and then copy out her boss's words on the typewriter. Any initiative by her to enrich the legal language by adding a creative touch, or "a greater variety of graphic adjectives," meets with rejection by the boss, who insists that she sticks to her passive role. So, all day long, she continues to "click, click, click, like the machine that I was" (10), until finally resigning from her job to escape from its "dullness and monotony" (12). On impulse, Juliet joins an anarchist farm in the countryside, where she hopes to cultivate the land with her own hands. This choice of an anarchist farm is significant because, more than just a whim, this desire to work close to nature with one's bare hands, together with law-defying anarchists, speaks to a yearning for an organic, natural, unmediated way of life that is sharply contrasted with typewriting's heavily supervised, mechanical work. That this escape back to nature should come right after Juliet's first contact with the typewriter underlines the monotonous, dehumanizing impact of mechanized speed.

At the same time that Allen's novel portrays the plight of the typewriter girl with sympathy and touches of realism, it also carries on some of the more familiar prejudices of the conservative masculine press. One of them is that when the story portrays in detail the postindustrial, Taylorized clerical world, including first the legal office Juliet works in and later the publishing firm she moves to, it is the typewriter girl who is represented as particularly in danger of mechanization. The male clerks in the legal office may be of lower class than Juliet, but they are described in terms predominantly animalistic rather than mechanical. One possesses "foxy" hair, hairy hands and large goggle-eyes, one has features "modeled on an oyster's," and the last one has a "pulpy" face (6, 7, 9). All three are rude and stupid, but the way they banter away incessantly about horses and girls in a most leisurely, lazy, and inefficient manner points more to some raw, animal qualities untamed by civilization, whereas by contrast Juliet is presented as an efficient machine clicking nonstop and without interruption. The male clerks seem to develop a genius for fooling around and avoiding work, but women like Elsie and Juliet are presented as patient, passive, and malleable, enduring stoically the long hours and heavy work without loss of attention or productivity.

The novel presents the typewriter girl as both mechanized and also highly erotic. Juliet has to endure the blatant sexualization of her body by the male clerks and the lawyer boss. When Juliet goes for the interview, the male clerks eye her up and down as if "I was a horse for sale," and their perfunctory question as to her typing speed "bore reference more to my face and figure than to my real or imaged pace per minute" (7). The lawyer boss is even more blatant, "scrutinizing my face, my figure, my hands, my feet" like a Sultan in "an Arab slave-market" (8). Later, Juliet has to reject both the advances of the male clerk and the leer and smile of the boss who intends to make her his mistress. This intention actually becomes reality when Juliet later moves to the publisher's office and does indeed become the love interest of her publisher boss, who wants to jilt his upper-class fiancé for her sake. Though the novel portrays this as true love, it does show that the body of the typewriter girl is always highly sexualized for its allure, as well as for its perceived disruption to marriage and sexual order.

What gives the novel its particular interest, though, is that Allen's typewriter girl is more complicated than her oft-depicted image as the struggling urban worker or sexualized machine woman. As the narrative develops further, other voices come to the fore, prime among which is a rather ambivalent approach to the relationship between the typewriter girl and the creative writer. The novel describes Juliet's second job at a literary publisher's and her daily dealings there, which encompass not only taking dictation and typing correspondences. Her duties also lead to some personal contacts with writers. In most circumstances Juliet is just an unobtrusive typist working quietly in the background while writers talk with her boss, but, in one particular case involving a famous writer, Sidney Trevelyan, whose name is a "familiar piece of public property" like "Charing Cross or Hyde Park" (62), the creative writer and the typewriter girl are suddenly thrust together.

The famous writer could not get his way with Juliet's boss about a cheap edition of his new novel, and decides to vent his rage on Juliet, who is typing nearby.

"[S]norting like a war-horse," he shouts at the top of his voice—'Send her away! I tell you I can't stand her. I won't have her scribbling there and making notes of all I say'" (63). This outburst happens not just because she is an easy target as a lowly secretary, but also because he claims that the note-taking, copying typewriter girl is threatening to steal the well-spring of his celebrated originality (63): "She's a paragraphist, the vilest spawn on God's earth, a paragraphist! What do you mean by setting spavined shorthand writers to report my *obiter dicta*?" (63).

This scene propels to the foreground the polar opposition between the typewriter girl and the creative writer. Sidney Trevelyan is the very picture of the creative genius. "An Heir of the Plantagenets" (61), he is portrayed in terms typically reserved for the flamboyant artist of Dionysian excess: "He burst into the sanctum, a whirlwind of a man, large, loose-limbed, masterful, with a restless gray eye, and a huge mop of brown hair, shot with threads of russet" (62). On top of his "two yards of humanity, double width" and an "elephantine weight," he also boasts of a "rich strident" voice, "diffusing itself very loud in clear thrill accents ... which one turn of a note would have made unendurable" (62). Shouting all the way from the stairs, he lets loose an endless volley of "volcanic" mock-disparagement of the publisher (63), calling him a blood-sucking "Barabbas," fattened with the "bones of authors" and the "spoils of the Egyptians," and a "sultan in Shelley's Hellas," "lolling in Eastern opulence, bathed in Cyprian perfumes, and fanned by obsequious Circassian odalisques" (62). This Byronic genius may be given to overblown theatrics, but it fits the image of the sublime, rules-disdaining artist who is far superior to the passive typewriter girl or even the profit-minded "Barabbas" publisher.

But the narrative goes on to reveal him as the opposite of the lonely, persevering genius who insists on his auratic originality against corruption and mechanization. Sidney glorifies himself as the high-flying "eagle" that "should circle about gleaming icy peaks in clear ether," and angrily dismisses the reading public as Philistines, "groveling beasts, prone in the mud they love," who do not appreciate his new three-decker novel (63). But he guards his own money jealously, begrudges his publisher's commission, and greedily seeks "a fresh raid against the purses of the Philistines" by asking the publisher to issue a cheap edition, too soon after the failure of the three-decker (63). He blasts his critics as "ignorant parrots," who could only copy and repeat and have "no wings" themselves. But he is bitterly resentful that they have pronounced his latest work as "artificial" and "unnatural," the very opposite of his touted originality (63). He claims lethal hatred for "copying" typists, but is not above "copying" from classical literature himself when he peppers his conversation with name-dropped texts and references. As this tantrum-throwing, falsetto-voiced, larger-than-life writer puts on a show of the wounded genius in order to extract the highest price, the boundaries between performance and interiority, copying and originality, and genius and peddler are cast into much doubt.

Sidney first notices Judith the typewriter girl as an erotic interest. She is, in his words, the publisher's "obsequious Circassian odalisque," one of those "large-eyed houris" with "voluptuous bosoms," who "strew your restless pillow with opiate flowers" (62). This stress on subservience and sexual appeal soon gives way to fear and anxiety when his offer of a cheap edition is rejected by Juliet's boss on the grounds that it will very likely fail. His subsequent outburst against Juliet is a clumsy effort to displace his own nagging suspicion of his mediocrity unto the typewriter girl, the ultimate symbol of uninspired imitation. As Leah Price points out, this pairing of the creative writer and the typewriter girl serves to underline the impossibility of separating creative gifts from the sale of "copy" in the modern ambience (136). The copying typewriter girl does not steal his organic creativity, but in his insecurity against her perceived threat he is exposed as the hack he really is.

The polar opposition between the two is further debunked when Juliet the typewriter girl later becomes a burgeoning writer in her own right and straddles both roles. After Juliet tells her publisher boss of her adventures in the East-end slop-makers and the anarchist farm, he urges her to write about them as they are "ready-made stories" (71). Better still, he encourages her to write a short story about "the modern girl who earns her own living in London": for example, "this little friend who uses your typewriter" (71). Far from being a passive, monotonous machine, the typewriter girl is actually interesting enough to be the worthy subject of a creative piece of literature, even if it is because "there is no more pathetic figure in our world to-day than the common figure of the poor young lady, crushed between classes above and below, and left with scare a chance of earning her bread with decency" (71). With Judith as the agentic author of such a story, she could cast her own experience in a critical light while imbuing it with both "heart" and creative imagination (70). Though in the end Juliet decides that this theme is too painfully close to herself and writes instead about her East-End experience, the fact that her first attempt at creative writing is later accepted by a periodical unconnected with her boss proves her real creative talent. Juliet receives twelve guineas for her "high-spirited if flippant" story from that editor (73), and, much buoyed by the success of her "literary firstborn," plans to follow that up with more creations.

Juliet's case may be special because, as a Girton girl fallen on hard times, she is still endowed with the privilege of education and knowledge necessary for her creative writing. But even for the under-educated Elsie, adjusting to this machine of speed does not merely lead to mechanization. Catching up with and mastering the fast speed allows the typewriter girl to rapidly improvise new powers of alertness and seeing, and match her response and energy to the speed of the typewriter. This interaction points to a mutually structuring and enabling relationship, as both the limits of the human body and the typing machine are pushed further and demonstrate a potential for adaptability and expansion. This points to the shifting boundaries between the machine of speed and the human agent, rather than their stark opposition. Much as the business rhetoric feminizes the profession and stresses its "blind," passive, and nonagentic dimension, typewriting and the ability to use more complex technologies does help women to enlist all their capacities and integrate different skills in the modern Taylorite office. A new type of actively alert women, powered by the combined energies of both mechanical and organic forces, is enabled by this participation in modern speed culture.

This new, machine-accelerated female subjectivity is in better display in another scene in the novel. When Juliet's very first experience of typewriting at the lawyer's office proves stultifying, she decides to leave for the idyllic anarchist farm by cycling all the way from London to the Surrey countryside. As she roams the rural landscape, the wind in her hair and scenes flying by, her cycling is presented as freedom and escape:

> How light and free I felt! ... I felt it that brisk May morning as I spun down the road, with a Tam O'Shanter on my head, and my loose hair travelling after me like a Skye terrier. "This," though I to myself, "is truly my Odyssey. To play at being a latter-day Ulysses in London, among those crowded streets, is like a child's game, too much make-believe. But mounted here on the ship of the high-road, scudding gayly downhill, or luffing against headwinds on a steep upward slope, I feel myself the heroine of a modern sea epic. (18)

Here the pastoral, organic values of the countryside are certainly presented as a relief from and a contrast with the repressive discipline of industrial speed. But it must be noted that Juliet does not escape from modern speed culture per se, but instead embraces another machine of speed: the bicycle. The bicycle takes Juliet to unspoiled nature but also enmeshes her deep in an active and energizing form of mechanized speed. Juliet's great pleasure and satisfaction when riding over the green fields does not come from a complete rejection of mechanized speed, but from her ability to harness the assembled energies of both the mechanical and the organic.

Cycling across the Weald of Surrey, Juliet comes across two other forms of mobility: the train and the horse. When trains "dashed under bridges with long streamers of steam," these "unabashed monsters of burnished brass, snorting death from their throats, such as would have terrified the timid Achaean sailors," give quite a shock to some horses nearby, which "reared and quivered at the ungainly monsters" (19). The train rumbles brutally over the green fields and terrifies the horses, which are symbols of a natural, organic, preindustrial world. But Juliet's bicycle seems to make the best of the two worlds. This "undaunted steel palfrey" takes no heed of the roaring train and merrily speeds on. Not dwarfed by the train, the bicycle offers Juliet, "the braver daughter of an iron age," an exhilarating experience of speed that utilizes the achievements of industrial mechanization and also enables a degree of freedom and human agency (19). Juliet is portrayed as a true modern heroine and an "unabashed" daughter of the industrial age, because she seems to possess a new, amalgamated subjectivity engendered and enabled by the partnership between machine and nature. This "braver daughter of an iron age" does not reject modern speed culture, but is capable of being better prepared to adjust to its challenges.

Allen's own writing experience also offers a further example wherein the human–machine interaction represented by typewriting does not lead to the one-sided erasure of the creative mind or obstruct its agentic working. Allen may suffer the ignominy of being referred to, by Joseph Conrad, as "a man of inferior intelligence" whose work was "not art in any sense" (qtd. in Morton 64). He himself does not seem to have a very high view of his literary calling, either, admitting that he has turned to literature from his favorite science because literature pays much better: "I never cared for the chance of literary reputation except as a means of making a livelihood for [the wife] Nellie and the boy" (qtd. in Morton 57).

But as a bestselling writer known for his skillful use of the typewriter to produce his many literary works and reviews, Allen does seem to successfully combine the writer-function with the typist-function, pointing to an enlarged scope whereby the mind and the body integrate new, machine-aided skills of speed to mutual benefit. If, in the case of the piano, the freewheeling, improvisational pianist could play the dual role of passionate artist and mere automaton, and project an auratic, unique self by harnessing the mechanical sounds of the industrial machine and the mechanical skills of discipline and uniformity, then the writer sitting at the typewriter could equally synchronize and coordinate a complex assemblage of capacities and energies, both industrial and organic. At his table in his Surrey home, where his Royal Bar-Lock typewriter sat beside a German microscope, a gift from Charles Darwin to acknowledge his services to science, Allen would type nonstop for four hours every morning from nine o'clock, "in one long even click," throughout his career (F. Harris 94). One friend remembered a scene when Allen, to demonstrate to his friends who had gathered to see him use his typewriter, composed an overdue review on the spot by typing 500 words directly from his mind (Price 138). As a fast and improvisational writer, Allen partners up particularly well with the typewriter, with the machine of speed seemingly facilitating his thoughts and making them flow faster. In one interview Allen seems to suggest that he is trying to make his mind follow the fast speed of the typewriter: "I haven't tried to work very fast, or my brains wouldn't keep pace with my fingers" (qtd. in G. Richards 268). Allen's nephew, the poet and publisher Grant Richards, writes in *Novel* in 1892 that Allen turns out "novel after novel, with machine-like regularity, and at a pace which the casual observer might imagine would militate against their quality, but which the critic will tell you has not in the least interfered with the general level of artistic excellence which he has kept from first to last" (265).

Richards might be defending his uncle, but the typewriter does not just help Allen's writers' cramp and facilitate his writing speed; it also seems to positively impact on his creative output. In a frenzied sixteen-year writing career before his death at the age of fifty-one, Allen produced seventy-two books and an enormous number of articles on a whole variety of subjects including literature, economics, biology, evolutionary science, and feminism. The way he writes ceaselessly and regularly does seem to parallel the automatic, reliable flow of the clicking typewriter, but the effortless ease of his writing, its witty humor, and impressive, encyclopedic knowledge also proves the working of an impressive intelligence. Frank Harris, editor of *Fortnightly*, the leading liberal journal to which Allen contributed twenty-nine lengthy articles and review, writes that:

> He [Allen] could be described with more "ists" than anyone else I ever saw. He was an atheist and pacifist and socialist, a botanist and zoologist and optimist, a chemist and physicist, a scientist of scientists, a monist, meliorist and hedonist ... A walk with him was an education in botany and zoology, and he had no whimsies or quirks; he was always reasonable, good-tempered, vivacious, bright, and interested in every human interest ... He was, also, astonishingly articulate; he wrote excellent prose, and could turn you out a first-rate article on almost any subject from the growth of the idea of God to the habits of the caterpillar, at a moment's notice, and without perceptible exertion. (94–95)

By using his typewriter as the mediator of his creative writing, and by "having a regular system" of disciplined and repetitive practice, "working at stated hours without interruption" (G. Richards 268), Allen is able to produce an impressive amount of work. Allen's role as the popular bestselling writer may be lesser than that of the genius, but this synchronization of mechanical and creative energies points to shifting boundaries between the organic and the mechanical.

To think that the typewriter was the much-maligned symbol of dehumanization in the late nineteenth century, it would be with a touch of bemused surprise that one finds, 100 years later, that the typewriter is now viewed with some sort of nostalgia. In the digital age, when communication technologies such as virtual reality or cyberspace dwarf those of the late nineteenth century and compel new ontologies of subjectivity, the typewriter is seen as a symbol of a more embodied, integrated, and even organic past, "the traditional world of letters and literature," in stark contrast with today's increasingly disembodied, hi-tech reality.[4] This is corroborated by Katherine Hayles, who writes in her influential *How We Became Posthuman* that the typewriter is a mechanical technology of inscription that

---

[4] In "Gibson's Typewriter," Scott Bukatman writes about the surprise that people had when learning that William Gibson wrote *Neuromancer* on an old manual typewriter, the novel that launched the word cyberspace and is often cited as one of the two seminal texts in the history of cyborgs and cyberspace along with Donna Haraway's Cyborg Manifesto essay. The surprise is mainly over the fact that the typewriter is viewed as archaic and nineteenth-century, whereas Gibson's novel is dedicated to the coolness of hackers and the newest technologies of the twentieth century (627–29).

maintains a "proportionate" relationship between signifier and signified (14). This is different in nature from the computer as digital technology, where the signified and signifier can no longer correspond in a one-to-one relationship. While the typewriter entails the physical act of striking a key and producing a directly corresponding letter, computer mousing is more random and a touch may trigger a whole multitude of visual images and texts. The circulation of signs thus has "little relation to the material world" (14).

Though Hayles uses this example to suggest the posthuman potential of the digital age and the new possibilities of thinking about self and other, body and technology, and reality and illusion, the typewriter as a symbol of the Machine Age is seen to denote a sense of greater immediacy, materiality, and presence, to be contrasted with the greater dislocation of information from the body in our current cyber-age. This view presumes that typewriting involves a greater correspondence between signifier and signifier, between the touching of the key and the letter impressed on the paper, and between the body and the word produced. It could certainly be interestingly compared with Kittler's earlier anxiety over exactly the opposite—namely, the typewriter's severing of the body from the writing. Such drastically differing insights on the same apparatus points to the need to historicize any discussion of the human–machine complex as it evolves over the years.

3

Venus on Wheels

The New Woman Cyclist and Conspicuous Speed

In Grant Allen's *The Type-Writer Girl*, the New Woman heroine Juliet is both a typist and an avid rider of the bicycle, another machine of speed closely associated with middle-class women in the *fin-de-siécle* period. Just as the 1895 *Pick-Me-Up* article, quoted in the Introduction, names the bicycle and the typewriter as two telltale signs of the New Woman ("To Time: An Apostrophe" 2), many women of the time typewrite for work and for their livelihood, while taking to the bicycle for recreation and leisure. Cycling is another important aspect of modern women's daily life wherein her body interacts with modern speed culture. Yet, while both typewriting and cycling propel women into the modern public space and train women to be faster, the speeding body of the New Woman cyclist, as the more visible symbol of the unconventional, sped-up New Woman, incurs more outcry than her typewriting. All the initial objections to women's cycling focus on the public visibility of her speeding body.

Since its early days, cycling was linked with men, and almost all the early cyclists and racers before the mid-1890s "bicycle craze" were young affluent men, driven to cycling for its promise of heroic adventure and athleticism (Herlihy 22). For women, despite a few early reports of women racers and velocipede-riders, for the most part cycling was inaccessible and discouraged. In 1892, when the Safety bicycle was already popular with male riders, the *Cycling* magazine of London printed an article strongly condemning women racers for their lack of female modesty:

> When a record-breaking craze takes hold of wheel women, we fear the end of the tether is within reach, and female cycling is doomed. There is a prescribed limit beyond which her modesty and deportment should absolutely forbid her to step: and moreover beyond which she becomes an exhibition that excites neither envy in her compeers or admiration in the opposite sex. The record-breaking woman cannot be graceful; the peculiar action of cycle propulsion at high speed will not permit it in her case, and as she poses in scorching attitude, twists her pedals as rapidly as she is able, and in fact centres all her attention and energy towards the attainment of speed, she cannot fail to be other than an object of ridicule. (qtd. in Ritchie 156)

The New Woman and Technologies of Speed in Fin-de-Siècle *Literature*. Eva Chen, Oxford University Press.

Women and scorching, or the fast and furious riding of the bicycle, are alien to each other because, for one, the "peculiar" propulsion through ceaseless pedaling would, if carried too far during scorching, turn her into "an object of ridicule" and deprive her of any claim to feminine decorum. As one commentator opines in the *Wheelwoman* on December 19, 1896, "the poet's ideal of exquisite womanhood is utterly destroyed by the sight of these perspiring, red-faced, lank objects, working their legs treadmill-fashion in mere blatant feminine vulgarity" ("Sorrows of Marie Corelli" 7). The author goes on to write that while "[m]en look sufficiently hideous and undignified on a wheel, women are worse than hideous; they are immodest" (7). In rhythmic pedaling women's ankles and legs would be partially revealed, and during the races held inside velodromes some women racers were known to throw "one leg or both legs up" at full speed, exposing themselves to the lascivious leer of male watchers (qtd. in Simpson 52). Cycling also requires women to wear shorter, less cumbersome, and more practical clothes, and the New Woman's Rational cycling costume was a focus of conservative attacks (Marks 200). A further objection, often couched in moral and medical terms, focuses on the sexual stimulation and moral abandonment brought by the bicycle's speed. Conservative doctors had always objected to female exercise and its supposed harm on the female reproductive system ("Woman As An Athlete" 636).[1] The thrill of the speeding bicycle would further "intoxicate" women to commit immoral acts and "swell the ranks of reckless girls who finally drift into the standing army of outcast women," warned Charlotte Smith, founder of the Women's Rescue League in America, in 1896 (qtd. in Guroff 43). One physician urges women cyclists that if they do have to ride, they should avoid the risks of female masturbation by riding "slowly and erect":

> The moment *speed* is desired the body is bent forward in a characteristic curve and the body's weight is transmitted to the narrow anterior half of the saddle, with all the weight pressing on the perineal region ... If a saddle is properly adjusted for slow riding and in an usual effort at speed or hill-climbing, the body is thrown forward, causing the clothing to press against clitoris, thereby eliciting and arousing feelings hitherto unknown and unrealized by the young maiden. (qtd. in Garvey 76; emphasis added)

This vociferous objection to women's cycling, however, soon gave way to a different voice by the middle years of the 1890s. Women's cycling pioneer Lillias Campbell Davidson comments on this sudden change of public opinion in her

---

[1] The conservative doctor Arabella Kenealy bemoaned that cycling has deprived girls of their feminine charm and made them mannish and barren, prone to nervousness because women's bodies could not take the strain of too much exercise. Women cyclists, on the other hand, insisted that cycling made women healthier. Lillias Campbell Davidson, an early cycling pioneer, asserted that, though "[i]t took doctors a long time to look with anything like a friendly, nay even a tolerant eye, at women-a-wheel," "doctors have seen the error of their ways, and know better now" ("A Few Cycling Dangers" 206). For more on early attacks on the New Woman cyclist, see Marks, and Wosk 101–8.

cycling manual *Handbook for Lady Cyclists* (1896), the first book "devoted solely to the service of the up-to-date lady cyclist" ("Preface"):

> Cycling women were regarded with a kind of pious horror by society and by the public at large. It was openly said that a woman who mounted a bicycle hopelessly unsexed herself; she was stared at and remarked upon in town, and hooted and called after in country districts. It was supposed that no woman would take to so masculine an amusement unless she was *fast*, unwomanly and desirous of making herself conspicuous. (10; emphasis added)

Fifteen years later, however, it is in fashion to be "fast." "It is no longer the woman with moral courage who cycles" now (10), but instead it would take "some little moral courage to remain an anti-cyclist when to do so stamps one as dull, unfashionable, and hopelessly out of date" (10). Davidson herself, when riding in the early 1880s, had to avoid controversy by cycling only in the early mornings on empty streets. Once she had to turn down a side road to avoid the town vicar ("Overlooked No More"). Davidson went on to found the Lady Cyclists' Association, the first in the world, and wrote the first ladies' page for the Cyclist Touring Club magazine the *CTC Gazette*. But she is still surprised by the "sudden change" in public perception of women's cycling (*Handbook* 10). "Fifteen years ago the women who cycled might have been counted by tens," she writes, but "today they number their tens of thousands—nay, hundreds of thousands" (2).

The very same public visibility of women's speed, previously the focus of conservative outcry, is utilized by capitalist commodity culture and recast as glamorous and fashionable within a matter of a few years. As Davidson points out, women's cycling is now the most fashionable thing to do, and is embraced by high society and emulated by those down the social scale:

> All the smart world rushed to wheels, and the would-be smart world hastened to follow ... Cycling is at present a fashionable craze—it has taken a more vehement hold upon the smart world than any mania before. It is becoming, through its smart patronage, admired and desired by all other women. (10, 11)

To cycle now is no longer to shock or offend, but to impress and display. Significantly, Davidson herself, as a New Woman cycling pioneer, actively encourages this fashionable image and urges the woman cyclist to regard fashionable display as the most important duty of women's cycling:

> To look well is as much the ambition of every lady cyclist as to ride well, for every woman who looks well awheel not only benefits the world at large by adding an item of beauty to it instead of one of ugliness, but she forms the best advertisement for the sport to which she owes so much in the eyes of all her fellow women. (21)

Davidson's pleading reveals that, to many New Women, glamorizing the woman cyclist helps effect greater public acceptance of women's cycling and bring more freedom to women. But her words also underline a crucial function of speed in the modern scene: its use as commodity and status display. In the mid-1890s, the bicycle quickly grew into a central icon of an accelerating modern commodity culture wherein speed itself becomes a precious commodity and is used to display classed identities. Just fifteen years earlier the New Woman cyclist was viewed as scandalous and transgressive. But by the mid-1890s, she is no longer the mannish, offensive Amazonian rider much ridiculed and attacked by conservative masculine press. Instead, she has evolved with an accelerating commodity culture to stand for the epitome of feminine elegance and the height of glamor and fashion. When the fashionable New Woman rides a bicycle, her speeding body becomes the primary site wherein modern speed culture joins hands with an accelerating commodity culture and expands into consumption and personal life. Many New Women cyclists encouraged this change. As Davidson makes clear, to look well is as important as to ride well. The fashionable woman cyclist, "sit[ting] erect," (95) "graceful, elegant, and womanly in the saddle" (114) in all her splendid finery, offers the best advertisement for cycling's function as "pretty," "charming" display (21, 22).

In order to look glamorous and display her charms, the right way to ride a bicycle is as important as wearing the right fashion. "There is really no more graceful and charming sight than a pretty woman, prettily and suitably dressed, riding a bicycle as it should be ridden," Davidson goes on (22). The way "it should be ridden" is to avoid looking "loud, fast, and simply a fright," but to stick to a measured, elegant speed (115). A woman should refrain from scorching because "[o]verspeed is always injurious to women" physically, and "a woman's nervous system suffers a hundred times more than a man's from the excitement and tension of the race itself" (95). More importantly, as she writes elsewhere, a fast speeding women, "if she dashes frantically along hot, dusty, and purple of visage," would "frighten" the public and do "infinite harm" to women cyclists' elegant image ("Cycling for Ladies" 91).

This image change demonstrates that the woman cyclist of the mid-decade boom years has increasingly metamorphosed into a glamorous, elegant, and privileged consumer of speed. The speeding body of the New Woman cyclist indeed epitomizes a narrative of female emancipation, but at the same time it also shows the working of speed's commodifying function, whereby her transgressiveness is recast as fashionable and tamed under a consumerist framework. When the public equates cycling with "smart society" and wealthy women, bicycle speed, done in the right way, now acts as the most visible display of privilege and entitlement. The bicycle's fast movement, noisy bells and brakes, as well as the performative nature of riding compels public attention and demonstrates the freedom and privilege of speed to every envious onlooker.

Because of the bicycle's high costs, its public visibility, and its primary use for leisure and recreation in the mid-1890s, this machine takes on a unique role to demonstrate the new use of speed for status and commodified display. This chapter proposes to examine this new meaning of speed by first analyzing the evolution of the bicycle as a machine of speed. It would then explore how the popular press, advertisers, and particularly cycling magazines work to persuade the public and transform the image of the New Woman cyclist into one of status display and fashionable consumption. The chapter then studies the literary representations of the New Woman cyclist in the works of H. G. Wells and George Gissing, to further uncover the hidden class hierarchies behind women's cycling. As bicycle-aided speed becomes the ultimate symbol of conspicuous display for the rich, and of upward mobility for the less privileged, the class exclusions behind the progressive image of the New Woman cyclist are glaringly displayed. Like literary representations that have pored over the trials and aspirations of the New Woman as she is sped-up and disciplined by typewriting work, the texts studied in this chapter also highlight the complexities at work when the New Woman throws herself with enthusiasm into cycling, both in challenge of established gender norms and in complicity with a modern commodity culture, wherein new rules and hierarchies apply.

Automobility and the Wheels of Speed

In 1896, *Cycling World Illustrated* characterizes the bicycle as "[a] mechanical instrument [that] consists of two wheels and a connecting framework capable of being ridden, driven and steered by human agency" ("What is a Bicycle?" 81). As a form of self-propelled transportation that frees people from the uncertainty of horses, the bicycle took its earliest form in the wooden-wheeled, hobby-horse walking machine invented by the German baron Karl Von Drais in 1817, which covered twice the distance and speed of a normal stride with each impulsion (Herlihy 21–22). Then, in 1861, Pierre Michaux developed the velocipede ("fast foot"), or boneshaker, a solid iron machine that applied pedals and cranks directly to the front wheel and turned it into a veritable vehicle. The velocipede was popular in France and spurred cycling races all over Europe, often to large crowds. In the 1870s and 1880s the high-wheeler or "penny-farthing" took over, with its large "spider" drive wheels and diminutive rear wheels, further proving that fast human-powered transport was possible. The "Ordinary," as the high-wheeler later came to be known, utilized the latest technology in wire wheels and rubber tires, weighed much less, and was able to cut the time needed to cover one mile to just over three minutes (163).

By the 1870s the British bicycle industry was fast asserting a dominant position, after the French industry was severely hampered by the continental trade blockage of the Franco-Prussian War. The Midlands factories were already advanced in the latest metalworking and machine-tool production methods, but had suffered an earlier decline in the weaving and clock-making businesses. Bicycle production, first for the French market but increasingly for domestic and other markets, soon revived business. The British manufacturers made constant improvements to the French model, first by using a C-shaped spring, then adding a step to help mounting, and reducing the rear wheel to reasonable proportions (Smethurst 46). The Ordinary was "a wonderful combination of speed and silence," as a contemporary source marveled, and one such sample displayed at the Crystal Palace in London in 1869 was rightly called the "Phantom" for its stealth speed (qtd. in Herlihy 163). But the biggest problem was still its difficulty in use. Its huge wheel, often five feet in diameter in order to maximize speed, made both steering and mounting difficult. The smallest road obstacle would send the rider falling head first over the front handle-bar. The extraordinary athleticism this requires and the high incidence of accidents meant that the bicycle at this stage was mostly used in racing as a means of sport, or as an expensive toy for young, athletic, affluent men.

By the 1880s, the need to reach a wider public propelled one Coventry producer, John Kemp Starley of Coventry Machinists' Company, to come up with a Rover Safety bicycle, so called because by positioning the rider between two equally sized wheels and closer to the ground it was much safer and easier to ride for almost everyone (Bijker 37). At the 1885 Stanley Show, the Rover Safety quite stood out, and its price of £22 cost more than an Ordinary but less than a typical tricycle, which had been the safer alternative to the Ordinary (Herlihy 235). Starley came up with his "Tangent" system for tensioning the spokes through a pair of levers attached to the hubs and rims, which later became the standard design for bicycle wheels, but he also incorporated other people's innovations from over the years, including ball-bearings, chains, steel tubing, and rubber-clad wheels.

The improved Rover Safety model of 1886 was the definitive modern bicycle, with equal size wheels of 30" geared to 45", tangential wire spokes, continuous block chain rear drive, and a saddle post as an integral part of the diamond frame (Smehurst 47–50). The later invention of inflatable or pneumatic tires by the Scotsman John Dunlop in 1888 gave greater speed to the Safety bicycle and further sealed its popularity, as people of all ages and both genders could now enjoy cycling with relative ease. From this point on, the bicycle was transformed from a clever gadget into a practical, popular vehicle.

Since its very first days, the bicycle was associated with speed and racing. The velocipede invented by Michaux weighed 70 lbs and could only achieve 12 miles per hour at the best, but it was already seen as an exciting breakthrough, allowing men, as the Paris correspondent of the New York Times reported in 1867, to have the "appearance of flying through the air" (qtd. in Herlihy 78). Commenting on the direly felt need to have a means of speed and automobility that lived up to the progressive spirit of the modern age, the reporter went on to express a dissatisfaction with the traditional carriage: "Is it not absurd, is it not a disgrace to the inventive age we live in, to see a man obliged to employ, in order to get through the street, a great vehicle, as large almost as a house? So let us have the velocipedes" (78).

As a machine of adventure and heroic athleticism, the velocipede triggered great public enthusiasm. Huge crowds gathered to watch intrepid cyclists striving to brave limits and beat records for faster speed at mile races and endurance trials, the latter held over long distances and often across national borders. The first properly documented contest, organized by the Olivier brothers' cycling business of La Compagnie Parisienne de Bicycles, took place in Paris in the suburb of Saint Cloud on May 31, 1868, when cyclists rode over a distance of 1,200 meters on a gravel path between the fountain and the entrance gate of the park. It was won by the Englishman James Moore, "at the speed of lightning," according to *Cycling Record*, in 3 minutes and 50 seconds, to the wild excitement of the aristocracy of Tout-Pariss who had gathered to watch the event (qtd. in Dauncey 28). Racing soon flourished in Paris and the provinces, with one race in Bordeaux in 1868 drawing a reported crowd of 3,000 spectators (Smethurst 50). Another famous race was the Paris–Rouen of November 7, 1869, again won by Moore, who covered 123 kilometers in 10.5 hours (Dauncey 29).

The fever for races soon spread to other countries, and the first cycle race in Britain took place just one day after the Saint Cloud race was won by Arthur Markham. The bicycle historian Wiebe Bijker points out that racing-led technological improvement was the instrumental impetus pushing the bicycle down the direction of the "speed criterion," as the size of the front wheel kept expanding to 48"–50" in diameter to reach faster speed (Bijker 45). Soon the record for a mile was reduced to just over 3 minutes (Smethurst 40). The British favored road races over track races inside velodromes, and in the 1870s and 1880s cycle racing as a spectator sport became especially prominent, typically covering between 1 and 25 miles and attracting thousands of spectators. Walter Goodall George rode his 54" Coventry Ordinary from Worcester to Calne in one day in 1883, a distance of more than 100 miles (Smethurst 38). The arrival of the pneumatic tire turned the Safety bicycle into the fastest cycle on the road, and a new record of 25 miles per hour and a mile record of below 2 minutes was set in 1893 (Herlihy 252). For the first time in history, the bicycle proved itself faster than the best speed by a trotting horse even over short hauls, offering a form of self-propelled, machine-aided speed that was both fast and accessible.

The heroism of these bicycle racers and the heated press fanfare over their exploits rubbed off on public perceptions of the bicycle, endowing the machine with magical powers. As early as 1883, the cycling journal *Wheelman* glorifies the bicycle as "Another chivalry to-day"; the cyclists "ride no steed but trusty Wheel," and "No garb of steel doth them array," "Yet gallant knights and true are they" ("A Ballade of this Age" 100). Between 1895 and 1897, as the "bicycle craze" caught hold of the general public, more than 750,000 bicycles were produced annually in

Britain (Rubinstein 51), and sales in America increased from half a million bicycles in 1895 to one million in 1896 and two million in 1897 (Macy 25). Hundreds of thousands of these cyclists sought to better the feudal knight-errants on the prosthetic power of the steel horse. "The annaled praise of feudal days hath faded like a mist," declared "The Song of the Wheel" in 1897, replaced by the "Flight of machine where once was seen knight-errant brave and gay" (455).

Many cyclists embraced cycling for exercise, recreation, and physical and spiritual regeneration. Arthur Conan Doyle, for instance, wrote a glowing account of the regenerative benefits of cycling in 1896: "when the spirits are low, when the day appears dark, when work becomes monotonous, when hope hardly seems worth having, just mount a bicycle and go out for a spin down the road, without thought on anything but the ride you are taking" (Doyle, "Cycle Notes" 38). The popularity of the bicycle and the social perceptions of its benefits tap into long-held Victorian concerns about the tolls of industrialization and urbanization. Since the mid-nineteenth century there were mounting calls to associate sports and exercise with redemptive building of the character—calls fueled as much by the religious ideas of muscular Christianity as by a Darwinian-inflected evolutionary belief in the survival of the fittest (Mangan 5). The change in mechanistic views of the human body also led to a new perception of the body that needed rest and recreation to combat the exhaustion and fatigue of labor (Rabinbach 2). These concerns fuelled positive perceptions of the bicycle, and even the medical discourse heaped praise on cycling as an ideal antidote to the ills of sedentary living. The bicycle was celebrated as strengthening the muscles evenly; stimulating the heart, lungs, and digestive system; and, most importantly, curing that very modern disease, neurasthenia, or nervous exhaustion, produced by the frenzied activity of modern professional life (Whorton 65). As is proclaimed in the article "Cycling versus morphine," published in *The British Medical Journal* in 1895, the bicycle relieves modern people from becoming "a race of nervous dyspeptics," and works better than the artificial sedation provided by narcotic; "a long spin in the fresh air on a cycle induces sweet sleep better than their favorite drug" (qtd. in Whorton 66). Cycling, in short, had advanced "the sanitation of this country ... [by] a hundred years" (qtd. in Whorton 64).[2]

The bicycle is thus linked with the outdoors, fresh air, and freedom—concepts perceived as preindustrial and at odds with those of mechanized urban modernity. Yet the bicycle is also fundamentally a machine of speed and the latest technology of modern machine culture. The mechanistically enmeshed nature of the bicycling experience mirrors the quintessential modern experience of ceaseless change,

---

[2] There was also opposition to the bicycle, but the dominant view was positive. For more on the medical opinions, see Whorton 61–88. It must be noted, though, that doctors were more divided on cycling's impact on women. Some were conservative and warned that the development of muscles detracted from women's feminine sensitivity and harmed their reproductive system, but as the bicycle became more popular, more doctors came to recommend the health benefits of exercise and fresh air for domestically bound women.

nervous stimulation, and spatial–temporal compression. The bicycle's speed offers faster and easier access to the outdoors and the countryside, but these values of unpolluted organicity are accessible through the help of the very machine such values seemingly oppose. In this sense, the bicycle offers both a release from and also a potential source of anxiety and tension for the human subject—both a means of escape from industrial modernity and also a sublime expression of its very essence.

As a form of mechanized speed, cycling still carries certain risks and dangers that might prove threatening to the public. Bicycle historians point out that the obsession with cycling speed, which gave rise to the prevalence of scorchers on the roads, is one of the main reasons behind the initial public opposition to the bicycle. These scorchers were often arrested for their "impulse to overtake any and every moving object which may be in front of him," for they startled pedestrians and carriage-horses, two main road users at that time ("The Dangers of Cycling," qtd. in Whorton 68). Cycling manuals denounced the urge for speed as foolish and preached the wisdom of "lengthen[ing]" "time and space" by "rest[ing] by the wayside," but the very need for such admonishment suggests that those bicycling "fools" who "measure pleasure by the miles" were way too many (Mecredy and Stoney 107).

The fast-moving and dangerously close-by bicycle awakened latent fears of the violent clash between the machine and the organic body, fears first emblazoned on the public mind by the train accidents of the mid-nineteenth century. Much of the early opposition to the bicycle uses a rhetoric that echoes earlier Victorian accounts of the danger of the train: "Pedestrians backed almost into the hedges when they met one of them, for was there not almost every week in the Sunday newspaper the story of someone being knocked down and killed by a bicycle" (Thompson 18). In the 1890s, a new heading of "Death by the Wheel" appeared in newspaper obituary columns, as more than one recorded cycling accident per day took place in London and New York (Whorton 68). Public outrage was such that there were loud calls for bicycles to have their own roads, "like railway trains" (Thompson 18).[3] These early objections, however, soon abated as cycling entered a new stage by the mid-1890s.

Speed as Fashionable Display: Glamorizing the Woman Cyclist

By the mid-1890s, with the acceleration of commodity culture and the development of the Safety model, which made cycling easier and safer for most people, the bicycle became an increasingly coveted commodity for the middle classes.

---

[3] An 1893 Leeds court case involved a carriage keeper who struck at a passing bicyclist with his whip, lassoed him round the neck, dragged him to the ground, and ran over him with the carriage, because the bicyclist failed to ring his bell and frightened the horses. He was fined £30 but insisted that "to us gentlemen who drive spirited horses, you cyclists are a great nuisance." Quoted in Bathurst, 31.

Bicycle speed, associated since its earliest days with record-breaking and derring-do, was now increasingly a matter of consumption and conspicuous display for those who could afford it. In the mid-decade boom years, the bicycle emerged as the most heavily advertised commodity, capturing the top spot for poster advertising and accounting for nearly one-fifth of all advertising space in magazines (Garvey 69, Hanlon 90). It became a ubiquitous presence in the visual landscape of the era, appearing everywhere in print and gracing "posters and postcards, magazine covers and cigarette labels, sheet music and card decks"—and even ads for other products that "had nothing to do with bicycling" (Coutin 18). This remarkable feat underscores speed's transformation into a fashionable commodity, prized for its ability to signify consumption power and elevate the social status of those who possess it. The elegantly attired woman cyclist, in particular, becomes a celebrated symbol of this new change, embodying the intersection of glamor, mobility, and modernity that speed has come to represent.

By the early 1890s, a significant portion of the middle-class male population had already embraced the Safety bicycle. In order to expand sales and increase profitability, the bicycle industry began to turn its attention to the untapped women's market. To allay public anxiety over the mannish New Woman cyclist and her disruption of feminine decorum, they tried a number of measures, including promoting female-specific cycle saddles such as the so-called "hygiene" seats, designed to avoid undue stimulation of sensitive parts; other measures included taking out the cross-bar and lowering the gears of the wheels, in order to make a specifically feminine bicycle distinct from that designed for male users (Hanlon 74; Hallenbeck 24–28). By fixing the handlebars several inches higher for women's bicycles than for men's, they made it harder for women to bend down and scorch fast by forcing them to sit upright (Garvey 9). Bicycle advertisers also emphasized bicycling's health benefits, and promoted these as necessary in preparing women for socially approved functions like motherhood (Hanlon 76–77). But the most successful strategy was to aestheticize the woman cyclist in ads and posters, and highlight her elegance, glamor, and fashionable appearance.

Prior to 1853, advertising in Britain remained a largely traditional and localized affair, with small-scale businesses comprising the bulk of advertisers. This was in part due to the significant tax levied on advertising during this period, which limited the ability of businesses to effectively market their products or services to a wider audience (T. Richards 86). In the subsequent decades, as more exhibitions and department stores began to use lighting and stage settings to stimulate the visual register and instigate a desire for consumption (Leach 9), advertising also became visually exciting and adopted sophisticated associational techniques as the industry developed into a modern, mass-scaled one (Beetham and Boardman 157). The bicycle ads of the 1890s were the first to use such techniques on a wide scale, becoming "trail-blazing pioneers" in a watershed moment in the history of modern advertising (Garvey 69). Previously heavily technical, these bicycle ads began to present mostly female cyclists in stylish and evocative settings. Rather than depicting the woman cyclist in realistic or social settings, they often portrayed her, posing prettily with her machine, in idyllic, scenic environments with a decorative, garden-like ambience. This approach not only emphasizes the fashionable and refined nature of the woman cyclist, but also imbues bicycle speed with symbolic, fantastical powers.

Many of these ads employed the help of famous or aspiring artists. The British producers hired artists of renown such as Childe Hassam and Charles Dana Gibson to produce beguiling illustrations for cycling magazines (Figure 3.1), while American manufacturing firms used William H. Bradley and Edward Penfield to design more sensual and colorful posters, often using distinctive Art Nouveau

Figure 3.1 *The Wheelwoman*, Dec. 4, 1897, cover. The British Library Archive.

techniques of swirling lines and stylized curves to convey an image of elegance and glamor (Petty, "Peddling," 33; Coutin 36) (Figure 3.2). In both cases, the beautiful, fashionably dressed female cyclist rides her bicycle prettily, her hair and gown flowing lightly, suggesting a measured and elegant speed that works best to highlight her beauty. This speed is also highly sexualized, as her mobile body is enveloped by a lush and verdant display of floral and foliar imagery, imparting a potent sense of alluring seduction and sensual enchantment. The constant use of the flying goddess trope, to complement the brands of women's cycles like "Sirius," "Capella," and "Triumph," suggests not only speed's links with freedom, flight, and

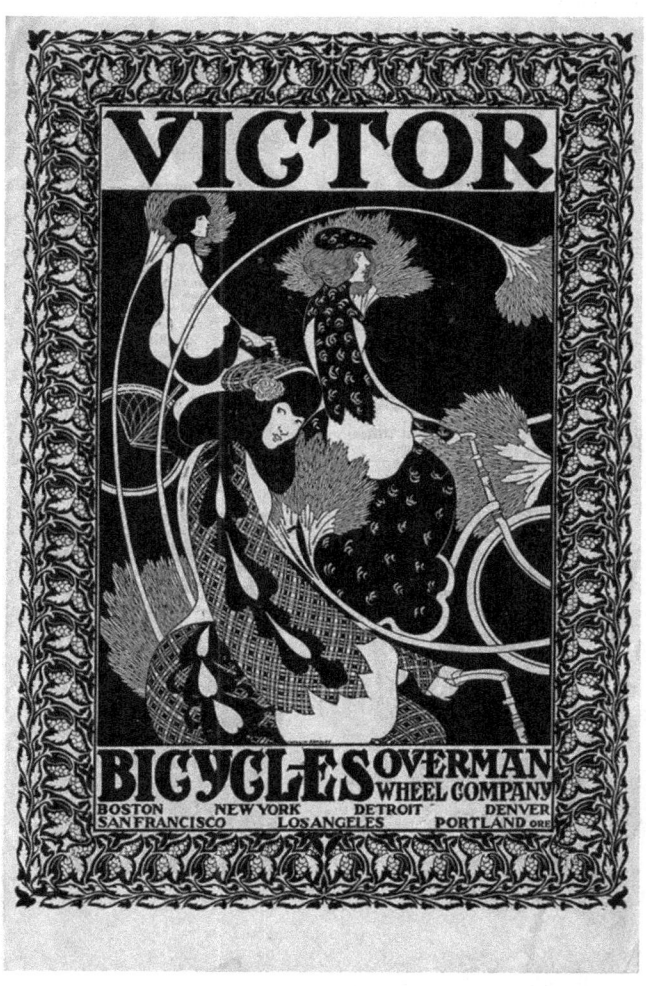

Figure 3.2 Victor Cycles, 1896. https://commons.wikimedia.org/wiki/File:William_Henry_Bradley-_Victor_Bicycles.jpg

escape from ordinary life, but also its expansive function in terms of beauty and glamor, as it elevates the cyclist from woman to goddess.

In these ads, the mechanical machine of speed is displayed like an artwork, juxtaposed with fashion costumes and lush foliage in a dazzling fantasy world manipulated to appeal to the tastes and dreams of the reader. The viewing public is elevated into what Kracauer, commenting on the fantasy world of the department store, calls a "fairy grotto," a "magic" realm, "exempt from natural laws," and "preserving marvelous illusions" like the "stage" (22). The ultimate objective, of course, is to instill in the public a newfound appreciation and positive response toward the image of the female cyclist, and to reimagine her as a figure of feminine elegance and fashionable display, rather than the masculine Amazon of brute strength and athleticism.

The manufacturers' efforts to glamorize the woman cyclist tap into wider trends in the *fin-de-siècle* years that increasingly position the bicycle as a coveted commodity and the latest fashion statement for a mostly middle-class clientele. By the mid-1890s, improvement in technology widened its appeal to other segments of the public, but the bicycle's continuing high costs meant that cycling was still a mostly bourgeois recreation. Rubinstein writes that membership of the Cyclists' Touring Club, the biggest one in Britain, shot up from 14,166 in 1894 to 60,449 in 1899, but the members were still mostly from "the titled, the fashionable, and the professional and business classes" (50). In 1898 there were more than 2,000 cycling clubs in the UK, 300 of which were in London alone (50).

London was the commercial and cultural capital of cycling in Britain, as bicycle sales, practice, exhibitions, advertising, journalism, schools, and clubs were all concentrated in London, and two national cycle shows, the Stanley and National Cycle Shows, were held there annually. To ride a bicycle and enjoy its elegant speed was a pivotal part, in those boom years, of the highly emulated London air and London lifestyle, and style and status were just as important as progressiveness in the appeal of that London air. *Lady Cyclist* estimated, on July 10, 1897, that there were more than a million bicycles in London alone, amounting to a third of the overall national number (277). Of all lady members of the Cyclists' Touring Club, half were London residents (Hanlon 15).[4] Many titled ladies were prominent cyclists, and their frequent appearances in interviews and photos in cycling magazines further highlights the bicycle's links with the privileged and the wealthy.

---

[4] The Cyclists' Touring Club was founded in 1878, and catered especially for the upper-middle class. Its members increased dramatically from 14,166 in 1894 to 60,449 in 1899, before dropping steadily afterwards as the bicycle craze waned. See Rubinstein 50. The Club also established the first cycling club magazine, which blossomed from an early club circular first published in 1878 to a full-blown cycling magazine—the *CTC Monthly Gazette*—in 1884. In 1890, it introduced the first "Lady's Page" and invited Davidson to be its lady columnist. See "The History of Cycle Magazines, 1878–1900."

One Humber bicycle ad, regularly printed in the pages of the *Lady Cyclist* in 1896 and 1897, lays particular emphasis on Lady De Veer's aristocratic title, and the envy and emulation of observers admiring her elegantly cycling figure (Figure 3.3). "How gracefully Lady De Veer rides," exclaims the man in the ad; "yes indeed," replies the lady by his side, "but then you see, she rides a Humber" ("Humber Bicycles" 278). Only a Humber bicycle, the ad suggests, is classy enough to display Lady De Veer's fashionable figure to the best advantage.

The final stamp of fashion and status is sealed when cycling became the highlight of London Society's annual season in the mid-1890s. By 1895, London's Battersea Park had become known as the ladies' cycle park, when debutantes went for their Sunday promenades on bicycles rather than horses. *The Times*

HE: "*How gracefully Lady De Vere rides!*"
SHE: '*Yes, indeed, but then you see she rides a Humber!*"

Figure 3.3 *Lady Cyclist*, Jan. 2, 1897, p. 278. The British Library Archive.

noted in November 1895 that "This year has witnessed a great development of cycling among ladies, and the parks, especially Battersea, have become quite a parade-ground for them" (qtd. in Hanlon 114). *The Pall Mall Gazette* also noted in August 1895:

> Battersea Park has now an individuality stamped upon its fair face—an individuality as clearly defined as that of Hyde Park. A lovely roadway of hard gravel ironed to the smoothness of a shopwalker's shirtfront by a thousand pneumatic-tyred wheels; a row of rosy-cheeked English girls coquettishly perched on the frailest, daintiest contrivance of glittering wire, purring along this said ironed roadway, a poetical flow of many tinted draperies, hair golden, black, auburn, red, chestnut, flowing free or striving to break from its tight coils; flaunting hats, modest caps, every kind of headgear in fact. And this endless chain of beauty forever circling by green lawns where row on row of lookers-on sit in wicker chairs or had County Council benches to enjoy the scene. Not only is Battersea Park the park of the cycle, but peculiarly the park of the lady cyclist. (115)

By 1986 when Hyde Park opened its own cycling parade, the north bank of the Serpentine became known as the "Ladies' Mile," with 2,000–3,000 cyclists seen riding along the Serpentine in Hyde Park, according to *The Queen*'s report on March 21, 1896 (514). Even the Queen's drive to take up residence in Buckingham Palace on March 6, 1897, a spectacle in its own right, lost some of its attraction as the crowds who had gathered in Hyde Park were distracted from the main event by the fashions displayed by the cycling ladies nearby. "The dresses were very good, very narrow stripes predominating, black and dark grey, with a white hair line, finding especial favour. Red, I thought a little 'off'; still, it was used much in hats ... Jackets are evidently to be worn very short this season" (qtd. in Hanlon 120–21). Lady cyclists were now a top-billed spectacle, looked up to and emulated as leaders of fashion.

Women's cycling is now treasured more for its function as conspicuous display. Ladies' bicycle accessories particularly put beauty above functionality, including bicycle parasols, canopies, cycling shields, aprons, handle-bar-mounted flower baskets, and diminutive-sized lamps, bells, watches, and compasses (Hanlon 88–89). These accessories certainly impede the speed of the bicycle, but they are most handy when the lady rides slowly and for effect. One advice article in *Lady Cyclist* goes so far as to hold up the bicycle itself as the epitome of fashionable elegance, to which the female bicyclist must constantly aspire. Entitled "Why Lady Cyclists Should Dress Well," the article opines that lazy or ugly women would be shamed into dressing better when standing beside a beautiful bicycle: "Even women with dowdy figures and appearances might have her blunted senses aroused if she be shown how her dowdiness, directly contrasted with the graceful lines of her machine, is increased a thousandfold" (9).

Women's movement activists also joined in and actively promoted the glamorous, fashionable image of the New Woman cyclist. Feminists celebrated the bicycle for bringing about women's emancipation, but they were also eager to emphasize the woman cyclist's femininity and elegance in order to assuage public unease. This fashion focus was partly a response to frequent public ridicule, especially in the early years, of the ugly, "unwomanly" New Woman cyclist. Many feminists felt it a mission or duty to aestheticize the woman cyclist and highlight her fashionable display. By emphasizing that this was always an appropriately female role, they sought to effect greater public acceptance. One writer, for instance, insists that the New Woman cyclist is far from that caricature who would "assume an attire which leaves her sex a matter of guess work" ("The New Woman: What She Really Is" 504). Unlike the "pushy, shrill-voiced, aggressive female" who "assumes a masculine swagger" and "demands her own right at the risk of trampling on those of others," the New Woman cyclist is instead elegant and feminine, "not at all different from what nature intends her to be" (504).

Other New Woman cyclists insist that bicycle speed, used as spectacle and display, does not detract from a woman's feminine nature but actually increases a woman's sexual appeal. One New Woman reader, who calls herself "advanced," "strong-minded," and "most eccentric," writes in to *Lady Cyclist* with the declaration that "though I love my 'cycle,'" it must "play second fiddle" to her very feminine "weakness to appreciate masculine admiration and interest" when cycling ("Pros and Cons" 118). For her, the pleasure of cycling lies primarily in displaying feminine beauty and attracting male attention, so much so that she is against wearing bloomers and supports long feminine skirts that only slightly reveals the cyclist's ankles, because "everyone knows the charm a pretty ankle has for a man" (118). A cycling woman may be progressive and advanced, but she must still be "guided by that beautifier of life," and "do our utmost to be as pretty, graceful and womanly when mounted as we are in our tea-gowns at home" (118). Lady Colin Campbell even blames ugly, unfeminine cyclists for the initial public prejudice against the woman cyclist: "Bicycling itself is not unfeminine ... [i]t is the fact that one is ugly and ungraceful when riding it that makes one unfeminine." To look fashionable and beautiful becomes almost an imperative and a duty, because this will help "mold public prejudices and opinions" (9).

When the New Woman writer Sarah Grand made several appearances as a famous lady cyclist in mass magazines like the *Lady Cyclist* in 1895, *Hub* and *Cycling World Illustrated* in 1896, and *Lady's Realm* in 1897, she also encouraged the identification of the female cyclist with the fashion model, and commented frequently on the latest Parisian cycling fashion (Heilmann *New Woman Fiction* 34). In her interview with *Cycling World Illustrated*, she revealed that she learned cycling at a cycling academy in Paris, where she saw "women of all ages, sizes, and weight managing their bicycles with perfect facility, and evidently enjoying exhilarating exercise" ("Chats with Cyclists: Madame Sarah Grand" 3). For her

Hub interview in the same year in the magazine's "Women of Note in the Cycling World" section, Grand posed with her bicycle outside her Kensington home, and devoted almost equal space to the fashion side of cycling. Conceding that she rides in a skirt in England to avoid disapproval, Grand was nevertheless highly critical of the cuts available in London that "convert the wearers into caricatures and are appalling to the cultivated eye and taste" (qtd. in Tooley 419). She is not averse to demonstrating a familarity with the latest fashion trends, and is especially appreciative of stylish Parisian bicycling costumes which accentuates the "good points" while concealing the "less pleasing" (419). "I think it is one of a woman's first duties," she declares in the *Lady Cyclist* interview of 1895, "to consider her personal appearance" and prioritize beauty and elegance ("Lady Cyclist at Home" 205). Grand herself certainly made a point of appearing elegant and feminine in her person. The reporter for the *Lady Cyclist* describes Grand as "the extreme opposite of all that is masculine, coarse, or loud":

> She is tall, and exceedingly graceful, with a soothing, sympathetic voice and a wonderful smile; and as she comes forward clad in a soft clinging gown of some dark material she is as unlike the much caricatured 'new' woman as it is possible for any beautiful, delicate creature to be. (205)

Elsewhere in her prose work "The New Woman and the Old," Grand also stresses the elegant beauty of the fashionably clad New Woman along lines similar to popular bicycle ads. The New Woman is "a young creature, slender, elegant, admirably built, her figure, set off to the best advantage by the new cycling costume, being evidently undeformed by compression of any kind" (69). This New Woman cyclist is not just fashionable and beautiful, but very feminine, "happily married, with a young child, and keen not to spend too much time talking to the narrator because she is intent on 'hurrying home to put my baby to bed, and get my husband's tea'" (69). In the same way that cycling ads and posters stress feminine elegance to assuage the mannish, menacing image of the woman cyclist, Grand separates the New Woman from the "Old Woman who shrieks" (70) and is "solemn" and "deadly dull" (71), and urges feminists to embrace "womanly" elegance (73) and "beautiful," "fine physique" (70, 75) as a political strategy to effect greater public acceptance.

By aestheticizing the woman cyclist and highlighting her elegant display, feminist activists link women's cycling to reassuring traditions while at the same time claiming new possibilities. This is a shrewd tactic because, for one, feminine display is traditionally an important means of showcasing middle-class respectability. An emphasis on fashion subsumes the otherwise menacing woman cyclist under familiar feminine roles, and also aligns her with the tides and progress of an increasingly consumerist modernity. The New Woman cyclist may be new and daring in mastering speed and staging an expanded subjectivity enabled by free mobility, but she still follows patriarchal norms which prioritize women's beauty and youthful attraction. With the bicycle's conspicuous speed acting as an essential index to one's modishness and a commodified form of progressive modernity, the New Woman has utilized and manipulated this bourgeois consumerist construction to further their political cause.

But in doing so they also make use of speed's new role as a marker of class, as this display is very much predicated on middle-class status, privilege, and exclusivity. The bicycle and the right look come with a high price, and even cycling's celebrated role in loosening the codes of heterosocial interaction is partially attributable to its exclusive nature. Because cycling is expensive and available largely to the middle class, this class restriction makes cycling seem safe for women, as one is likely to meet only middle-class cyclists. In a modern urban environment of chance encounters and ephemeral appearances, bicycle speed becomes a reliable indicator of class and status, and access to that speed translates into an assured way of meeting one's social equal without the need for introduction. Women cyclists may encounter men on more equal terms, but this equality is predicated on their shared power as consumers of ostentatious speed. Bicycle speed is now an increasingly sensuous, luxurious, and pleasurable experience of middle-class life that has brought women greater freedom along gender lines, but it also helps to erect new hierarchies along class lines.

Cycling Romance: An Out-and-About Heroine

As bicycle manufacturers and advertisers, as well as New Women activists, work to glamorize the image of the woman cyclist, cycling press becomes the best venue to help shape and transform public opinion. The bicycle and the popular magazines, as Sarah Hallenbeck points out, enjoyed a "symbiotic" relationship in the middle years of the 1890s (74). New Women cyclists gave frequent interviews, posed for portraits and wrote letters and columns for these magazines, and bicycle manufacturers also advertised heavily there. Advertising for manufactured goods had traditionally used huge billboards erected in thoroughfares (Adburgham 232), but bicycle manufacturers switched ads to the mass press, giving the latter a "measure of recognition" as a major medium of advertising (Petty 33). The mass press, in its turn, responded by accentuating a new periodical format where the magazines integrate the bicycle ads, now their biggest source of revenue, with their editorial contents in a shared discourse of consumption. In the more commercialized, ad-packed, product-centered cycling magazines, editorial materials blur with the bicycle ads, as magazine editors "actively solicited and commissioned" stories, reports, and other "topical, timely materials" (Garvey 82). The ultimate purpose is to promote the ads and steer the reader toward a new view of cycling as glamor and status display.

During the height of the "bicycle craze," almost all general magazines had their cycle correspondents, reporting on the latest bicycle races, tours, newest models, and accessories. The preeminent women's magazine, *The Queen*, for instance, probably the best source for women's cycling among noncycling magazines, ran a weekly column on cycling from the summer of 1895 onward. Between July and December that year, it published 39 articles on cycling, and in the year 1896 about 100 articles altogether.[5] While male-catering cycling magazines—including *Cycling, Tricyclist, Bicycling News, Cyclist, Bicycling Times, Wheel World, Wheeling, Scottish Cyclist, Irish Wheelman, Amateur Wheelman,* and *Hub*[6]—saw increased sales, cycling magazines targeting women also sprang up. In the inaugural March 1895 issue of *Lady Cyclist* (1895–97), the publisher Charles P. Sisley, who also published *Cycling*, wrote that "ordinary cycling papers are unable to devote sufficient attention to cycling for ladies, and with the rapid growth of this branch of the pastime, it is only natural that it should have its special and exclusive organization" ("When in Doubt" 42). The new journal sold at 3d per issue, and was so sought after that it soon changed from a monthly to a weekly as of June 27, 1896. Another advertising-supported ladies' weekly, *Wheelwoman and Society Cycling News* (1896–99), appeared on May 23, 1896, and sold at an annual subscription rate of 5s. *Cycling World Illustrated*, published biweekly between March 18 and September 9, 1896, also featured lady cyclists on all its covers and most of its editorial and advertising materials.

These women's cycling magazines particularly reflect a consumerist bend and a visual focus designed to promote women's cycling as fashionable and glamorous. Mass magazines of the 1890s have in general become increasingly visual, in a sharp departure from early- or mid-nineteenth-century journals that appealed mostly to bourgeois male readers and favored long discussions on politics and social issues (Sillars 72). For women's magazines in particular, glittering ads and illustrations and later photos take up more than half of the pages by the 1890s, while editorial materials are shorter and more varied, favoring a "visual" mode of reading involving maximum change and an ever-mobile pace always seeking the next stimulation. Even feminist magazines share this pursuit of glamorous display, with ads and illustrations appearing alongside suffragette slogans and calls for feminist meetings.[7] When women's cycling magazines cropped up in the mid-1890s "bicycle craze," the pages are crammed with an endless array of bicycle ads and accessories, photos of beautifully dressed lady cyclists, and the latest fashion tips

---

[5] This information about *The Queen* and the cycling magazines is based on my research in the British Library in July 2017.

[6] The most popular magazine, *Cycling*, reported a circulation of 50,000 copies in its November 20, 1898 issue ("50,000!" 425).

[7] The first issue of *The Woman Worker*, for instance, a penny magazine published by the National Federation of Women Workers, has five pages of ads out of a total of sixteen pages, and arranges its slogan "WOMEN SHOULD VOTE" in a similarly eye-catching format alongside an ad for Fenning's Children's Powders.

and news of fashion sales. The act of reading is therefore very much like the act of window-shopping, with the textual space mirroring the commercial space of London in a ceaseless parade of commodities and spectacles. By turning themselves into a visually titillating and desire-stimulating "virtual emporium" (Fraser, Green, and Johnston 172), these cycling magazines impart the message that to dress well and be in fashion is one of the chief pleasures of cycling.

Lady Cyclist, for instance, carries twice as many advertisements for patented underwear, cosmetics, skirts, jackets, boots, and hats for women cyclists as it does for the bicycles themselves. *Cycling World Illustrated* is a delight to the eye, with well over half the space devoted to the latest Parisian cycling costumes, millinery, dainty cycling accessories, and proper manners and etiquette for women cyclists. A September 16 issue, for instance, chats excitedly about a Parisienne cyclist attired in "a costume of dark blue silk, consisting of a *culotte* cut quite straight and short and trimmed with three rows of narrow silver braids" ("Parisienne Cycling Modes" 9). A "marvelous powder" is also recommended to lady cyclists to be sprinkled on their hair to add luminousness. The anonymous reporter, camouflaging as an English lady writing home from Paris, is particularly enthusiastic about an expensive, small leather case which could be attached either to the handle-bar of the bicycle or to the waist-belt, or "worn across the shoulder á la bandoulière," because it usefully contains cosmetics as well as "a small button-hook, a tiny pair of scissors, needles, cotton and a stiletto" in case of tears to the bicycling costume (11).

These editorial materials increasingly blur with the bicycle and accessories ads, and fortify the image of cycling as a preeminent platform for conspicuous display. In this new editorial format, which facilitates a form of magazine reading in constant dialogue with and often corroborating the product-pitching of the ads, even the romance stories join in. Romance stories had long been a staple in Victorian women's magazines, and when the bicycle became popular in the mid-1890s a particular type of romance stories cropped up, which typically featured middle-class women cyclists who meet and marry ideal men as a result of their cycling. Several traits distinguish this new type of stories. They were mostly published in the cycling magazines which blossomed during the "bicycle craze," and when these magazines folded after the bicycle boom waned by the end of the decade, the stories also faded from the scene. In terms of content and layout, these stories are an integral part of the product-specific and ad-reliant cycling magazines and are much more commodified than other periodical literature. Liberally interspersed with ads and illustrations, they are often "commissioned" and chosen by the cycling magazines to promote the bicycle and actively advance an overall discourse of consumerist display (Garvey 82).

Still, by featuring women cyclists in outdoors settings and exposing them to the excitement as well as the dangers of expanded mobility, these stories may prove radical even for the typical Victorian women's magazines, which prefer "larmoyanty love-tales" and celebrate domesticity as a feminine ideal (Beetham 22). Within the cycling magazines themselves, these stories also prove to be more sophisticated than other editorial materials like reports and advice columns. They achieve greater persuasion and sensitivity by seeking a measure of realism, and place women's cycling in plot lines where real sociocultural problems are acknowledged. At the same time, they also seek to offer imaginative pleasure and a happy fantasy of love and marriage, which ultimately resolves all conflicts and manages to stretch to the uttermost what is acceptable. The stories register conservative anxieties by acknowledging that women's cycling is still a subject fraught with controversy, but they strive to assuage its disruptive image by subsuming it under the tried and proven formula of heterosexual romance and the new discourse of fashionable consumption. Ultimately, they prove to be the most subtly effective part of the magazines' consumerist agenda, as they manage to convey the message that access to the right kind of bicycle speed enhances, rather than detracts from, a woman's elegant femininity and her chance for happiness.

Cycling romance first appeared sporadically in illustrated magazines with a long tradition of covering women's leisure activities, like *Susan: The Badminton Magazine of Sports and Pastime*. They also showed up in family magazines like *The Strand, The Windsor, The Idler*, and *Bow Bells*. These are much longer than in the illustrated magazines, taking up nine to ten pages, and would appear in issues with a strong focus on cycling in their both ads and their editorial content. When women's cycling magazines came on the scene, cycling romance became a regular feature. *Lady Cyclist* published one or two love stories in almost every issue from March 1895 to July 31, 1897, when it merged with *The Wheelwoman*. The latter was more focused on reports and comments in the earlier issues, but published more stories in 1897 and 1898. The stories are mostly penned by female authors, often under pseudonyms, a format replicated in other editorial content such as comments and reports. On January 8, 1898, *The Queen* wrote that "[b]icycling stories are becoming quite the thing now," and "one can scarcely take up a magazine without coming across a story in which the ubiquitous bicycle figures in a more or less prominent fashion" (92).

Because cycling is still linked with the New Woman and all her controversial connotations, cycling romance often features women's cycling as a central conflict in the narrative plotline, which needs to be specially worked on. All the stories aim toward a measure of realism and set cycling up as a source of contention dividing the lovers, with the male lead most vociferously protesting its harmful impact on the heroine. A 1897 story in the *Lady Cyclist*, for instance, features a male lead who even harbors murderous intentions toward female cyclists. When he sees the "degrading spectacle" and "hideous picture" of two girls "unabashedly" trying to ride bicycles, "his annoyance was extreme, and he felt it only needed the presence of a revolver to urge him to commit a desperate deed" ("Vagaries of Fate" 310). In another, a male cyclist calls himself "a sensitive plant," "a very mimosa of retiredness," and a "shy" and "timid" man without "an independent opinion upon anything in the wide world," but his "one firm line of moral demarcation," "the only subject" he could "wax fluent and self-assertive" and "confidently express an opinion over," is his abhorrence of women cyclists and their detestable rational dress ("Wanted—A Bicycle" 713). The very titles of the stories, like "The Conversion of Ernest Warren" (1895), "The Hate that Changed" (1895), "A Cause of Quarrel" (1897), "The Reformation of Laurence Hope" (1897), and "Discord and Harmony: The Story of A Musical Ride" (1897) acknowledge the antagonism toward women's cycling and the effort needed to overcome such opposition.

As a genre, romance stories recognize problems, differences, and multiple subject positions, and explore the anxieties of femininity, before finally constraining such femininity within the orthodoxy of marriage and motherhood (Modleski 46, Ang 105). In traditional romantic stories published in Victorian family magazines, obstacles to the heroine's eventual happiness usually reside in her lower social and financial standing as she falls in love with a man "her social superior" (Beetham 73). It is her irreproachable, decorous femininity—in stark contrast to the dangerous, transgressive femininity often embodied by the "bad woman"—that eventually wins for her the love of the hero. In the 1890s cycling romance, however, the heroine's penchant for bicycling brings her dangerously close to the domain of transgressive femininity, at least from the point of view of the male protagonist. It is her very distance from, rather than embodiment of, the ideal femininity celebrated by the hero that becomes the central narrative conflict. Many of the male protagonists express a nostalgic longing for submissive, modest femininity, and insist that their beloved do not become one of those "fast," "forward," "unfeminine," and "unbecoming" women cyclists ("From a Man's Point of View" 16). Bicycling, in this sense, becomes a point of division along gender rather than class lines, constituting a major obstacle to the happiness of the main couple or the resolution of the romance plot.

This is a conflict that seems to arise only with women cyclists. Romantic stories about male cyclists appeared sporadically in the 1870s and 1880s during the time of the Ordinary bicycle. In these early stories, a gentleman high-wheeler goes for a ride in the country and meets a demure maiden in a cottage, typically after he has had an accident and knocks at the cottage door for help. The housebound maiden, like in the 1888 story "How Dick Managed It," demonstrates her natural nurturing and potentially wifely qualities, enchants the gentleman cyclist, and secures a marriage proposal by the end of the nursing session. The pursuit of bicycle speed for the male characters is perceived to be a naturalized part of their masculine heroism and adventurous spirit. In "The Vicar's Daughter" published in *The London Reader* in 1883, the bicycling gentleman carries on the age-old image of the active and mobile man of the world, who appears to the waiting and domestically bound maiden like a knight-errant in steel. To the naïve, homely, unsophisticated daughter, trapped by her tyrannical vicar father in a Sleepy Hollow existence, the hero's possession of high speed and mobility is an indispensable extension of his admirable masculinity and power, a brave means effecting her rescue that is controlled by the man but irrevocably beyond her own reach.

In the 1890s cycling romance, however, women are themselves the controllers of that speed, freed from their passive domesticity and actively riding out and running into men. More often than not, they are the party responsible—presumably due to inexperience or endearing innocence—for a cycling accident which invariably turns into a love encounter with their future husbands. A new, active, and more emboldened femininity is therefore advanced in these cycling stories—a femininity that is first of all predicated on the women's possession of bicycle speed. Victorian women's mobility had already expanded with the arrival of the railway in the mid-decades of the nineteenth century; by the last decades of the century, many middle-class women were able to navigate the public urban space on foot or by omnibus without the need for chaperones.[8] This greater female mobility, however, was invariably seen as threatening and disruptive by masculine conservatives.[9] The bicycle entails an even more agentive, individualized manipulation of speed, and the bicyclist of the mid-1890s is able to go to places farther away from the prying eyes of the public. This gives rise to greater freedom, but also to increased risks for transgression.

In the cycling romance of the mid-1890s, all the heroines enthusiastically embrace the active speed of the bicycle. In the 1897 "Catastrophe," the heroine takes her bicycle on a train that leaves London for the countryside and then braves an evening ride in the dark country for 8 miles all by herself. In "A Country Ride" (1896), another lady cyclist uses the same method to see a friend 60 miles away from London and gets back home by the same evening. She is out and about on her bicycle so much that her husband suspects her of secretly meeting her former lover. In "Overthrown" (1897), the female protagonist rejoices in her solitary bicycle ride in the country and thinks nothing of staying the night, all by herself, in the village inn: "Such a September evening! And such a road! Fair English scenery just touched by autumn, and my trusty wheel answered like a living thing to my slightest touch, as we sped into the little village where I intended staying" ("Overthrown" 745). Bicycle speed offers much greater individual freedom than previous modes of transport, as one lady cyclist finds out: "It is splendid to be independent of the carriage; one has so much more freedom without impatient horses and hungry coachmen" ("Woman of Today" 105).

Another story, "Trespassers will be Prosecuted" (1897), reverses the traditional order of gendered spatiality when the lady cyclist becomes the unwitting trespasser and invades into the land of the male protagonist. The female cyclist is now the

[8] For more on how the acceleration of commodity culture at the end of the century helped broaden women's mobility in the urban streets, see Nord and Parsons.

[9] For male objections to the female walker or *flaneuse*, see Parsons 43–81; for male anxiety over women's use of the railway, see Martin's discussion of *Lady Audley*, p. 132.

actively mobile and speeding party, while the male love interest is land-bound, static, and waiting. In "The Conversion of Ernest Warren" (1895), the cycling Mabel further takes on the role of the knight-errant, saving her lover who nearly falls down a cliff. Ernest is at first "horrified" when he learns that his Mabel is "not the tractable little woman he expected her to be," because she has learnt to cycle and joined the ranks of the hated "New Woman" cyclists who "wear men's clothes, smoke cigarettes," and are "unwomanly and unlovable" (40). But when he accidently falls down a cliff when out walking one day and clings on to a rock in desperation, it is Mabel's fast cycling and her active mobility that allows her to get to that desolate, out-of-the-way spot, and discover her lover's plight when no one else is around. Again, when Ernest is trapped and motionless, it is Mabel's machine-aided speed that finally saves him: "Thank God! I have my bicycle here!" She quickly seizes her bicycle, "mounted like a flash," and speeds to the nearest village to get help. Then she cycles back to the cliff ahead of the helping neighbors, who have to come on foot, and saves her lover with a thick rope tied to her waist. This is a task that no ordinary maiden could perform, but with Mabel's regular cycling and the exercise and energy this affords, she is able to stand with "the rope-end coiled around her dainty waist, her feet planted firmly on the ground, and a look of love and determination on her sweet face which intensified its intense beauty," while her lover clings on to the other end of the rope before help eventually arrives (43). After this trauma Ernest is, of course, completely converted. He admits his "error of reasoning" and professes to love her forever more, for "being the fearless girl you are" (43).

Not only are the women cyclists more sped-up and mobile, but the circumstances of their love encounters are also changed. Like most short stories published in magazines in the 1890s, the short length of cycling romance dictates that it forsake the complicated plot of serialized fiction and gear up all its narrative elements toward one experience, one moment of truth, in order to achieve what Edgar Allan Poe calls "a unique singular effect."[10] For Poe's detective stories, that moment comes at the final ending when all pieces of the puzzle fall into place. But since readers of romantic stories are more invested in the process of falling in love, wherein lovers meet, sparks fly, or misunderstanding occurs, the moment of revelation in cycling romance does not usually come in the final obligatory happy

---

[10] Poe defines the short story as a work that has a "unity of effect" in his 1842 review of Hawthorne's *Twice-Told Tales* (qtd. in Chan 4).The short story consolidated its form in the 1890s when fiction published in the mushrooming mass magazines was more likely than not short stories. The *Strand* and the *Yellow Book* published only stories to the exclusion of serials, long a staple of Victorian periodicals. The genre's basic conventions of economy, realism, and unity of effect are as much dictated by aesthetic considerations as by the economic imperatives of the magazines where almost all of them were published. As Winnie Chan points out, the stories unify the plots around a revelation and work toward an ultimately inevitable truth at the ending. The Sherlock Holmes detective stories, published to such a success in *The Strand*, are a good example. These commercially developed conventions, coupled with the focus on isolated experiences through a limited point of view, anticipate modernist narratives (1–4).

ending, but when the heroine runs into her future husband whilst cycling, often as a result of accidents or punctures.

In these moments, which take a central place in the stories, the accidents arise because the woman cyclist is not yet a master of bicycle speed. But this challenge of speed adds drama and excitement rather than fear, because it is presented as manageable with repairs and basic knowledge. More importantly, it even becomes desirable and thrilling because it facilitates love encounters and enhances opportunities for romance and marriage. The lady's interaction with mechanized speed provides a means for her to demonstrate her helpless, feminine nature to the gallant gentleman cyclist who would fix the puncture and rescue the lady. Such moments of revelation reinforce stereotypes of the weaker, inexperienced women, but the meticulously described scenes also harbor other meanings that set the genre apart from more traditional romance. The love encounters, for instance, invariably take place in the outdoors, on the street or the country road, and on more equal terms between two fellow bicyclists who enjoy a more relaxed heterosexual code of behavior without the need for proper introduction. Access to bicycle speed, as the critic Patricia Marks points out, has changed the "conventions of courtship and chaperonage" and hetersocial interaction (174).

In "Romance of a Bicycle" (1896), published in the family magazine *Bow Bells*, a mother enquires curiously of her daughter for any interesting person she has met during her afternoon bicycle ride. She is not at all perturbed to find the daughter has ridden with and talked intimately with a Mr. Nicholas, of whom she herself knows a little. Her only opinion is that "the little I have seen him I think he is very nice, and certainly very good-looking" (289). In "A Double Marriage" (1897), a lady is much shocked when a friend thinks that their cycling club is for ladies' only and not a mixed one, for "nobody except the veriest old maid would dream of a club for ladies only nowadays." "We are," as she claims, "much more advanced than that in these educational times" (196). This more relaxed code of interaction has also come about, of course, because bicycle speed has become a reliable indicator of class and status. With cycling being affordable mostly to the middle class, bicycle speed becomes safe for women because one is likely to meet one's social equal without the need for introduction.

In "The Result of an Accident" (1897), similar experiences with bicycle troubles lead a gentleman cyclist to offer help to a lady cyclist who is waiting to transport her wrecked bicycle onto a train. Both smile understandingly and speak freely, for who would expect a lady cyclist to "look at etiquette from the *slow* standpoint of English maidens in such crisis like this?" (128; emphasis added) This sentence suggests that the most visible mark differentiating the modern woman from the traditional is speed, and that the traditional woman is particularly seen as hidebound and narrow-minded because she is "slow." In "A Romance of the Wheel" (1896), things get more heated when the "modern-minded" lady cyclist notices the "straightly-built," "well-formed" legs of the male cyclist resting in a country inn, a "splendid" "magnificent" "Apollo" and "King Otho" to her admiring eyes. She has been on a week-long cycling tour all by herself, and would have liked to take the initiative to speak to him after seeing the "CTC" badge the man wears: the Cyclists' Touring Club, of which she is also a member. Shared membership is "clearly a bond of union" to "warrant an introduction," which would very likely develop into a love encounter if only the young man has not affected a "disgusted" look because of her rational costume. He is later, of course, to come round and fall in love with her after an accident (18).

In these stories, women's access to bicycle speed certainly disrupts the male characters' view of ideal femininity. Yet, more often than not, the male protagonists end up accepting their lovers for who they are: "a woman of today" ("Woman of Today" 104). As is suggested by the titles, it is often the men who are converted or reformed, after trying unsuccessfully to change their lovers into what "is impossible to their nature" ("Conversion of Ernest Warren" 43). This recognition of a modern, out-and-about, and sped-up femininity does not mean, however, that cycling romance celebrates radical feminism or the New Woman's iconoclastic calls for social and political emancipation. Cycling romance portrays women's restlessness with static domesticity and their enthusiasm for a more active, mobile lifestyle. But, ultimately, any suggestion of overt disruptiveness associated with "unfeminine" fast speed is downplayed and smoothed over, giving way to a more elegant, controlled experience of cycling that acknowledges the woman cyclist's newness while also recuperating her within familiar traditions. This taming of women's otherwise threatening use of speed has greater urgency, because cycling romance is an integral part of the cycling magazines' overall mission to boost the popularity of the bicycle and effect greater sales. The stories seek to recuperate the woman cyclist by persistently emphasizing on her beauty, youth, and stylish elegance. While all romance portrays women as young and beautiful, cycling romance adds a consumerist twist and links feminine beauty particularly to fashion and display, and to women's participation in modern commodity culture, wherein speed becomes a commodity and a crucial status symbol. The greater freedom brought by bicycle speed is thus aligned with a wider consumerist choice, with which women could enhance their beauty, sexual appeal, and romantic prospects.

In all the cycling stories, the heroine's reassuring feminine beauty melts the heart of the male protagonist, and alleviates any initial objection he may harbor. In "A Romance of the Wheel," the disgusted young man with those Apollo-like legs " underwent some subtle change" when he sees the "grey eyes" of the heroine (19); he forgets all about his previous "unfeigned disgust" over the "filthy spectacle" of a rational-dressed female cyclist (18), curses himself as "a Mrs. Grundy in trousers," meditates on the writing of a "Treatise on the Defence of Rational Dress," and finally begins to compose a "song to a Diana, with a touch of a grey-eyed Pallas Athene about her," his "newly-made Queen of the Beauty of Things"

(21). Fortuitously, the lady's wheels suffer a puncture five miles from the nearest inn, allowing Apollo to forego all "mental preliminaries" and help the lady "as a knight of old." His "entirely unnecessary ardour" is, of course, finally rewarded with reciprocated love and an agreement of marriage (21).

In "A Good-Looking Young Man" (1897), Lawrence, the male cyclist, is annoyed when he is run into by a lady cyclist at the street crossing, but "there are distinctly mitigating circumstances, when, for instance, the lady is young and beautiful, with a timid appealing look in her blue grey eyes, and a complexion like a rose leaf that deepens prettily as she pleads for forgiveness" (682). In "The Hate That Changed" (1895), a young "misogynist" aristocrat is alarmed by the sharp bells of two lady cyclists, hates the sight of their rational dresses, but is transformed when, after his horse is frightened by the bicycles and throws him to the ground, he is nursed and bandaged by one of the girls (Figure 3.4). Those feminine nursing skills and her "grey eyes" are enough to change his hate and secure a vow of love after his recovery (33). In "Wanted—A Bicycle" (1899), the shy "mimosa" man who has firmly sworn against rational dress because "skirts are the prerogative of women," immediately declares that the costume is "really a becoming garment," and that his previous views about the "demoralizing effect of trousers" are but "so much windy prejudice," after meeting a "pathetic and engaging" young female cyclist, "as pretty as a carnation" (715). The young lady has had her bicycle stolen, and could not face the prospect of walking home alone without her bicycle. The mimosa man hastily offers to escort her, and does not at all mind being seen walking down the street with a woman clad in rational dress. "[G]iving no thought at all to the sweet irony of circumstance that implies him an apostate to his creed," he finds himself in "an enchanted dream" (716). By the end of the day, he is ready to "take oath" that not only does the rational bicycling dress have a "complete raison d'être," but that any woman who doesn't wear it is a "frump," and any man who hates it is a "blackguard and a decadent" (717).

In "Vagaries of Fate" where the male lead harbors murderous intentions toward women cyclists, the sight of the "beauty" and "pretty figure" of the cycling heroine is enough to make him crane his neck after her in a most "undignified position," and pronounce her clothes to have "good taste," her ankles "not thick," nor her feet "clumsy" (311). Making "an exception to his unbounded intolerance of cyclists," he returns diligently to the same spot the next day anxiously waiting for the girl cyclist, and is so desperate for an introduction that he fancies something heroic, like "dashing into the road and snatching her from under the feet of a runaway horse or to rescue her from the jaws of a mad dog"—"anything that would lend him a halo of romance" (311).

These stories' emphasis on the women's transformative beauty and feminine grace shifts the focus of ideal femininity from innate, nurturing qualities to visual impact and specular display. This is partly due to the fleeting nature of the lovers' encounter, wherein they meet as strangers while cycling speedily. It amounts to

THE LADY CYCLIST.   29

" *Gentle hands removed the mutilated coat from his left arm, and Nancy produced from her pocket a business-like pocket surgical case with a roll of lint.*"

Figure 3.4 Illustration for "The Hate that Changed." *Lady Cyclist*, March 1895, p. 29. The British Library Archive.

a sped-up version of the quintessential modern urban experience of the transient, the fleeting, and the contingent, in which context and depth fade away and appearance and spectacle dominate. Speed accelerates the need to highlight the visual register, and emphatically links the heroine's feminine attraction to fashionable consumption and conspicuous display. In the cycling romance, all the heroines are portrayed to be fashionably dressed, their enviable figure, elegant posture, and beautiful dress displayed to best advantage when they ride slow and upright on the wheel (Figure 3.5). This speed-enhanced beauty is the key to the triggering of the romance plot and the drastic change of the male characters' attitude.

While feminine charms and bodily display have always been celebrated in romance stories as a whole, cycling romance stands out by suggesting that only cycling's conspicuous speed brings out the best and most beautiful in these women. Many heroines seem to go for cycling more because they "looked so well in the dress" ("A Cause of Quarrel" 250). The stories go into meticulous detail over what the characters wear and where they for the right occasions, lingering over the woman cyclist's "short, tailor-made frock," the neat hat "which suited her

Figure 3.5 Illustration for "Trespassers Will Be Prosecuted." *Lady Cyclist,* July 31, 1897, p. 393. The British Library Archive.

to perfection," and the "daintiest imaginable shoes that were a delight to behold" (250). By facing half-tone, full-page ads for bicycling costumes and accessories alongside with the romance stories, or liberally interspersing them in the middle of the narrative, the magazines create a consumerist fantasy whereby the desirable femininity promoted by the stories is instantly promised by the consumption of the advertised products. This blurring of advertising and stories leads to better "results" for the advertisers (Beetham 193), and underlines the slippage between ideal commodity and ideal femininity—both objects of the reader's fetishistic desire (Figure 3.6).

Figure 3.6 Ad inserted in "Violet's Venture," *Lady Cyclist*, April 3, 1897, p. 713. The British Library Archive.

In "The End of a Club Run," published in *Lady Cyclist* in April 1895, the story's illustration, depicting the hero embracing the lady cyclist, appears facing an ad for cycling accessories such as boots, hats, and dresses, suggesting that love is to be got by consuming these accessories. In *Lady Cyclist*'s August 1896 issue, an ad for Dunlop Tyres depicts a lady cyclist flirting with a male cyclist while being peeped at by two younger girls. This ad is inserted within the romance story "Another Man's Wife," and uses the same painting style as the story's illustrations. The caption of the Dunlop ad—"Flirting? Oh! No, merely exchanging opinions about the superlative excellence of DUNLOP Tyres"—corroborates the romance plot of the story and implies that the smooth-running Dunlop tires particularly enhance a girl's prospects for love (see Figure 3.7).

In "A Bicycle Story" (1896), the husband, himself a famous cyclist, is "a bit of a tyrant" and adamantly refuses to allow his wife to cycle, insisting that "a woman's place is at home." When his wife surprises him one day riding in the park with her cousin, it is her "nice, trim figure," her cycle costume which "became her wonderfully," and particularly the fact that her "graceful" riding "attracted much attention" in the fashionable park that finally persuades the husband (368). In "Discord and Harmony" (1897), a husband claims that he "would never say a word against bicycling again" after seeing his wife leading the musical cycle ride, "on a machine decorated with flame-colored azaleas," "her graceful figure" swaying "in perfect rhythm with the music as she circled round," to the enthusiastic applause of a "large and fashionable audience" (904). A member of the royalty even patronizes the show and compliments his wife, which makes him really "quite proud" (905). Publicity, fanfare, and conspicuous display of status is crucial to the success of women's cycling.

Cycling's elegant speed does not just bring out the best and most beautiful in women, it even trumps other traditional markers of feminine desirability for marriage. In cycling romance, courtship and marriage are ultimately presented as a consumerist choice that is expanded by a woman's access to bicycle speed. In "Paul's Ring, or A Bicycle," a story published in *Lady Cyclist* in 1897, country girl Ellie's desire to emulate the rich and glamorous life of her friend, the heiress Vera, culminates in her decision to purchase a second-hand bicycle. Ellie, an orphan adopted by her country doctor uncle, can only afford crude, country-made clothes, while Vera wears nothing but the latest fashion from Paris. Yet the competition between the two girls escalates not over pretty clothes, but over a bicycle. Ellie's envy seems especially roused when Vera takes up cycling. "Oh, it was hateful! And now to crown it all Vera has a bicycle" (815). Vera loves cycling around with a dashing captain from a crack regiment that has newly arrived in the village, a man Ellie has also set her heart on. The captain has previously shown attention to Ellie, despite her dowdy clothes, but is now courting Vera after her purchase of the bicycle. In merry laughter they cycle far and away, while Ellie is stuck at home and can only watch and fret. Interestingly, Ellie's envy does not lead her to wish for new

"OVER THE GARDEN WALL."

Flirting? Oh! no, merely exchanging opinions anent the superlative excellence of DUNLOP Tyres.

Figure 3.7 Dunlop Tyres ad in "Another Man's Wife," *Lady Cyclist*, August 1896, p. xxi. The British Library Archive.

clothes, but instead for the mobility and speed of the bicycle. Here, speed outshines pretty clothes and stands more potently for a new marker of sexual attraction. Only cycling, it seems to her, could elevate her desirability and help her steal that dashing Captain from Vera. "She would have a bicycle too at any cost. She would ride too—" (815).

This desire burns more fiercely when she is shamed by Vera: "Why don't you beg, borrow or steal a bicycle so you could come with us?" (815) In desperation, Ellie makes a decision which further underlines cycling's links with marriage prospects. She pawns an engagement ring given to her by her uncle's assistant, Paul, a man she has promised to marry but is not quite satisfied with. A marriage with steady, reliable, honest Paul would bring no change to her slow, circumscribed life in the village, but the dashing captain from town epitomizes the ceaseless excitement of modern London life, to which the speeding bicycle offers the key. Ellie would not, of course, beg, borrow, or steal a bicycle, but she could purchase one by selling her ring, exchanging one hope of love and marriage for another. The ring is only good enough for a used bicycle, yet even second-hand the bicycle is more desirable than the ring. Although Ellie eventually wakes up from her fantasy and good old Paul takes her back, this story nevertheless suggests that, instead of masculinizing women and hampering their marriage prospects, bicycle speed actually makes women more desirable and marriageable. Even Vera, the heiress, calls her eventual marriage with the dashing captain a "bicycle match," a "bicycle marriage"—one that is made and facilitated by the pair's shared love of cycling (817).

Bicycle speed makes women more desirable, while slowness and lack of speed is equated with reduced marriage choices and prospects. This latter point is painfully driven home to a matron who complains to a journalist that she has to learn cycling at her ripe old age so that her three daughters won't lose their chance of marriage. Young men nowadays no longer call at one's house, and "two of my husbands' nieces, who are not anything like so pretty as my three girls, had got engaged whilst bicycling." Since speed and mobility prove even more attractive than "pretty" looks in enticing a husband, she has to let her daughters cycle too and come out of traditional domesticity to catch up with the faster pace of modern life ("Women on Wheels"). In cycling romance, a similar contrast is staged between slow, quiet, traditional domesticity, and a new, faster, more mobile and exciting life represented by cycling women. The genre does not reject or criticize the former, but simply presents the latter as offering greater choice and variety. This enhanced choice applies to beauty and fashion, and also to romance and marriage—all essential to the construction of ideal middle-class femininity. The equation of bicycle speed with this increased consumerist choice proves most effective in popularizing women's cycling.

New Woman Literature and Speed as Conspicuous Leisure

By the mid-1890s, the joint maneuverings of bicycle manufacturers, the cycling press, and women's activists had glamorized the woman cyclist and turned cycling into an elegantly feminine pastime for middle-class women. Women's access to cycling speed was no longer transgressive or improper, but instead the best advertisement for a modern commodity culture wherein spectacle and status display is increasingly important. In this sense, the New Woman cyclist's much touted progressiveness is predicated upon a conspicuous consumption of speed that excludes other poorer, slower members of the public. This hidden class dimension and the new hierarchy speed constructs is glossed over in the popular cycling press, but literary representations of the New Woman cyclist, including the works of Wells and Gissing, demonstrate a more critical awareness of speed's function as privilege and status display.

Like most New Woman writers, Gissing and Wells were also avid cyclists themselves and took up cycling during the mid-1890s "bicycle craze," when the bicycle was credited to bring along, as *The Times* writes in 1898, "a social boon" and "a social revolution" (qtd. in Rubinstein 71). Wells learned to ride in the Surrey countryside in 1895, when he was preparing to write *The Wheels of Chance*"; soon, he and his wife Jane were riding on "a tandem bike of a peculiar shape made for us by the Humber people and we began to wander about the south of England" (*Autobiography* 543). Wells proved to be a most dedicated cyclist, continuing to cycle long after the bicycle craze waned and most of his peers had abandoned the sport. He wrote of riding "out of the cold skirts of a wintry night into a drizzling dawn along a wet road" to try and find a doctor for a dying Stephen Crane (qtd. in Withers 10); by the early 1900s he was still doing cycling tours of France and Holland (13). In two letters from 1911, for instance, he mentions "having been away on a cycling tour" for two months and "bicyc[ling] part of the way home" from France with his two sons. If it was not "for rain and punctures" he would have done the entire ride home from France (13). This preference for cycling only stopped when Wells switched to motoring, a newer and faster machine of speed.

Gissing also learnt to ride with Wells's help. At one of these lessons, Gissing met his third wife, Gabrielle Fleury. Gissing had met Wells at the Omar Khayyám Club in November 1896, and the two quickly became friends. During the cycling lessons they attended soon after, Wells records that Gissing fell down "shrieking with laughter" when Wells told him to "[g]et onto your ironmongery" (*Autobiography* 482). Two years later, Gissing bought his own bicycle for £14 (Price and Badoleto 241).

Unlike many female New Woman writers, Gissing and Wells make cycling an important topic in their works. In their focus on the New Woman's daily activities in the modern public space, cycling becomes another crucial part, other than typewriting, of the New Woman's new, unconventional life. Cycling speed's exciting appeal, its promise of freedom and self-expansion, as well as its inherent class exclusions and new use as status display, all receive detailed treatment as their stories present the complications of women's cycling in a critical light. Often shunning the fantasies of happy endings common in the commercial cycling romance, these literary representations are more alert to the socioeconomic exclusivity of cycling as a pastime for the rich and fashionable. They present the speeding New Woman cyclist as progressive and modern, but also point out that such speed comes at a high price and is not available to everyone.

This is seen, for instance, in Gissing's story "A Daughter of the Lodge" (1901), where consumption of the bicycle and its much-desired speed becomes a new marker of status that sets up finer distinctions and hierarchies even among New Women themselves. In this story, Gissing deftly sets two New Woman characters in opposition to one another, exposing the true nature of each through their relationship with the bicycle. In the end, it is the character who is able to consume the bicycle and utilize its speed who emerges as the authentic New Woman, while her counterpart, who cannot afford a bicycle, is revealed as an impostor and socially humiliated.

The story presents Lady Hilda as the typical, conventionally perceived New Woman. Hilda is the twenty-six-year-old daughter of Sir Edwin Shale of Brent Hall. With her privileged background, "athletic person," "tall, strongly built" physique, "face of hard comeliness," and "magnificent tawny hair," she is a walking example of the mannish, Amazonian New Woman much-lampooned in the popular masculine press. "All her movements suggested vigour"; "she shook hands with a downward jerk, moved about the room with something of a stride and, in sitting down, crossed her legs abruptly" (172). A confident woman with a "force of character" (167), Lady Hilda, dressed in her short skirt, easy jacket, and brown shoes, seems to be taken straight out of the 1896 *Punch* cartoon "Rational Costume," where an exasperated "Vicar of St Winifred-in-the-Wold" mistakes two Rational-dressed New Women for men (rprtd. in Adburgham 157).

The other New Woman, May Rocketts, is the main protagonist of the story and the elder daughter of Sir Shale's lodge-keeper and former gardener. Despite her humble origin, May has shown from an young age a desire for higher learning and an ambition to rise above her circumstances. Clever and gifted, she "had an intellect which sharpened itself on everything with which it came in contact" (167). Soon, the village school and the high school in the neighboring town are not enough for May's mental development. At the age of twenty-two, after a stint as governess, May gets a job in London as secretary "to a lady with a mission—concerning the rights of womanhood" (167). May does not mention to her parents about the "very modest" salary of her job, but she has managed to achieve independence and a "livelihood" that depends "upon her brains" (167). She keeps very busy doing her secretarial work, writing and dispatching letters, staying up late reading books, and "occup[ying]" herself "a good deal" with women activists in London, many of whom she knows on a "first-hand" basis (172). When she comes back home for a brief stay several years later, her posh, ladylike appearance and "strange," progressive talk puts her homely parents into "a state of nervous agitation," so that they "could neither say nor do anything natural to them" (168).

Like Gissing's New Woman character Rhoda in *The Odd Women* (1893), who similarly rises from a provincial background to become the managing partner of Mary's feminist typewriting school in London, May gravitates toward London and blossoms in the broadened horizon that the London ambience and feminist work has opened up for her. And, like Rhoda, May is "well dressed in a severely practical way; nothing unduly feminine marked her appearance, and in the matter of collar and necktie she inclined to the example of the other sex" (168). She mitigates this severe appearance, however, with her naturally "soft complexion," "bright eyes," and "light, quick movements" that add a "picturesque value" to her person (168). She talks "with the tone and gesture of one who habitually gives orders," greets her parents with dignity and "no excess of feelings" (168), stuffs her luggage with books and periodicals, and immediately asks for a London newspaper. When told that her rustic parents keep no such newspapers, May is bewildered—"How do you live without it?"—and decides to run into the town that very afternoon (169).

Gissing has long emphasized the importance of a cosmopolitan setting like London, "at the centre of things," which has enabled London women to profit from broadened horizons and new opportunities ("Letter to Ellen" 116). Writing to his sister Nelly in 1889, twelve years before writing this story, Gissing asserted that the cosmopolitan, progressive ambience of London was the key to why London women towered above girls in the provinces:

> Now you remember the problem we once talked over. –Are these London women of larger brain than women the country? ... They know everything that appears in our day, & can talk intelligently on any subject current in intellectual circles. Well, the explanation of course is that they have always lived in intellectual society. It is not remarkable brain-power that distinguishes them, but *opportunity*. Had you lived in the same way, your attainments would be no less than theirs. These people learn most of what they know in conversation ... On their tables lie all the new books, - either purchased or from Mudie's. They live at the *centre* of things. ("Letter to Ellen," 115–16)

Gissing was talking about Olive Schreiner and Edith Sichel, New Woman intellectuals in London whose knowledge and intelligence impressed him. In "A Daughter of the Lodge," May has certainly expanded her "attainments" by her years in London amidst the circles of intellectual women. The story refers to May's confidence in her wide knowledge when she pronounces the local "country medico" a "duffer," declares that she herself has been "going in a little for medicine lately," and takes upon herself to diagnose her father's rheumatism (168). Her London experience and "first-hand information" about the women's movement also allows her to be admitted as an equal to the drawing-room of Mrs. Lindley, a local "progressive" lady on the same social rank as Sir Shale, who is eager and "grateful" for any latest news from London (169). When her mother expresses surprise, May smiles indulgently and asks "When will you come to understand what my position is?" (169).

Indeed, May believes herself to be even superior to Lady Hilda, to whose benevolence the Rocketts owe their residence at the lodge. When the family talks about

Lady Hilda, who has just cycled past the lodge and is quite annoyed that they have failed to open the gate for her, May responds with coldness and "a smile of ineffable contempt" (168). Lady Hilda may be the "feudal superior" to her parents (167), but May believes that her knowledge, intelligence, and years in London have elevated her above the country-bred Lady Hilda. Her manners are so confident that even her simple parents privately agree with her, too. They do not like the haughty and "disdainful" Hilda, and believe that May's "bearing and talk" and the "brilliant qualities which were flashed before their eyes" make her "more of a real lady" (169).

May's belief in the superiority of her knowledge and experience reflects what the nineteenth-century women's movement had always advocated. In *The Odd Women*, feminists like Rhoda and Mary are convinced of women's ability to "emancipate" themselves and bring about a revolution in the social order if they could elevate themselves through education, employment, and active use of their intelligence (245). As the category of the New Woman broadens to include a greater army of lower-middle-class women, work, autonomy, and education, rather than birth, are increasingly the hallmarks of New Womanhood. May's case offers a most powerful testimony to the impact of this feminist cause, as she comes from even humbler circumstances than Rhoda or Monica, who are at least of genteel birth, and has proved herself to be capable of transcending even more daunting constraints.

But Gissing's story also reveals that such elevation seems to rest on fragile grounds. When May goes to see Mrs Lindley in the neighboring town, she is able to "k[eep] the lead in talk"; "she glowed with self-satisfaction, feeling that she was really showing to great advantage, and that everybody admired her" (172). This talk, emblematic of a London New Woman who, as Gissing wrote in his letter, seems to "know everything" and excels at erudite conversation (115), is soon interrupted when Lady Hilda also arrives, dressed in her cycling costume. May still keeps on valiantly, pretending not to know her, but the sight of the Rational-dressed Hilda soon turns the conversation to cycling. When Mrs. Lindley asks May if she cycles, May has to admit with some awkwardness that she has never found the time to learn. At this moment, Lady Hilda's "abrupt and rather metallic voice" cuts in and strikes a fatal blow. In a tone of seeming "gentle irony" but really aimed to expose and humiliate May, Hilda laments that "It's a pity the machines can't be sold cheaper," and that it is such "awfully hard lines" that "[a] great many people who would like to cycle don't feel able to afford it" (172). May is flustered and ashamed and loses her command of voice, because Hilda has insinuated that it is her poverty, not her lack of time, that has prevented May from cycling.

Gissing's tale was published in 1901, but this talk of the prohibitive costs of the bicycle places its setting squarely within the cultural phenomenon of the mid-1890s "bicycle craze." In those boom years, the expensive bicycle and its conspicuous speed had overtaken others as the most important display of New Womanhood. It is exactly May's lack of ability to consume and display this conspicuous speed that debunks her claim to true New Womanhood, however hard she has tried to use other means like manner, talk, or knowledge to prove her newly elevated position. That Hilda decides to use the bicycle in a roundabout way to bring about May's downfall suggests that she, too, is aware how cycling differentiates the New Woman from her would-be imitators. As the conversation soon turns to cycling and the prices of different bicycle models, May is unable to join the chatter and makes a hasty exit in great vexation. She is "stung intolerably" by Hilda's hint about "the prohibitive cost of bicycles," which is "harder to bear because hitting the truth" (173). May has been able to transcend her humble origins to stage a successful performance of New Womanhood, but this performance has collapsed because the ultimate accessory of New Womanhood is beyond her reach. She is revealed to be an impostor, and, as Hilda would certainly "make known her circumstances," May's future acceptance into the drawing-room of Mrs. Lindley is in jeopardy (173).

In this 1901 story, written eight years after *The Odd Women*, Gissing's earlier optimism about the revolutionary impact of new forms of women's work in big cities like London seems to have given way to greater ambivalence. Work, autonomy, and an urban lifestyle does help the New Woman transcend traditional boundaries, but this comes accompanied with new hierarchies and new differentiations. In London, one's family origin may not matter as much, but status and class still play a key role, now mediated through the new force of consumption power. May's secretary position allows her to be on "first-hand" terms with famous London feminists, but her very modest pay deprives her of any significant consumption power and denies her full membership of New Womanhood.

This use of the bicycle as a marker of class differentiation is already hinted at, though in a light-hearted and flippant manner, in the *Wheelwoman* story "A Borrowed Bicycle," published in 1897. The story mocks the ambition of a servant called Bridget, who dares to imitate her mistress by "borrowing" her bicycle without permission and batters it while learning to ride. Though her shins are bruised and her face so hurt that she has to "tie it up in a handkerchief" to pretend she has a toothache, Bridget revels in the envious gaze of the passersby as she rides in the streets (23). When a policeman questions her she puts on a bold face and insists that this is her own bicycle. The mistress, after finding out the truth, is "white with passion, and could hardly get out the words," (23) firing Bridget on the spot. Bridget reacts with perplexed anger, because the mistress chooses to fire her not for "staying out half-an-hour late every Wednesday night, ... for forgetting my cap, nor for talking to my young man, nor for giving an answer," but for "simply taking a loan of the mistress' bicycle" for several hours (23). "Borrowing" the bicycle constitutes a greater reason for dismissal than Bridget's regular neglect of her duties, because the bicycle is expensive and costs a lot to repair. A more important reason, however, is that in riding the bicycle and enjoying its class-specific speed, Bridget has become an impostor who transgresses her class boundary.

In Gissing's "A Daughter of the Lodge," the privileged New Woman Lady Hilda makes a similar appeal to the bicycle's class connotations. Bicycle speed is now a telltale accessory of the emancipated New Woman, but this ability to use speed to construct her progressive identity is often denied to other, less privileged women. At the end of the story, the bicycle again figures in May's final downfall. After walking three or four miles to get back to her father's lodge, May meets Hilda again at the gates of the Hall. This encounter and May's subsequent humiliation would have been avoided had it not been for the superior speed of the bicycle. May has left Mrs. Lindley's gathering midway through, and is so "flushed and wrathful" at Hilda's stinging words that she loses track of time and misses the only train home. Unable to afford a cab ride, May is forced to walk all the way home, arriving at the gate of the Hall at close of evening, "tired, perspiring, irritated" (173). Just at this moment, "a bicycle-bell trilled vigorously behind her," and Miss Hilda cycles up and orders her "imperatively" to open the gate. May refuses point blank, forcing Hilda to dismount and open the gate herself. "I couldn't imagine you were speaking to me," May answers Hilda haughtily, believing herself to be a New Woman on an equal footing with Hilda; "I suppose some servant of yours was in sight" (173). May's pride would not allow her to obey Hilda, but the situation is certainly exacerbated by the contrast between a tired, slow, rather disheveled May and a cool, fresh, and speedy Hilda—a contrast arising from Hilda's access to the luxury and convenience of bicycle speed. Access to this speed allows Hilda to overtake May at the finish line; it also enables Hilda to assert her superior status when she orders May to open the gate and reconfirms May's servile position.

In the end, May's defeat in literal speed parallels her defeat in social status, when Hilda orders an immediate eviction for May's whole family because of May's refusal to open the gate. The family, with her old, rheumatism-tortured father no longer able to work, have been living in the lodge at the goodwill and mercy of Hilda's father. May's mother tearfully accuses her "conceited" and "overbearing" manners for ruining the family and leaving them homeless (174). Faced with the horror of her parents in a workhouse and her only sister going into service, May is forced to swallow her pride and tearfully begs Hilda for mercy. By entering Hilda's house through the servants' entrance and meekly addressing Hilda as "my lady" (174), May admits her servility in relation to "her feudal superiors" (167). The "last blow" to her mistaken belief in her own refinement comes when she finally leaves the hall and gets out into the yard. The footman, waiting outside, greets her and asks her with a grin, in a spirit of commiseration and fellowship, "any good?" (174) This proves more than anything that in the eyes of the footman—and, indeed, everybody else—that May is simply no better than himself, both being dependent on the pay and whims of their masters.

Without waiting for the final decision from the Hall, May, having "wept out the bitterness of her soul," leaves for London by an evening train (174). She claims that "I'm in a false position" in the country and that her leaving would free her family of "any more trouble" (173). But she is going back to her London position, which is probably no less "false." In London, May seems to have made herself a success as a New Woman of advanced talk, confident manners, and erudite knowledge. Yet the story reveals that her New Womanhood itself is often no more than spectacle and show, constituted through the display of names, objects, and chatty gossip that she drops here and three to dazzle her audience. As a London New Woman, May turns out to be no less superficial than Mrs. Lindley, the local fashionable lady for whom everything "progressive," whether a new religion or a new cycling costume, "stirred her to just the same kind of happy excitement" (172). May shines in Mrs. Lindley's drawing-room not just because she could provide the latest London news and gossip about famous women activists, but also because May's talk is "exactly what [Mrs. Lindley] liked, for it glanced at innumerable topics of the 'advanced' sort, was much concerned with personalities, and avoided all tiresome precision of argument" (172).

This performance, designed not for the benefit of serious societal change but for the benefit of personal social advance, underscores the fact that May, just like Mrs. Lindley, is wearing her New Woman identity as a commodity and a form of conspicuous display. And it is no wonder that, in this display, her inability to consume the ultimate commodity of speed leads to her defeat and humiliation. To May and her "progressive" circles, conspicuous consumption and the right kind of display are the new markers of New Womanhood—markers that will ultimately exclude May because of her limited consumption power.

The Young Lady in Grey and the London Shop-Hand

H. G. Wells' *The Wheels of Chance*, published in 1896 at the height of the mid-decade bicycle boom, similarly uses the bicycle to expose speed's new function as a marker of status. Whereas in Gissing's story the contrast is between a privileged New Woman and her lower-class imitator, in Wells's novel the New Woman cyclist Jessie, the "young lady in grey," is paired up with an under-exercised and over-worked London drapery worker, Hoopdriver, who makes a reckless attempt at cycling even though he could barely afford it (12). The novel describes seventeen-year-old Jessie as a New Woman brought up on "that deleterious ingredient of our book boxes" called "the New Woman Literature," (110), who is resolved to "Live my Own Life," and be "a free woman" (69). She escapes from her comfortable home on her brand new, expensive Safety bicycle, joins her seducer (a married Oxford man, Bechamel), and cycles with him toward London, where Bechamel promises to find her a journalist job. Along the way, she comes across Hoopdriver by accident, who later sees through Bechamel's scheme and helps Jessie to escape from him and her chasing family. The novel is often viewed by later critics as a social romance (Hammond 121), or as a work that links women's cycling with women's freedom and sociopolitical iconoclasm (Wånggren 77). But, in its depiction of the contrastive cycling experiences of the New Woman and the London shop-hand, Wells's book also lays bare the privileges and class differentiations behind the New Woman's transgressive cycling.

In his *Autobiography*, Wells reveals that he composed the plotline at the same time that he himself was learning to cycle in 1895: "I rode wherever Mr. Hoop-driver rode in that story" (543). Many of the insights about cycling in the novel, including the reference to Hoopdriver's bruises and trepidation as a beginner, as well as the assertion that to "ride a bicycle properly is very like a love affair— chiefly it is a matter of faith" (*The Wheels of Chance* 9), are very much Well's own. Wells himself called the novel "a very 'young' book"; "indeed, in some respects it is puerile" ("Preface" ix), but at the time of its construction he thought it "far more carefully written than anything I have done hitherto" (*Correspondence* 257). Con-temporary reviewers agreed with him. *The Athenaeum*, for instance, declares that although cycling romance has been "tried pretty often in the cycling newspapers," this novel "is the first that has got into book form" and "the first to achieve success" as "artistic work," because it has an "ingenious" humor and its characters are "so sympathetically" portrayed ("*The Wheels of Chance* Review" 752).

In its thematic issues, *The Wheels of Chance* collates almost everything asso-ciated with cycling in the *fin-de-siècle* period, including cycling as exercise and rejuvenation, cycling as a potential means for elopement or a love encounter (a staple in the commercial cycling romance), and cycling's links with status and the New Woman. Cycling is the impetus that kick-starts all the main plot twists, and cycling tropes and themes mark the key stages in the two protagonists' relation-ship and propel it forward. Hoopdriver, for instance, meets Jessie as a result of a near bicycle collision, renews their acquaintance when mistaken by Jessie for her gentleman companion Bechamel because of a similar-looking cycling jacket, finds out about Bechamel's evil scheming when all three put up for the night as cyclists in a country hotel, runs away with Jessie by stealing Bechamel's bicycle and deny-ing him the power of the chase, and finally gets overtaken by Jessie's chasing family riding on their faster and more powerful tandem bicycle. Cycling, therefore, is the driving narrative force in the whole novel.

The naïve, young cyclist Jessie is, as Brenda Tyrrell points out, Wells's first attempt at portraying the New Woman, about thirteen years before his most famous New Woman heroine, Ann Veronica (50). In the wake of the very public debate in May 1895 in the pages of *North American Review* between anti-feminist sensation writer Quida [Marie Louise de la Ramée] and New Woman writer Sarah Grand as to the meaning of the New Woman and the many complicated, often conflicting representations in the popular press, Wells, through Jessie, gives vent to all the frustrations and yearnings of a sheltered New Woman while also satirizing the vacuous nature of her idealism. Many of Wells' protagonists of these years are what he calls, in his Preface to the novel's 1925 Atlantic Edition, "caricature-individualities" (*Autobiography* 499), whose aspirations are "thwarted by the defects of our contemporary civilization" (*Works of H. G. Wells* ix). Hoop-driver, for instance, laments how different things could have been "If I'd been exercised properly, if I'd been fed reasonable, if I hadn't been shoved out of a silly school into a silly shop"; "I'm not such muck that I might not have been better—with teaching" (*The Wheels of Chance* 67, 100). Seventeen-year-old Jessie, in her turn, is restless with her domestic life in a "pleasant," "refined" home, where "my stepmother takes me shopping, people come to tea, there is a new play to pass the time, or a concert, or a novel" (69). "It is horrible," "like a little speck, whirling on a wheel, suddenly caught up" (69). Finding a voice and stirrings for change in Olive Schreiner and George Egerton (92), Jessie declares that she would "Own myself," "be Unconventional," "take my place in the world," and "shape my own career," (69, 70)—abstract phrases and slogans "you may have heard before," as the narrator rather drily comments (38).

However, she is soon to be bitterly disillusioned when trapped by the perfidious Bechamel, who intends to turn a false promise of job into a de facto elopement. "Think, if you want to. It's your cry always. But you can't save yourself by thinking, my dear girl," exults Bechamel as he succeeds, for their second night at a hotel, in registering their names as husband and wife (51). New Woman literature, the kind of "daring," "antimarital" novels that Jessie's stepmother also writes (62, 93), does "Teach new Ideas, new Lessons," as the step mother later confesses, but it is only meant to "want people to THINK as I recommend, not to DO as I recommend" (82).

Wells's views on the New Woman are complicated. While he sympathized with women's frustrations with marriage and domesticity and signed a declaration for women's suffrage in 1909 (Rønning 190), his advocacy for women's freedom focuses on sexual equality, justified on biological grounds and the need to produce the best offspring for the nation and race. As is seen in his New Woman novel *Ann Veronica* (1909), women should take the same equality as men in terms of sexual desire and the freedom to choose their lover, but women should also obey nature's call as mothers and the evolutionary place for women as breeders of a better race (Snyder 20).[11]

Wells's portrayal of the military feminists in *Ann Veronica* is ruthless, describing them as "barkings, yappings, roarings, pelican chatterings, and feline yowlings, interspersed with shrieks of hysterical laughter" (205). In his portrayal of the New Woman cyclist, he agrees with the greater freedom cycling brings to women, but also seems to suggest that more is needed to bring about real, meaningful changes

---

[11] Wells believes that biology laws underpin all forms of life including human sexual desire, and that all obstacles, including concerns of moral propriety that force women to marry against their instincts, should be eliminated so that natural selection could take over to ensure the best evolution of the human race. When Ann's lover Capes says "You have converted me to—Lester Ward" (284), the American sociology claiming the innate superiority of the female species throughout the animal kingdom, this view is still limited to an emphasis on women as mothers and justified on women's regenerative role. This has led some feminists to claim that Wells's feminism is "running second best to eugenics and the needs of the state" (Stubbs 189).

in women's life. As Ann Veronica's father complains to his dissatisfied and insouciant daughter, "Did I stand in the way of your going to college? Have I ever prevented you going about at any reasonable hour? You've got a bicycle!" (34). The young Jessie in *The Wheels of Chance* also thinks that taking up her Safety bicycle, donning a rational dress, and just riding away to London would be enough to bring the independence and change she earnestly longs for. Jessie's cycling embodies all the liberating potential that feminists have championed in the bicycle: its expansion of women's mobility and mental and physical strength, and ultimately its contribution to women's wider employment prospects and financial autonomy. But her failure reveals that such freedom is conditional upon privilege and money.

Jessie despises convention and is "resolved to be Unconventional—at any cost" (70), but when she later finds that her escape has to come to an end because Hoopdriver has run out of money, she bursts out "I never thought of money coming in to stop us like this" (105). The realization of the high price tag behind "unconventionality" disillusions Jessie: "Is it possible—Surely! Conventionality! May only people of means—Live their own Lives? I never thought ..." (105).

Only a New Woman "of means" could afford the unconventionality and freedom enabled by bicycle speed. Jessie is able to run away from home and make use of cycling's transgressive freedom, because she owns a brand new, expensive Safety bicycle, which "couldn't cost much under twenty pounds" (14). Her five-day journey of freedom is sustained by Hoopdriver's saving of "a five-pound note, two sovereigns, and some silver" (9), which quickly dries up. The novel best illustrates the privileges behind the New Woman cyclist when it compares Jessie with the London shop-hand, Hoopdriver. Jessie enjoys the freedom and recreation of cycling as a release from her suffocating but privileged life of shopping, afternoon teas, new plays, and reading. But while cycling is a part of a New Woman's life and celebrated for improving women's health (Marks 200), it is usually beyond the reach of a toiling London drapery assistant like Hoopdriver, who most needs the exercise and recreation offered by cycling.

In *The Wheels of Chance*, Hoopdriver's decision to go on a ten-day cycling holiday is described as impractical and the result of an ill-considered impulse. It is "against all the conditions of his calling, against the counsels of prudence and the restrictions of his means" (3). As the opposite of the typical, moneyed protagonist in a mid-1890s cycling story, Hoopdriver could only afford an old battered bicycle, "an antiquity" "with a fork instead of the diamond frame, a cushioned tire, well worn on the hind wheel, and a gross weight of perhaps three-and-forty pounds" (11). Compared with the new, much pricier Safety bicycle, replete with its pneumatic tires and a diamond frame, this model was fast becoming outdated by the mid-1890s (Oddy 105). Hoopdriver is roundly laughed at by his fellow shop assistants, who, like his roommate Briggs, have "never been on a cycle in [their] life" (5).

The novel makes gentle mockery of Hoopdriver's reckless attempt to emulate his social betters by taking up this mostly middle-class recreation, but it also portrays with great sympathy the London shop-hand's desperate longing "to seek the wholesome delights of exertion and danger and pain" as a release from monotonous work. "Only those who toil six long days out of the seven, and all the year round ... know the exquisite sensations" of the freedom and refreshing recreation offered by a cycling holiday (6). As an "uncomplicated, half educated, commonplace, sentimental & well meaning shopman" (Wells, *Correspondence* 257), Hoopdriver grinds away every day in the "cheerless, shutter-darkened" draper shop (*The Wheels of Chance* 1). A "got-up imitation of a man" (96), he has weak knees, thin legs, a pallid complexion, a skimpy moustache, and an emasculated body "not used to muscular exercise" (2). In his *Anticipations*, published five years later in 1901, Wells would write with much regret that a lowly urban worker like Hoopdriver would be the best subject to benefit from the rejuvenating exercise of cycling. The bicycle "might have served its most useful purpose," if costs are lower and the filthy, muddy state of London streets could be improved, "in affording a healthy daily ride to the innumerable clerks," "shop hands," and "such-like sedentary toilers of the central regions" who are "positively starved of exercise" (24–25).

Indeed, the pallid, weak-limbed Hoopdriver is a member of the sedentary urban population for whom cycling would provide the most-needed exercise and regeneration. As Hoopdriver later explains to Jessie, drapery is "not a particularly honest nor a particularly useful trade ... there's no freedom and no leisure—seven to eight-thirty every day in the week" (99). "You look respectable outside, and inside you are packed in dormitories like convicts, fed on bread and butter and bullied like slaves ... one draper in a hundred don't even earn enough to marry on" (99). A drapery assistant may be higher in social rank than the "street-bred," "stunted," unfit, "easily wearied" Cockney "city type" with narrow chests and fickle excitability, whom the Victorian social reformer Charles Booth described in his social surveys from 1886 to 1903 (Masterman 7–8), but, like the unfit London poor, the expanding army of semiskilled service-sector clerks toiling for long hours in monotonous, sedentary jobs are in similar need of the fresh air and physical exercise recommended by Booth. Victorian reformers encouraged the ideal of rational recreation to combat the danger of an urban, sedentary lifestyle and improve the health of the people and the prosperity of the nation (H. Cunningham 90). But most of these "controlled, ordered, and improving" leisure activities were middle-class in nature and beyond the means of the poor (Mangan 5). A drapery assistant like Hoopdriver might avoid the urban poor's recreation of drinking, gambling, prostitution, and visits to the newly popular music hall, which offers bodily release but no physical or mental improvement (Beaven 90). But the most he could do is to indulge in the reading of popular "Romance and Knight-errantry" (53), the likes of "Doctor Conan Doyle, Victor Hugo, and Alexander Dumas" (41), which allows him to be "divinely forgetful of his social position" (53).

By buying an old bicycle and using up all his savings on a cycling holiday, Hoop-driver, the "mere counter-jumper," seems to be even more forgetful of his social position (115). But even on the wheels of this obsolete bicycle, Hoopdriver experiences an instant social elevation that has never befallen his lot before. Dressed in his "new brown cycling suit," consisting of "a handsome Norfolk jacket" and "thick chequered stockings," with "a neat packet of American cloth behind the saddle" for his change of clothes, and "the bell and the handle-bar and the hubs and lamp, albeit a trifle freckled by wear, glitter[ing] blindingly in the rising sun-light" (6), Hoopdriver is treated as an equal by a man in drab, "evidently a swell" (15). A nursemaid addresses him as "the gentleman wizzer bicitle" (9), and a road-side heath-keeper shouts "a bloomin' Dook" at him with ill-repressed jealousy (8). Hoopdriver couldn't repress a "silent laugh" and a sense of "sheer happiness": "His social superiority had been so evident that even a man like that noticed it" (9). This superiority, predicated upon the ostentatious speed of the bicycle, soon persuades him that he is now "a gentleman, a man of pleasure," "as good as a Dook, if not precisely in the peerage" (19). He couldn't stop thinking of the "the imaginary spectators [who] would fall a-talking of the fashionableness of bicycling—how judges and stockbrokers and actresses, and, in fact, *all the best people rode*" (85; emphasis added). And he is quite right, for the world is divided into two: those who own speed and brandish their prosperity, and those who lack speed and languish in slowness.

The novel abounds with other examples that underline the exclusive, privileged nature of cycling. When Jessie first meets the novice rider Hoopdriver on her way to meet Bechamel, the sight of her Rational costume unsettles Hoopdriver and sends him crashing to the ground. Hoopdriver has a nasty fall and cuts his finger, while the more experienced Jessie, speaking "with a touch of superiority" (12), assures him that it needs to be bandaged as it will hurt badly in a moment. She then whips out from a little side pocket of her rational dress "a small packet of sticking-plater with a pair of scissors in a sheath at the side," and expertly cuts out a large portion (12). This incident, the first of their many encounters on the wheel, establishes an empathetic rapport between the two, which deepens further as the narrative moves on. Such rapport and sense of comradeship, reflected in Jessie's kind enquiry after Hoopdriver's bruises and offer of help with his wounds, was common among early cyclists of the time, but at least a partial reason is that bicycles were still expensive and limited to mostly middle-class users who shared a sense of fellowship.

When Jessie at first mistakes Hoopdriver for a South African colonial, because of "that novel of Olive Schreiner's you know—'The Story of an African Farm'" (73), this inability to place the London clerk's exact social standing is a result of her youthful inexperience. But it may also be because the typical cyclist of the mid-1890s was still a person of means and leisure, so Jessie could be excused for not realizing he is just a shop-hand. Bechamel feels insulted that Hoopdriver should don the same brown cycling jacket as he, which, though a cheap imitation, really looks quite similar from a distance, prompting Jessie to mistake Hoopdriver for Bechamel and wave a handkerchief at him. All these narrative twists and turns are at least partially hinged on the exclusivity of cycling as an expensive recreation.

Even the relaxed heterosexual interaction enjoyed by the New Woman cyclist— a relaxation that New Women activists celebrate as one of the emancipating benefits of cycling—also comes about partly because of the exclusivity of cycling. Jessie is able to spend the first night at a country hotel as brother and sister with Bechamel, with great ease and no questions from the hotel management. The hotel barmaid, whose "modesty was much impressed by the young lady's costume," watches her with both envy and disapproval: "There'll be no knowing which is which, in a year or two. And her manner too! She got off her machine ... and in she marched. 'I and my brother,' says she, 'want to stop here to-night.'" The maid could never "fancy my brother letting me boss the show like that" (43–44), because such confidence and freedom enjoyed by the middle-class woman cyclist is very much class-specific. When Hoopdriver wsteals Bechamel's bicycle and runs away with Jessie, again taking advantage of the relaxed social code and registering at hotels under false names as brother and sister, the novel mockingly adopts the tone of a shocked Mrs. Lynn Linton, the late Victorian conservative noted for her animosity toward the New Woman:

> Here is the girl—what girls are coming to nowadays only Mrs. Lynn Linton can tell!—in company with an absolute stranger, of low extraction and uncertain accent, unchaperoned and unabashed ... Then this Mr. Hoopdriver of yours ... in illegal possession of a stolen bicycle, a stolen young lady, and two stolen names, established with them in a hotel that is quite beyond his means ... There are occasions when a moralising novelist can merely wring his hands and leave matters to take their course. (62)

The bicycle's potential for freedom and even transgression derives largely from its speed, which expands individual travel beyond familiar places and entails dynamic uncertainties as a result of the disruption of old spatial–temporal constraints. This engenders a sense of spontaneity and unpredictability that gives rise to unexpected encounters, brief liaisons, and transgressive performances. Notably, cycling was frequently linked in the popular press of the *fin-de-siècle* with illicit romantic entanglements between male and female cyclists, a source of intense societal anxiety (Marks 200, Garvey 84).

Yet such expanded possibilities of sexual transgression are jealously guarded by middle-class cyclists if infringed upon by outsiders. In Wells' short story "A Perfect Gentleman on Wheels" (1897), the plot also revolves around the main character's meeting of a "very pretty girl" at the side of a road who has punctured her tire (786). As the narrator comments wryly, "Now this is the secret desire of all lone men who go down into the country on wheels. The proffered help, the charming talk, the idyllic incident. Who knows what delightful developments?" (786) This perfect gentleman Cecil, "sole proprietor of Crampton's Meat Juice," is hoping to marry Madge, "with her half-share in Fenton's Safe Cure," but he is "not averse to dreams of casual romance," enabled by speed's transcendence of everyday constraints and its potential for adventure and transgression (784, 786): "To ride out from the familiar locality, into strange roads stretching away into the unknown, to be free to stop or go on, irrespective of hour or companion, inevitably brings the adventurous side uppermost" (786).

But Cecil is much offended when he is accosted by a lower-class cyclist on "a machine that went clank," a "bounder" who "had the cheek" to compliment him on his expensive bicycle, and claim the sense of fellowship common among cyclists (784). His indignation is even greater when, trying in vain to mend the pretty lady's tire, he is usurped by the bounder, who turns up with his clanking bicycle and immediately locates the problem, to the gratitude and appreciation of the young lady. "I didn't know you wanted to stop every man that came along," complains Cecil to the lady, bitterly resentful that his hope of romantic adventure is now stolen by the lower-class bounder. The bounder also rises to the occasion and makes a clumsy attempt at knight-errantry: "if you're going to be rude to this young lady, I shall just punch your 'ead" (790).

This rivalry between a lower-class bounder and a gentleman cyclist over the favor of a lady cyclist again comes about in *The Wheels of Chance*, between Hoopdriver, the London shop-hand, and Bechamel, the Oxford-educated journalist. Hoopdriver at first conceals his real identity and goes along with Jessie's naïve conjecture about him being a South African colonial, venturing further to add that he is an ostrich farmer who once shot a lion in Africa and chased cattle robbers. For five days he is able to claim the company of the normally "inaccessible" New Woman Jessie on false pretenses and a stolen bicycle (112). Saving her from the grasp of Bechamel, he tries to play the knight-errant to Jessie's lady in distress, and is wild with joy that "[a] most delightful and novel human being had flashed across his horizon" (12); "he realized all that those days had done for him ... Love he wouldn't presume. It was worship. If only he could have one more chance" (112).

But Bechamel is not that naïve and sees through Hoopdriver's cover at first glance. Long before Bechamel recognizes that Hoopdriver has discovered his scheme and is out to foil him, he is already insulted when first seeing Hoopdriver on his old bicycle. "Greasy proletariat," mutters Bechamel as he rides past, not just because Hoopdriver is wearing a cheap imitation of his own expensive cycling jacket. "Got a suit of brown, the very picture of this. One would think his sole aim in life had been to caricature me. It's Fortune's way with me. Look at his insteps on the treadles! Why does Heaven make such men?" (18) Bechamel is further offended when Hoopdriver dares to address him with comments on the weather and the road. In an apparent effort to claim the "brotherhood of the wheel" and the "wide sympathy that binds all cyclists together," Hoopdriver assumes the "air of one born to the wheel" and greets him with "A splendid morning, and a fine surface," (18). Such a lower-class "blackguard" is in no place to contravene and intrude into the class-specific pastime of cycling, a privilege that only he and Jessie could lay claim to (111).

When again running into Hoopdriver while visiting a castle with Jessie, Bechamel cries out "Damn!" in irritation, and loudly complains that one "Can't get alone anywhere" (23). However evil his own intentions are toward Jessie, he envisages a united front of class privilege with her, a privilege he now believes is threatened by the lowly shop-hand. As he subsequently warns Hoopdriver, "I object—we object ... to your proximity to us" (40). The low-class cyclist is too close to him and Jessie, and threatens the monopoly on space and speed that middle-class cyclists enjoy. That monopoly also extends to cycling's potential for sexual transgression. Bechamel has no qualms about taking full advantage of this potential and forces Jessie to accept their outing as an elopement, but he is much riled when exposed and thwarted by Hoopdriver, who replaces him in the role of companion and possible lover to Jessie.

This jealous protection of speed's class privilege again crops up, perhaps in a darker and more ominous tone, in "A Romance of Four Wheels," a story published in the *Strand* magazine in 1897. When the "self-contained" and "independent" Miss Anastasia goes for an extended cycling holiday, she deliberately chooses a "very out-of-the-way" route to avoid "the Madding Crowd" (497). She is at first offended when the hotel landlady mistakes her and the only other cyclist, a gentleman, for a couple. Anastasia prides herself on her independence without the need for escort or chaperone, but the landlady's mistake suggests that the bicycle, still relatively rare in that locale, links the two cyclists both in terms of hobby and class. Class identity becomes more important later in the story when a tramp attempts to rob and assault Anastasia. While this incident, threatening dangerously to develop into a sexual crime, may act as a warning to the lady's headstrong independence, it also significantly unites the two cyclists against the tramp and his obvious class differences.

As a pedestrian and a member of the rural poor who could only gape from the roadside at rich cyclists, the tramp would not normally enjoy the advantage of speed over a cyclist. But as a local, he knows a short cut to intercept Anastasia at a turn in the road:

> Anastasia put on all the speed that she and her machine were capable of. Faster and faster she flew along, and all the while the man was drawing nearer to that gap in the hedge she could see. If she could but get there first, she would defy him to overtake her. (500)

In this competition of speed, Anastasia's bicycle almost prevails over the running tramp, except at the last minute she crashes her bicycle and is thrown to the ground. The tramp gloats about his triumph, shouting "You almost gave me the slip" over a prostrate Anastasia (500). But he is immediately denied his advantage when the gentleman cyclist rides up and rescues the lady. The threat from a lower-class man cements the love union of the two middle-class cyclists, as Anastasia, who "would have annihilated any man for daring to propose to accompany her" yesterday, now gladly accepts the company and later marriage proposal of the gentleman cyclist (500). In this story, love is actually engendered and intensified not by cycling itself, but by threats and challenges to cycling from outsiders and inferiors, underlining the crucial importance of a shared privilege and class identity, much in need of defense, to the pleasures of speed.

4

Its Beauty, Danger, and Feverish Thrill

Speed as Excitement and Rejuvenation

In 1899, several years after the mid-1890s "bicycle craze," the noted New Woman cyclist, suffragette, and Rational dress campaigner Miss Nelly G. Bacon turned her enthusiasm to motoring. She had celebrated the bicycle as early as 1886, "this dainty mechanism of steel," for "invit[ing]" women to such "a new world" (qtd. in Hanlon 39). By 1899, as the leading British car journal *The Autocar* discloses in its September editorial, Miss Bacon was busy planning for a ladies' automobile club, after women members were rejected by the Automobile Club of Great Britain (835). The editorial takes an indulgent attitude toward this "indefatigable young person," but in its background notes on Miss Bacon it reveals that years ago she "was very indignant" when the National Cyclists' Union "discountenanced bicycle racing for women," even though women-only races were thriving in America ("Notes" 835). The article suggests that both in Miss Bacon's earlier passion for cycling and in her new interest in motoring the love of speed and racing is a major motive. Miss Bacon is not the only New Woman who embraced the motorcar for its faster velocity and greater range after the bicycle boom had waned. Many early women cycling pioneers threw themselves with equal ardor into motoring by the end of the 1890s, often choosing the powerful but unreliable petrol car over the steam car because of its greater speed (Scharff 76).

This instance, in a roundabout way, demonstrates that, in the midst of the earlier bicycle boom, not a few New Women cyclists went into cycling for its speed and stimulating thrill. Until the advent of the motorcar in the last years of the nineteenth century, the bicycle was the fastest vehicle on the road and the best means of offering the pleasures of speed as a dynamic, adrenaline-packed force. In the same way that these New Women became car enthusiasts in the very early stages of the motoring movement, they had welcomed the bicycle during the previous "bicycle craze," and not just because it allowed "our English damsels" to "glide along like a graceful swan" (qtd. in Hanlon 39). More importantly, they wanted to experience speed as a new modern pleasure, an "*excitant modern*" available to the public through modern technologies of speed (Schnapp 3). The female cyclist may be urged by manufacturers, etiquette manuals, and the popular cycling press to ride in a slow, elegant, and restrained manner, but many seem to long for a taste of the thrilling excitement and rejuvenating expansion activated by speed. This is

The New Woman and Technologies of Speed in Fin-de-Siècle *Literature*. Eva Chen, Oxford University Press.
© Eva Chen (2024). DOI: 10.1093/9780198922285.003.0005

a dimension to women's cycling that should not be ignored, even if the forces of commodification reign supreme.

This dimension has always been a major appeal of speed. In the case of the bicycle, the cross-fertilization between agentic power and mechanical energy further triggers a transcendence of old limitations and the attainment of a heightened level of intensity and power. Because the force that powers the bicycle comes from the rider's muscles, a force then extended and amplified by the machine, the cyclist does not just respond to speed but is also a self-generator and controller of speed. This more visceral and participatory experience of speed helps restore a sense of agency and compensatory freedom to the human subject, even if such freedom is mediated through the very product of mechanizing industrialization. Cycling both replicates the rhythms and ceaseless stimulation of industrial modernity and constructs these as within the control of the human subject. This leads to a more agentic experience of modern speed culture which promises to compensate for the oppression of industrial speed. As the rider has to battle the weather, air resistance, terrain, and fatigue and pain of the human body, cycling induces an experience of speed as exhilaration, excitement, and overwhelming freedom, precisely because it is bruising, arduous, and dangerous: "[A] wholly new experience" of feeling speed as a thrill and a physical sensation is made possible (Duffy 4).

This chapter argues that such compensatory freedom and empowering excitement provided by the active speed of cycling is also available to the New Woman cyclist. During the mid-1890s "bicycle craze," many women cyclists worked with and complied with a modern commodity culture that turned her speeding body into a best platform for conspicuous display, ultimately reinforcing a new set of hierarchies and class differentiation. But there are still those who defy the pressure for restraint and elegant display. Even for those who conform, cycling speed's potential to help fuel a modern, speed-empowered identity is still within their reach. Such an identity is indeed class-specific, as is shown in Chapter 3, but it allows for some progress along gender lines when the New Woman makes use of this active speed to better adjust to the challenges of modern speed culture.

This chapter will first uncover journalistic sources that unveil women's love of cycling speed despite a mainstream emphasis on elegance, restraint, and fashionable display. It will then turn to literary representations and start with Mrs. Edward Kennard's novel *The Golf Lunatic and His Cycling Wife* (1902). In this book, Kennard reverses the gender connotations of speed, and contrasts a lady cyclist's enthusiasm for speed and adventure with her husband's insistence on home comforts and slow-paced indulgence. The chapter then focuses on Grant Allen's *Miss Cayley's Adventures* (1899), another of his New Woman novels, wherein he portrays his heroine's triumphant use of speed to win a major cycling competition against men. Finally, Gissing's story "The Schoolmaster's Vision" describes cycling speed as an active force that unleashes sexual energy; by mastering cycling speed, the New Woman cyclist is able to manipulate this aggressive, speed-liberated sexual energy in a role that is traditionally only reserved for men. This invigorating potential of speed, as this chapter hopes to prove, is essential for the New Woman to construct a new, retooled subjectivity that is at ease with and prospers in modern speed culture.

Racing Women

Ever since the very early days of the high-wheeler era, public disapproval of fast, "unfeminine" speed afflicted women cyclists. Still, this did not deter a small number of women from taking part in races and touring competitions to beat records, display derring-do, and generally relish the thrill of unrestrained speed (Smith 127). The first documented account of women racing occurred in November 1868, when between 4 and 12 women (witness accounts differ) entered a velocipede race from Paris to Rouen amid a total of 100–300 competitors (Simpson 50). An English woman calling herself "Miss America" finished in 29th place, about 12 hours behind the final winner the Englishman James Moore (Fishpool).

Early races of women high-wheelers were reported in Paris's Hippodrome stadium in the 1860s and later in America in the 1870s (Herlihy 205; Dauncey 35). By the late 1880s, more women took part in marathon cycle races in America, and the best record achieved was in Boston in 1882, when Louise Armaindo took on John Prince, the American champion, got a five-mile head start, and lost to Prince by barely a minute (Herlihy 205). In June of 1894, the American Annie Kopchovsky, who assumed the name Annie Londonderry as part of a sponsorship deal for a spring water company, became the first woman to ride around the world. "[P]acking a pearl handled revolver and a change of underwear," Annie completed the ride in fifteen months and won a prize of $10,000, after her return becoming quite a celebrity and appearing in advertisements "for everything from milk to perfume" (Zheutlin 2, 4).

Even in popular women's cycling magazines, where the main thrust is to glamorize cycling as elegant, restrained and ideal for fashionable display, still an occasional appreciation for the thrill of speed steals in here and there, most obviously in the readers' letters and less so in some of the ads. In the October 1895 issue of the *Lady Cyclist*, a poem seems to urge its women readers to go for the attractive grace of slow riding, and warns them against scorching and women's racing: "Is it the girl who doth ride a pneumatic/Over the roads at a furious pace;/Who, with a voice that is bold and emphatic,/Tells about records, who lives but to race—/Is this the girl that men worship and honor,/And to whose feet they will willingly go?/Tell us the masculine verdict upon her:/Little bird dismally whispereth, 'No'" ("Ideal Lady Cyclist" 283). But in the ad for the ladies' "Witch" Safety in the March 1895 issue, a woman cyclist is shown speeding with great pleasure, the wind blowing through her hair and ribbons (Figure 4.1). In "Along the Brighton Road" in the May 1895 issue, a girl beats a record in the London–Brighton race, waves her hat in triumph, and lets her hair fly long and high, suggesting a great pleasure in her fast speed (241).

An illustration for the magazine's September 1895 issue also shows a scorching lady outpacing a two-horse-driven carriage, with the caption "Down! Down!" capturing fully the visceral thrill of speeding (Figure 4.2). In the October 3, 1896 issue, a lady cyclist writes in to pronounce her friend Ethel "ungraceful," because Ethel has just returned from a cycling holiday and has had her bicycle adjusted "a la 'scorcher,'" so that her handles are set up low and seat high. In a slightly mocking tone, the lady reports that she "told Ethel we should expect her to beat the record now" as she "looked so fearfully earnest" ("Letters of a Lady Cyclist" 633). But in the magazine's November 28, 1896 issue, the front cover inside ad, captioned

Figure 4.1 *Lady Cyclist*, Mar. 1895, p. 181. The British Library Archive.

Figure 4.2 "Down! Down!" *Lady Cyclist*, Sept. 1895, p. 258. The British Library Archive.

"Charley's Aunt Rides Beeston Tyres" (Figure 4.3), imparts a more ambiguous message. Though the ad features an old woman speeding away, reinforcing the familiar message that this is something that attractive, elegant ladies would never do, the mischievously happy face of the old woman stealing a look over her shoulder tells otherwise. Confirmed by the words in the ad—"A good judge is she not? Since she is still running. Can't be beaten!"—the ad suggests an illicit pleasure in speeding that only the initiated are in the know of, just like Charley's Aunt.

In the May 1st, 1897 issue of the *Lady Cyclist*, an editorial piece "Speed v. Pleasure" urges women not to give way to "[a]n idea which seems to prevail to a great extent among women riders that the whole delight of cycling lies in speed" (211). But this also suggests that the editor is well aware that scorching is becoming increasingly popular among women. In the December 19, 1896 issue of the

Figure 4.3 Beeston Tyres, *Lady Cyclist*, Nov. 28, 1896, inside cover. The British Library Archive.

Wheelwoman, one writer feels "sorry" for Marie Corelli, a popular writer of melodrama known for her disapproval of scorching, because "[i]t is clear that she has never experienced the poetry of motion or the fine freedom of coasting down an incline of forty-five degrees with a pleasing uncertainty as to the road ending in an open ditch or a corduroy bridge" ("Sorrows of Marie Corelli" 7). In a condescending tone that suggests that the writer herself is well attuned to the

exhilarating freedom and rejuvenating expansion of cycling speed, the article concludes by saying that "Marie is sour; her system is jangled, out of tune, harsh, and
she ought to learn to ride the wheel as soon as possible" (7).

The Joy of Speed: *The Golf Lunatic and His Cycling Wife*

This joy in speeding, half suppressed in the commercial cycling press, blossoms in
bolder touches in some New Woman literature of the period. One such example is
Mrs. Edward Kennard's bestseller *The Golf Lunatic and His Cycling Wife* (1902),
about a middle-class female cyclist who is so addicted to cycling that she later
becomes a cycling correspondent for three cycle magazines. The novel was published in 1902, but its portrayal of flourishing bicycle journals and middle-class
fascination with cycling sets the story very likely in the mid-1890s. Mrs. Kennard had always shown a keen interest in writing about sporty, energetic women,
and her earlier novels published in the1880s featured female characters who love
horses and hunting (S. Wintle 72). In the 1890s, reflecting the popular interest in
the bicycle, she moved on to women bicyclists and even penned a *Guide Book for
Lady Cyclists*, published in London by F. V. White & Co. in 1896. Her support
for female cycling and the Rational dress is evident in this guidebook, where she
writes "If it were the fashion in this country for ladies of good standing and position to wear knickerbockers, and if they could appear as freely in them as in France,
without shocking the non-cycling portion of the community, then, no doubt much
might be adduced in their favour" (p. 44). Kennard carries on her appreciation of
speed and "fast" women in her next novel, *The Motor Maniac* (1903), wherein the
lady-cyclist-turned-motorist heroine freely admits that "once you take to motoring, it was all over with cycling" (42), because nothing beats "the glorious sensation
of racing" in a motorcar (59).

In *The Golf Lunatic and His Cycling Wife*, the cycling wife Cynthia attributes
her love of cycling to the rebellious spirit she has had since her childhood days.
Cynthia's mother had "tried her very best and hardest to mould me into the conventional young lady of her own early days" by teaching her "fancy work and the
customary useless accomplishments of girlhood" (5). But Cynthia proves to be
a girl with "an intense love of action," who wants to be "a great warrior," or a
Red Indian in Fenimore Cooper's books (4), rather than the "flighty little commonplace woman" she is expected to be (7). When she marries a husband who
is good-natured but rather silly and expects his wife to stay at home and play the
hostess to his many friends, Cynthia simply "took the flight" by mounting "my
beloved bicycle" and going away for "forty or fifty miles on my wheel" (62, 63):

> How dearly I loved those expeditions! It was such a blessed relief to roll along
> the peaceful country roads, think my own thoughts, and right my ruffled temper.
> However irritable I might have felt at starting, the sight of the green fields and
> wide sky, accompanied by the smooth gliding motion of my conveyance and the

sense of freedom it conferred, never failed to exercise a soothing influence upon me. (63)

Cynthia's cycling starts out as an escape from "restraint" and a release from the "bonds of Society" and domestic duties. The bicycle in these scenes serves as the much-acclaimed "freedom machine" liberating women from confining domesticity (Wånggren 77). But Cynthia soon begins to pursue cycling for the excitement and thrill of speed itself (63). After becoming a member of the Cycling Touring Club and contributing several letters to the Club, Cynthia is asked by the editor of the "well-known paper *Cycle Snips*" to write a monthly column on the latest bicycle models (66). Under the guise of trying and reporting on "every innovation placed upon the market" for the paper, Cynthia accepts the job with "unadulterated pleasure" and is able to indulge her own yearning for "experimentalization" and speed (67): "For a whole month I had a Collier two-speed gear, and changed the lever from fifty-six to sixty-six to my heart's content" (68). The lure of speed "was extremely fascinating, and apt to carry one away in the beginning ... until one gets used to it" (68). Once she gets used to it, she longs for "higher gears" and faster speed, and tries a new model with seven-inch cranks which allow her to climb ascents "with more ease than had ever hitherto been the case." Riding an "arduous" 56-mile distance to "Lowborough" one day, in gusty wind and with a succession of long hills to climb, Cynthia overtakes every other lady cyclist who is forced to walk their bicycles in the heavy wind. Barely able to contain her excitement, she declares herself "a convert," because "the sixty-eight-geared New Rapid came out of the ordeal triumphantly" (68). "Against the fury of the blast it made steady progress," and if the wind is favorable "the rider experienced the pleasures of cycling to the fullest extent" (69).

One chapter in the novel, aptly titled "Cycling Mad," reveals that Cynthia is not the only woman who is thrilled by speed, as a great many other women cyclists share her enthusiasm as well:

> The following month I was literally besieged with letters from various ladies, all requesting me to furnish them with further particulars. I discovered that a very large section of the feminine element liked going a good pace, and being able to keep up with their husbands and brothers. In fact, they showed a considerable hankering after speed. (69)

This "hankering after speed" shows that women cyclists are more than just the decorous and elegantly restrained lady cyclists portrayed in the commercial press and etiquette manuals. They are, in fact, participating with undisguised enthusiasm in the danger, energy, and thrill of speed, conventionally constructed as a masculine province. They besiege Cynthia with letters not because they are novices, but because, as experienced cyclists, they thirst for faster models and want a share of Cynthia's speed-enabled thrill.

In this novel, Kennard portrays Cynthia's old life as weighed down by the slowness and stasis of her woman's time. Her daily routine of dressing for meals, taking walks, playing the piano, and attending parties has only one aim and object: "to kill time" (6); "I grew restless," "my horizon was limited," and "I simply could not stay in the house" (71). Luckily Cynthia finds a "vent" for this insufferable frustration "in cycling" (72), and attains a higher, more intense way of realizing her potential through the active thrill of speed. "An intense longing seized me to go out into the sunshine and roll along the leafy lanes" (73). Out in the open and merrily speeding along, Cynthia celebrates the bicycle as a woman's freedom machine:

> What a field of new experiences the cycle opened up to modern womanhood! It freed her from a multitude of conventional shackles. She could wander at her will, go where she listed, stay where she elected; dependent on no man, no horse, no carriage, but solely on the clever bit of mechanism constructed by the ingenuity of human brains and hands. She owed them a debt of thanks, for nowadays she could fancy herself a beggar or a queen according to her proclivities. (63)

The self-proclaimed "unconventional individual" (73) soon yearns for greater excitement and challenge. Not content with her daily rides, she ventures on two long bicycling expeditions in the second half of the novel: one with her husband to Belgium for one month, the other with a female cyclist to Scotland for two weeks. Such expeditions are certainly quite unusual for a woman cyclist, and when first proposed to her husband he responds with disbelief and shock. Cynthia's husband has already complained of her Rational cycling costume: "How ridiculously short your skirt is, Cynthia! I call it quite indecent" (82). He is unhappy that his wife does not "dress like other women," and protests that he "can't see the object of making a guy of yourself" (84). Now he calls her "as mad as a March hare" if this tour is to go ahead (77). But it turns out that his chief objection is over the threat to his own masculinity posed by his wife's much better cycling skills and faster speed. "Where a bicycle is concerned you are not to be trusted, Cynthia," he complains, because "you scorch away from your poor husband and leave him toiling hopelessly in the rear" (75). "A woman has no business to go careering on before her husband," he goes on protesting, as "[h]e is the proper one to be at the head of affairs" (76).

This tacit admission that men's equation with and monopoly of speed comes about only after a deliberate suppression of women's speed does not seem to bother the husband too much, as he reluctantly agrees to the trip after winning a promise from Cynthia that she will be "as docile as a lamb" and always follow him from behind (75). He continues to assert his masculine prerogative on the grounds that "a fellow" can't be expected to bother with lowly details, leaving all the itinerary-planning, bicycle-cleaning, oiling, and puncture-mending to Cynthia (77). Throughout the journey Cynthia turns out to be the real force steering their pace and direction, as she meets every challenge along the way while relishing the varied sights and sounds of a changing landscape. Her foray into this new experience of speed and mobility would have been much more rewarding were she not constantly dragged down by her lazy, slow husband. Complaining nonstop of sores and tiredness, it is her husband who longs for the regular hours and "home comforts" of English domesticity, and who seems to embody the passivity and stasis always blamed on women (157–58). The novel in this way manages to reverse traditional gender connotations of speed and stasis.

Cynthia is able to avoid this slowing impediment in her second cycling expedition in Scotland, in the company of her friend Dora, who is a much more resilient and capable cyclist than Cynthia's husband. Like Cynthia, Dora's eyes light up at the mention of a cycling tour which, she declares, "was the dream of her life" (174). Though Dora's father calls the two women "a pair of lunatics" (178), and Cynthia's husband deems the trip "a wild goose chase" (172), the two women thirst for the "refreshing effect" and "novel experience" of the cycling tour, and are fully prepared for "roughing it a little" (172). This expedition starts out when Cynthia could no longer bear her husband's silly flirtation with a scheming seductress, who has persuaded him to pay good money for her house 300 miles away just on hearsay. Ever the mobile and energetic woman, Cynthia decides to cycle all the way there in seven days to see the house for herself, to the great astonishment of her husband. Dora, in her turn, has just emerged, much battered, from a disappointing romance. Cycling, to these two women, offers a release from men and confining home life, where "my susceptibilities ... were trampled upon every hour of the day" (176). It also nourishes a sense of female companionship and solidarity, where both enjoy the exhilaration and enrichment enabled by speed.

In these scenes, the narrative highlights a particular kind of energizing speed, one that comes only after much toil and strenuous overcoming of limitations. Throughout their journey, which the novel describes as "arduous" but also "triumphant," the two women brave strong winds, heavy rain, bumpy roads, punctured tires, bodily hunger and exhaustion, and derive a great pleasure from the speeding bicycle that is not just based on fun and excitement, but also individual triumph over duress (179). Feelings of great exultation dot the pages here and there. The two women "indulg[ed] in the most glorious run down to the vale which gradually unfolded itself to our vision in the far distance" (230). "[P]utting our feet up" in the mode of scorching, they relish the speed of the downhill ride while the scenes "flew by in a perfectly wonderful manner" (230). This speed brings intense pleasure, but the passage also foregrounds the hardship and toil of their struggle. The road seems interminable, the wind "raged indomitable," and the uphill ascents were "so steep we were forced to dismount and push our machines" (226). When Dora, on one ascent, could take it no more and begs for a rest and a cup of hot tea, Cynthia encourages her to "pull yourself together" (228) and "[b]race yourself for another effort" (229), because they refuse to be those women "who melt like sugar at a few drops of rain" (178). They should learn to "take the rough with the smooth," and the resultant pleasure would be doubly rewarding (228).

It is significant that in these passages in Kennard's novel such an arduous form of pleasure, gained after toiling against obstacles and triumphing over limits, seems to be interwoven with mechanized speed, whereby the human subject achieves both an organic and a machine-aided expansion of self. Dora is at first heartbroken and downcast before the expedition, but she is greatly "revived and regained her spirits" at the end (230). "What fun this is!" she exclaims; "Such a lovely coast almost makes up for all we have gone through" (230). Even the indefatigable Cynthia learns a lot, having "gained wider knowledge, fuller experience, [and] increased my area of sympathy" (254). At the end of the trip, Cynthia takes pride in her new, heightened self when she "feels curiously enterprising and independent," and is "exceedingly pleased with ourselves" and "proud of the muscles and energy" gained (180, 207). "Who will dare affirm that women can't get on together, and are helpless without a man to look after them?" (210). The speeding bicycle not only injects energy into women so they will no longer submit to "rotting and rusting from inaction" (211), it also cements a female bond based on a shared "ambition" "more ... than the average men" (72), an eager desire for the thrills and challenges of modern life. Thanking her "little wheel," "my Raleigh" "religiously," for being a "deliverer of the female sex" (211), Cynthia declares that "I had escaped from the narrow groove of everyday existence, and felt ready for any enterprise" (179).

This invigorated, expanded female self and fantasies of emancipation from mundane limitations are at least partially enabled by the two women's interaction with machine speed. Not all women, of course, emerge successfully from such interaction. Judith, the typewriter in Mitton's *A Bachelor Girl in London*, could find only momentary release in her thrilling bus rides with the driver Ireland, before bowing out in defeat. Allen's New Woman typist-cum-cyclist Juliet proves to be more resilient, and finds compensation and rejuvenation in the bicycle's active speed. In Kennard's novel, the New Woman cyclist Cynthia does not have to work for a living and is relieved of the need to face the coercive pressure of industrial speed. But in immersing herself in the active speed of cycling and its new energies and expanded freedom, Cynthia attains a higher level of confidence and is more ready to face the challenges of modern life, where speed and its many impacts infiltrate into every corner.

The bicycle's promise of limitless speed and individual control not only fuels exhilarating dreams of transcendence of limitations. Mastering this mechanized speed also entails hardships, both physical and mechanical, that are instrumental to the building up of greater resilience and moral fortitude. To Kennard, this character-building potential does not just derive from the physical travails and hardship of the cycling tour, but also from Cynthia's interaction with the machine of speed and from her mastery of its prosthetic power and mechanical challenges. The constant repairs, accidents, and efforts to tease out the best performance from her bicycle provides for a tortuous, taxing, and problem-ridden experience of speed. This experience promises to unleash new levels of resourcefulness and resilience, and enriches and expands her character.

This very positive presentation of the mechanical side of bicycle speed and its enabling impact on women is meaningful. In this novel, it is women like Cynthia, normally constructed as passive and alienated from mechanized speed, who embrace speed and derive fortitude, derring-do, and mechanical knowledge from their mastery of speed, while men like her husband wallow in the decadence of comfort and indolence. On their Belgian expedition, even Cynthia's husband has to acknowledge her mechanical skills when asked by an American tourist for help with his punctured bicycle. Recommending his "old missus to fix the thing up right for you in a few minutes," he admits that Cynthia is "a perfect wonder where a bicycle is concerned, and knows more about them than two ordinary men put together" (120). Later on Cynthia proves that mending the puncture needs not only a strict adherence to the instruction manual, which the American tourist has religiously followed, but also an instinct and resourcefulness developed from her hands-on experience with bicycle repairs. Even though she admits to "never having previously performed" this particular insertion of the plug to the puncture, she is able to solve the problem by semi-inflating the tire and leaving the puncture to stand and dry out (121).

Cynthia proves that it is women, not men, who have better mechanical skills, a theme repeated in Kennard's next novel *The Motor Maniac*, where, again, the heroine, not her husband, is the maniac for this new, faster machine of speed. Here the wife is not just adroit with puncture repairing, but actually goes down and dirty under cars, dressed in a "blue engineer's jacket" (190). When she is busy washing ball-bearings and doing the repair work, her husband, much shocked, calls her a "female mechanic," which is "scarcely a lady's job" (190). Kennard herself was a cycling enthusiast and motoring pioneer and is known to have driven a 40 hp Napier car, a De Dion voiturette, and a 15 hp Darracq in the early 1900s. This explains how her New Women characters know so much about bicycles and cars, and why her novels are among the few works penned by women writers that display a technical virtuosity unrivalled by many men (Marks 75). When the *St. James Gazette* wrote a review of *The Motor Maniac*, it may not have approved of Kennard's talent "as a story-teller," but it still credited her for "the technical accuracy for which her work is well-known" ("Rapid Review" 16). *The Graphic* review even declares that the novel proves "the point of the maxim that what Woman has done, Woman can do" ("*Motor Maniac* Review" 24).

Kennard is not the only voice that celebrates women's empowering mastery of speed and all its technical challenges. In women's cycling press, similar affirmations sometimes surface, though often under the guise of terms that seek to align such skills with traditional feminine accomplishments like nursing or sewing.

Girl's Own Paper, for instance, encouraged women to know more about the construction of their bicycles and "master the elements of cycle 'first-aid'" (qtd. in Hanlon 85). Lilias Campbell Davidson also urged women cyclists to "[t]ake care of the machine yourself," and "thoroughly understand the use of every nut and cog, and be able to right any small derangement that might occur" (85). Cycling and the later motoring require an active, whole-body engagement that propels women into direct contact with machine-aided speed. They have to develop an eye and an ear for the rhythm of the bicycle, diagnose mechanical faults, and learn to use tools for repair, in order to get the best performance from the bicycle. As is shown in Kennard's work, it is women like Cynthia who relish the new experiences brought by modern speed culture, while men like her husband remain stuck in the slow habits of the old.

"Pedaling away like a machine": *Miss Cayley's Adventures*

Mrs. Kennard's bestseller announces with enthusiasm that women are now, literally and symbolically, accelerated into modernity. But once launched into the giddy whirlpool of mechanized speed, the female body is also bound to be impacted upon and transformed by the constraints, energies, and desires triggered by the interaction between the mechanical and the organic. In Grant Allen's *Miss Cayley's Adventures* (1899), where he features another New Woman cyclist-cum-typist, Lois Cayley, this complicated simultaneity of emancipation and constraint receives a more detailed treatment. Contemporary reviews of this novel tend to be dismissive; the *Saturday Review*, for instance, declares that Allen "has gone over to the merrymakers," and that the book is "innocent of any serious import" and "[r]eplete with inconsequent absurdity as a modern farce" ("*Miss Cayley's Adventures* Review" 598). But the novel also contains plenty of Allen's characteristic sensitivity to issues of mechanization and human agency, particularly in those passages highlighting the excitement of fast speed and perennial movement.

Like Juliet Appleton in *The Type-Writer Girl*, Girton-educated Lois Cayley is an example of the mobile, adventurous modern woman who makes clever use of the technology of speed. She takes trains and ferries to cross the English Channel, rides a bicycle around Germany and Italy, works as a model/agent for an American bicycle entrepreneur, opens a typewriting and shorthand shop in Italy, and then travels to Egypt and India to work as a journalist. She even acts for a time as an amateur detective, and is always one step ahead of her criminal because of her adroit use of machines of speed such as the train and the bicycle. The novel records the exhilarating series of adventures Lois gets into, all of which come about as a result of chance opportunities that spring up when she is moving around, either by bicycle, train, or ferry.

Lois comes from a privileged background, but when her stepfather dies just as she is finishing college, she faces poverty and the need to earn a living. In the same way that Gissing's New Woman character Rhoda has rejected reaching, Lois also refuses to teach, because "I'm a bit of a rebel" and "not cut out" for traditional feminine jobs like teaching (*Miss Cayley's Adventures* 2). She has always been "before my time," and was cycling around at Cambridge at a time when "ladies did not cycle," and the bicycle was "a startling innovation" and "terrified" everyone (3). Again, like so many New Women heroines, Lois decides to go to London, because this "greatest and richest city in the world" offers plenty of "loopholes for an adventure" (4): "This city bursts with enterprises and surprises. Strangers from east and west hurry through it in all directions. Omnibuses traverse it from end to end ... folk sit face to face who never saw one another before in their lives, and who may never see one another again" (5). London as a metropolis of fast speed and variety, so dizzying and alienating to many, is eagerly embraced by Lois. Walking around Kensington Gardens, she stumbles upon a "Cantankerous Old Lady" who is in need of a companion to accompany her to Germany, volunteers herself for the job, and immediately sets out for her journey across the Channel to France and Germany. The novel portrays her as constantly on the move and engaged in different adventures, first thwarting the attempted theft of the Lady's jewelry by a fake Count, and then refusing to marry the Lady's rich nephew out of pride and a desire for independence.

The culmination of Cayley's active use of speed is in her third adventure, when she enters and wins a bicycle race as the only female cyclist and beats all of the male competitors. Cayley travels to Frankfurt after leaving the nephew and is riding around on a hired bicycle when she runs into an "inquisitive American" bicycle salesman (43). It is her "swift" cycling, her ability to "[soar] off at once, heedless of the jeers of Teutonic youth," that attracts the attention of the American (43). The American is in town to debut his Manitou—a crude version of today's mountain bike—and to claim the Kaiserly and Kingly prize money offered by the German Imperial and Prussian Royal Governments for the best military bicycle. He wants Cayley to be the model for his new invention and to enter the race from Frankfurt to Limburg, arranged by the Prussian government for this purpose, wagering that this would create maximum publicity for his bicycle. With characteristic humor and in vivid imitation of the American's broad accent, Allen describes the American bragging about his Manitou as "the biggest thing in cycles since Dunlop tires" (60), "geared to run up most anything in creation," and sure to "give these Meinherrs fits" and "knock 'em" out (49). Lois initially hesitates to accept his offer, because the shrewd American wants to keep his invention a secret and leave Lois in the dark until the morning of the competition. But she soon decides to take up the challenge, partly because of her irrepressible desire for adventure, and partly because she is determined not to rot and rust like the German old maids boarding at her hotel, who spend their days knitting and waiting in a "stuffed comatose" existence like "a placid fat oyster ... settl[ing] down on a rock" (46). "Adventures are to the adventurous. They abound on every side; but only the chosen few have the courage to embrace them. And they will not come to you: you must go out to seek them" (46).

On the day of the race, Lois puts on a "short serge dress and cycling jacket," and arrives at the city square thronging with professional male racers, who "eyed me superciliously" (52). She is the only woman there, and some men try to ban her from attending, protesting that this is not "woman's play" (53). When they finally set out for the race, she is at first left far behind by the greater speed of these male professionals, and jeered at and called on by bystanders to give up. "Give it up! Fraulein, give it up! You're beaten. You're beaten!" (54) But she keeps going and soon proves to be a more clever user of speed, for she refrains from scorching on level lands and only accelerates when climbing hills. With the four gears of the Manitou, she is able to ride up the steep hill smoothly "like a whirlwind" (56). The American has chosen Lois because she has quick "prehistoric feet," great "circular ankle-action" and the power of "clawing up again" her feet very fast to move the wheels (51). Here "strength of limb counted for naught" (51), but is replaced by speed and nimbleness from the human rider, for the bicycle can do all the heavy work.

One by one she overtakes the male cyclists "with a spurt" (55); "with hair flying behind," "I rode for dear life," sweeping past village after village. As she levels up with the last male cyclist, a German man who tried to ban her at the start, he darts her a look of disbelief and "unchivalrous dislike," tries to foul her by swerving deliberately, but ends up hitting the rock himself and almost falling down (56). Lois overtakes him and gains the summit, coasting down thereafter with "my feet up" all the way down the slope to the final destination, winning the long race "like a squirrel" (56). The news of her win is splashed all over the newspapers because a woman has beaten the men at high speed. This is the publicity long anticipated by the American when he chose Lois: "if a female wins, it makes success all the more striking and con-spicuous. The world today is ruled by advertisement" (50). And nothing gets greater advertisement than a woman winning a bicycle race—and a "high-tone" English lady at that (59). It would be "an international affair," and a "first-rate advertisement for the Great Manitou" (53).

Lois's win, as Patricia Craig and Mary Cadogan point out, is shamelessly exploited by the American entrepreneur (26). It also works to reinforce the implied derogation of women as slow and weak—for if a woman can ride that fast on the Manitou, who else couldn't? But Lois's win, widely covered in every news-paper, still manages to put women firmly in the middle of modern speed culture, and helps imprint the idea that women are joining their brothers in mastering speed and taking pleasure from it. Lois is certainly far from a mere victim. She gets £50 from the American for winning the race and shows herself a shrewd learner through doing business with him. When the American explains with some reluctance that he prefers to manufacture his bicycle in Germany rather than in

England, Lois quickly sees that it is because an English company would buy the patent and manufacture it for themselves. while in Germany he can do his own manufacturing and pocket greater profit. The American eyes her with admiration: "That's so! You hit it in one, miss!" (58).

He is even more impressed when Lois then takes the initiative and pitches her own proposal to him. When he proposes that she should have the Manitou and ride about as an advertisement for the new bicycle, she comes up with a better idea, suggesting that she should become his sole agent and get a 25 percent commission from every bicycle she helps to sell. She even volunteers to lure prospective customers by deliberately riding to and fro in front of them and then pretending to ask them for the time, to make her pitching look natural. The American's face "was one broad smile": "I do admire you, miss. You may not know the meaning of the word commission, but durned ef you haven't got a hand of the thing itself that would do honor to a Wall Street operator, anyway" (60). Even a Wall Street operator may not better Lois, for when the American suggests the exaggerated American way of advertising his Manitou in the name of "progress" and "evolution," Lois persuades him that a toned-down, more personal and chatty tone would better "rope in the Europeans" and "take 'em on their own ground" (62). His admiration is "undisguised": "Well, I do call you a woman of business, miss ... You'll jest haul in the dollars!" (62) Like her race win over those German professional men, Lois shows herself an agentic steersperson of both speed and any monetization of speed.

This portrayal of Lois's interaction with speed is rather positive, but Allen also tackles the more complicated dimensions of cycling. Miss Cayley as the female cyclist, for instance, is far from the romanticized subject of preindustrial, unmediated, organic agency. This is seen in the novel's reference to Lois's nimble feet as the reason for her win. The shrewd American claims that brute strength, amply possessed by the male bicyclists, "counted for naught" (51). It is Lois's nimble feet, her "lithe" movement (45), and "circular ankle-action" (51), meaning her power of "'clawing up again' promptly" (51), that best brings out the speed of the Manitou. "There is money in your feet. You'll take the clear-starch out of them," claims the American (49). Here nimbleness and quickness, coming from Lois's "prehistoric feet" of "tree-haunting monkeys," are gendered as female and constructed as an inherently female bodily trait that is better attuned to mechanized speed than the male body. As Cayley asserts, "The Manitou was built for me, and I was built for the Manitou" (51).

This emphasis on a woman's nimble body, already amply utilized when manufacturers and business owners tried to stress women's suitability to operate the typewriting machine, points to a belief in the particular congeniality of the female body to the machine, and their increasing conflation. Allen's *The Type-writer Girl* makes constant references to the female typist's nimble fingers, and the same reference to Miss Cayley's nimble cycling feet may serve to reinforce, rather than challenge, established ideas about gender and sexual difference. However, it must also be pointed out that in this novel Lois's portrayed affinity with the machine of speed could act as a metaphor for a new type of human subject, a subject inevitably changed by the interaction with the mechanical beyond the boundaries separating the body from the machine. Riding her bicycle furiously, Cayley comments that "We ran together like parts of one mechanism" (51). Then she sees her feet—the part of her organic body engineering the speed—almost mutating into some prosthetic attachment to the machine: "my feet" are "working as if they were themselves an integral part of the machinery" (55). Cayley ultimately finds herself losing tactile awareness, completely fused with the machine in an oblivion of speed: "Bump, crash, jolt! I pedaled away like a machine; the Manitou sobbed; my ankles flew round so that I scarcely felt them" (56). So murky is the line of demarcation that, as the human body becomes indistinguishable from the machine, the machine itself is described in animated terms. The Manitou is a "squirrel," in the same way that Lois is a squirrel: it can "sob," and "bounded forward like an agile greyhound" (49). It even threatens to commandeer the act of steering from the human subject, as "you had but to touch it, and it ran of itself" (49).

This invigorating assemblage of human agency and prosthetic technology allows Lois to revel in the thrill of conquering machinery and enjoying her expanded power. Here, both woman and bicycle are metamorphosized into a living, mutually enhancing hybrid: the Manito enabling the woman to fly, the woman manipulating the Manito and coaxing it into the best performance. This ability to unite human agency with mechanical precision means that Lois is far from mechanized by the bicycle, but instead their adrenaline-packed interaction ultimately serves to reshape and expand the human body, as it instills in her a more alert sense and new coordinated skills. This new, expanded female power is not simply located in the natural body itself, but as a result of the medley between the organic and the mechanical.

By allowing her speeding body to become a network of energized encounters with the mechanical, Miss Cayley thus attains a new selfhood activated and launched by the machine of speed and better attuned to the mechanical. Certainly, she offers a picture of prosperity as she later rides her Manitou and attracts great attention and new orders, many from other women excited by her sensational win and by her triumphantly speeding body. This female subject emits an image of power, which is reaffirmed in her later success in life in the second half of the novel. Riding feverishly and overtaking the male bicyclists whose own speed is also prostheticized through the aid of their bicycles, the New Woman cyclist proves she adapts better to and even revels in such fusion of body and machine.

The Eroticization of Speed

The link between women and speed also unleashes a new sexual energy and brings out another dimension: the eroticization of speed. In *Miss Cayley's Adventures*, a second reason the American chooses Cayley, apart from her quick ankles, is that she has got "style" and is a lady of "considerable personal attraction"—"jest the right woman" to promote the Manitou (45). This is perhaps an added dimension when women participate in modern speed culture, as the cycling woman becomes a vehicle *for* desire as well as *of* desire. Just like the typewriter girl, the fast body of the cycling woman has always had sexual connotations in the *fin-de-siècle* sociocultural scene, as she gives rise to, as was mentioned earlier, fears of illicit encounters with men and worries of a general loosening of moral standards. The public visibility of cycling and its use as a platform for conspicuous display further focuses attention on her sexualized body and short attire. But there is another source for her desirability, one that is derived from her links to the sexual energy brought by speed.

Fin-de-siècle press reported on cycling exhibitions where the audience was particularly drawn to and fascinated with professional lady cyclists, who would demonstrate great speed and skills while performing on indoor tracks in velodromes or as part of acrobatics shows. *The Hub* reports in 1896 that a troupe of French women, who were employed by the Royal Aquarium of London to give cycling exhibitions during their visit to England, were paid more than their male counterparts; they were "pounced upon" by agents and cycle makers and proved to be "one of the most powerful attractions we ever had" ("How Ladies' Cycle Races" 221). In those mid and late 1890s years, bicycle races were increasingly transferred from the road to indoor velodromes, due to concerns about public safety and because velodromes charged entrance fees and offered better views (Simpson 52). Men dominated these races, but women racers were also becoming more common. Feminists and women's dress reform movement supported women's racing, but most of the public watched for entertainment or out of a sense of titillation. As women's scorching on public streets was still largely discouraged, these exhibitions offered a chance to see speeding women cyclists who both impressed and aroused with their mastery of speed.

It is significant that in these exhibitions, as is the case in Allen's novel, speed itself is presented as sexually arousing, mediated through the attractive image of the speeding woman cyclist. This erotic appeal does not derive solely from her looks nor from her naturalized sexuality, but particularly from her cycling body— a body sped up by and in fusion with the machine. It is when Miss Cayley is cycling that she proves most alluring, catching the eye of every spectator. Here, a new form of sexual energy is ignited by the engine of speed and by a medley of the organic and the mechanical.

In George Gissing's story "The Schoolmaster's Vision," published in *The English Illustrated Magazine* in 1896, this eroticization of machine-aided speed gains more thematic importance. In Gissing's mid-1890s New Woman novels, the text may sympathize with women's struggles in the modern city, but it nevertheless blames women for their particular attraction to the speed and stimulation of modern culture. His detached, languid, and ironically contemplative male characters, staunch supporters of the stability and traditional values of a premodern world, often rail against "flashy," restless, and mobile women characters who prefer to "live in hotels and trollop about the streets" of a fast-paced modern city (*In the Year of Jubilee* 39–40). Many of his women characters are restless with the "ennui" of domesticity, compared with which even "the meanest of London streets shone as a paradise" (*The Whirlpool* 142). This dissatisfaction with the modern world of "sham and rottenness" (21) can be interpreted as a dissatisfaction with speed and the accelerated pace of modern life. Even literature and serious journalism are now threatened by "chit-chat" New Journalism, which provides a miscellany of "two-inch" columns, "bits of stories, bits of description, bits of scandal, bits of jokes, bits of statistics, bits of foolery" to a mass readership of short attention span craving only for fast change and new variety (*New Grub Street* 376). In "The Schoolmaster's Vision," this dissatisfaction is again in display when the story links the dangerously aggressive sexuality of the New Woman with the bicycle, and with the sexual energy of mechanized speed.

The story's main character is a schoolmaster of a boys' school, a staid, "arid," "disaffected" widower who is secretly recoiling from the monotony of his sedentary school routines (Rawlinson 174). He meets the mother of one of the boys, a young, fashionable, attractively vivacious lady wearing a Rational cycling costume, "with curiously short skirts," who "diffused about her an atmosphere of wealth and fashion" ("Schoolmaster's Vision" 131). Not the sort of decorous, nurturing women the schoolmaster is used to, she leaves her young boy in the care of relatives after the death of her husband, and enjoys life "in her own way" in France (132). The story implies that the mother, who is ready to marry again but has no wish to take on the care of her son, is a New Woman "of the newest type," and the bicycle she rides all the way to school from Bristol symbolizes her unconventionality, derring-do, and independence (132). Like the women characters in his other works, Gissing portrays the New Woman mother as restless, ceaselessly moving about, and enjoying the stimulation and thrill of modern life. The schoolmaster, by contrast, is associated with the slower pace of a preindustrial way of life in the countryside, disaffected with and observing from the side the dizzying bustling city of Bristol, "a murky cloud" "on the horizon" far away (130).

Yet even this "ideal of head-mastership," who rules by "spiritual awe (scornful of baser method)," and embodies the "bland union of erudition and high breeding," is fascinated whilst watching the New Woman mother nimbly mount her bicycle. Later in the evening he has a sexually charged, "feverish and phantasmal" dream in which he tries to catch up with the lady while cycling in a fantasy land (138). Cycling is thus equated with a sense of kinetic speed, dynamic excitement, and sexual arousal. The schoolmaster married young right after college, and the women in his life—both the wife who died six years ago, and the sister who now keeps house for him—are paradigms of "discreet," "loyal," "modest" femininity whom the schoolmaster treats with "tenderness" but also a whiff of "secret impatience" (131). Day after day he discharges his school and family duties with a "noticeable languor," repeating a fixed routine in a country school. Into this sedentary and rather "oppressive" life comes Mrs. Argent, "so fresh her complexion, so slim and lithe her figure, so spirited her whole aspect, that one would naturally have taken her for six-and-twenty at most." He has little time to express his disapproval of her neglect of motherly duties, but is instead mesmerized by her "gay," forward manners, her "delightful frankness," and especially her "curiously short skirts" and "wonderful feet," which he stares at with an "indecorous fixity."

Mrs. Argent's bicycling skills and nimbleness seem to most arouse him and "so wrought his imagination." On the spur of the moment and without prior announcement, Mrs. Argent has ridden all the way from Bristol, a "peculiar ... mode of travelling," given the distance, to see her little son. When she shows him how to cycle, "slowly, skillfully," the animation and excitement of the little boy mirrors the same emotions on the part of the schoolmaster, as he tries awkwardly to disguise the fact that he "thought more of Mrs. Argent than he cared to say." She is so quick, energetic, and spontaneous, flitting in and out, soon to go back to Bristol by the same mode of cycling, that he "would have given half his substance to be able to mount at her side." The schoolmaster could not cycle himself and, at leave-taking, he "watched her wheel out the machine and spring to her seat with perfect grace," standing by the gate "bareheaded as she swept away." When the little boy runs after her, shouting and leaping in her track, the schoolmaster is equally hankering after her cycling body. "[H]is eyes dazzled," and "his blood became a rushing torrent," as he longs to match her speed and not be left behind.

Later that night when he puts up in an inn, having wandered away from home restless and agitated, he has a dream wherein he finds himself suddenly "speeding through vast spaces" and cycling after her. He "pursued ..., ever calling, imploring, with wondrous vocabulary of passionate desire" (138):

> beside him sped – not a person, but a voice. A woman's voice, clear as a silver bell, ever rising to the note of merry laughter. And it seemed to urge him on, until the exhausting violence of his efforts made him aware that he was neither running nor flying, but riding on a bicycle. He marveled at his sudden skill in the management of this machine. "Do I ride well?" he shouted, against the wind that all but stopped his breath. And the answer was a gay, echoing laugh, which shook him with such delirium of passion that he started up from the bed, and half awoke. (138)

The sexual allure of the cycling New Woman is so powerful that it injects not just cycling skills, but also a rush of adrenaline and energy into the schoolmaster's languid body. She "inflamed his blood, and made his brain whirl with rapture." It is significant that the object of desire is no longer the body of Mrs. Argent but a disembodied voice, the voice of speed as it were, calling out to him, urging him and alluring him with all the promise of sexual fulfillment. Only the auditory sense is at play here, as the voice of speed defies the strong wind, the pull of gravity, and bodily limitations to deliver a kinetic fantasy of exhilarating release. Responding to the voice, he cries out a delirious wail wherein consummate speed is synonymous with the consummation of erotic desire: "[a]t the peak, you are mine!" (139).

This eroticization of speed departs from the usual literary representation. Commenting on the famous dog-cart scene in Thomas Hardy's *Tess of the D'Urbervilles*, Enda Duffy argues that the thrill of fast speed is traditionally linked with the energetic, aggressive sexuality of caddish, predatory men (119–20). The rakish Alec D'Urberville drives a frightened Tess downhill at full speed in his dog-cart: "[d]own, down, they sped, the wheels humming like a top, the dog-cart rocking right and left ... the figure of the horse rising and falling in undulations before them" (*Tess of the D'Urbervilles* 54). The demure and innocent Tess begs him to slow down, but he threatens to go faster unless she agrees to let him have "[t]he kiss of mastery" (56), which he finally gets. Speed in this episode is linked with male sexual conquest and aggressive power, while women are presented as passive and in fear of speed. In Gissing's story, however, it is the woman who relishes speed and is actively skilled in maneuvering at speed, while the schoolmaster awkwardly tries to emulate and catch up with her. Here, speed is still linked with aggressive sexuality, but is now gendered as female. Mrs. Argent's powerful erotic appeal, stimulating the schoolmaster into a feverish fit of mad longing, does not just come from her naturalized feminine body, but specifically from her speeding motion and her actively nimble, machine-aided cycling body. More so than in Hardy's dog-cart scene—in which the driving Alex relishes the thrill of speed but sits still, letting the cart transport him along—Gissing's cycling woman physically participates in and manipulates the generation of the speed of the bicycle. Her body is in a more intimate fusion with the machine of speed, even dissolving into a voice and becoming pure energy and speed.

In his mid-1890s New Woman novels, Gissing's women characters often end up meeting tragedy when they embrace the thrills of modern culture. But in "The Schoolmaster's Vision," it is the male body that is found wanting, and suffers the consequences of failing to catch up with the latest trends and technologies of the modern world. The schoolmaster keeps on dreaming:

> He was once more on the bicycle, but this time had no control of it; he wriggled, tumbled, could not advance a yard, and fumed in the anguish of feeling himself, of making himself ridiculous. Near him stood Mrs. Argent, holding her own machine as he had seen her just before she mounted to ride away from the school; but she wore a magnificent dress, such as would have become her on some brilliant occasion of festivity, her bosom bare, save for gleaming jewels, and her arms a glory of living flesh. She was beginning to show impatience. "Oh, can't you do better than that? You really must be quick; I can't wait for you." He made a desperate attempt to mount, but his eyes would not turn from the woman's beauty,

and again he came ignominiously to the ground. Then she gave a loud, scornful laugh; he saw her spring to the saddle, bend her shining head, and float away ... All at once he saw by the roadside a little boy, who, without moving, held out his hands after the woman, and cried to her, "Mamma! Mamma!" ... But in that moment the radiant figure passed out of his sight ... He heard the boy weeping bitterly, and he too wept. (141)

In contrast to the New Woman's triumphant mastery of speed, the schoolmaster's awkward incapacity and humiliating defeat parallels his lack of possession of a speed-mediated and speed-liberated sexuality. The lady is always on the move, travelling around Europe and meeting all kinds of interesting people—"politicians, learned men, celebrated women"—whereas the schoolmaster is stuck in his country school and his unvaried daily routine (132). The woman takes no time in finding a second husband and would not allow the duties of motherhood to spoil her enjoyment; the schoolmaster's biggest regret in life is to have squandered away his "richer opportunities" on a passionless marriage (134). For a brief moment in his dream, the schoolmaster's emulation of the speeding lady frees up his repressed sexuality. Rising like Icarus, intensely energized and ecstatic, on the prosthetic wings of his speeding bicycle, he imagines himself to be running away from an entombing state of vegetation. Soon, however, his poor cycling skills fail him, and he falls down, "plunged into the gloom of fathomless depths" (141). Both in dreams and in real life, the story equates slowness and the inability to master speed with impotence and sexual passivity, which are now assigned to the bruised, debilitated, and defeated male body.

Gissing is not the first person to link female sexuality with the mechanical, but he gives a new twist to the idea of the seductive machine woman. The cycling woman is indeed constructed to have a dangerous sexual allure, but here the schoolmaster also eagerly seeks to embrace the mechanical, rather than staying away and displacing all his anxiety onto the machine woman. The schoolmaster wants a part of that machine-accelerated sexual energy as well, and revels in that excitement for a while, only to be ultimately deflated by his lack of acumen. This suggests that the longing to be enraptured by the kinetic thrill of mechanized speed is a pervasively modern desire, which women seem to put to better use than men. The integration of the human body and mechanized speed releases a new type of sexual energy that is no longer the trait of a naturalized body alone, but one that is machine-aided and doubly exciting.

At the end of Gissing's story, the schoolmaster awakes from his dream shaken and debilitated. In his humiliation he decides to go back to his old routine in the secluded school, and warns his students to never give in to the seduction of the outside world. "There is a spirit abroad—a spirit of restlessness, of revolt. Be not misled by it" (144). In other words, the schoolmaster decides to bow out of the modern culture of speed and leave that stage to the lady. This story shows that if adaptation to speed is the quintessential trait in becoming the new modern subject, then women—as they embrace the bicycle and turn their cycling body into an interface between the organic and the mechanical—stake as much claim as men in this modern means of individuation.

In the Futurist celebration of speed, Marinetti sees the new, sped-up, adrenaline-packed modern subject as the "[m]an multiplied by the machine ..., a fusion of instinct with the output of a motor and forces that have been mastered" (*Critical Writings* 122). But, as we see in *fin-de-siècle* literature and its depiction of the mobile, energetic, and machine-accelerated body of the New Woman, women are also active participants in this new modern pleasure of intoxicating speed and blurred borders. This sped-up woman is no longer the romanticized woman associated with unmediated, organic nature, nor the passive machine woman used as a trope to displace male fears of mechanization. Instead, she is inextricably enmeshed in and constrained by the modern culture of speed, but also energized and expanded beyond the boundaries separating the body from the machine.

Afterword

In his illuminating essay "Crash (Speed as Engine of Individuation)," Jeffrey T. Schnapp writes that speed "play[s] a key role in engendering modern forms of individualism" (4). Whereas speed belonged to the domain of gods or angels in premodern times, "the gods or angels of the modern era will be found holding the reins or sitting behind the wheel, so identifying individuality with the possession of and mastery over wheels" (4). Schnapp is referring to the sense of agency, excitement, and empowerment experienced by drivers of the stage coach or the motorcar, the "new fantasies of attachment ... between rider and engine" (10), but this rejuvenating potential is triggered by all forms of modern accelerated speed. Machine-aided speed is the essence of modernity, and to have the capacity to administer this speed is to accelerate oneself into modernity and stake a claim to a new, sped-up subjectivity.

This celebration of the expansive, almost heroic power of speed must be counterbalanced by an awareness of speed's other functions. Virilio, for instance, describes the modern subject living in a sped-up, dromocratic society as a "picnoleptic," someone approaching a state of sub-epilepsy wherein s/he loses momentarily the ability to assimilate the prevailing contingency of things, or the ceaseless stimulation of traffic, people, and things moving in rapid succession (*Aesthetics of Disappearance* 19). In the interaction between the human subject and accelerated speed, alienation and passivity come side by side with the celebrated excitement and sense of empowerment.

British writers and commentators in the modern period have demonstrated varying degrees of alertness to the impact of modern speed culture. Many are influenced by the antimachine, pastoral tradition and unsympathetic to the ramifications of mechanized speed on human interiority. Modernist writers famously decry the pollution of the speeding motorcar and its association with the maiming, monstrous machine. In *Howards End*, E. M. Forster links the "throbbing, stinking" car with "dust," stench and the unfeeling killing of a cat by the wealthy, car-driving Wilcoxes on a trip from London (200). A particular objection is directed against the car's speed and its threatened erasure of depth and interiority. To Margaret Schlegel, terribly upset by this London trip, the car's "swift movement" has "robbed" the English landscape "of half its magic" (36, 197); it also "tried to rob from her" "the sense of space" (188) she desperately needs to hold on to a deep interaction with "the earth and its emotions" (200). Here the speeding car is also

The New Woman and Technologies of Speed in Fin-de-Siècle *Literature*. Eva Chen, Oxford University Press.
© Eva Chen (2024). DOI: 10.1093/9780198922285.003.0006

symbolic of a wider "craze for motion" and social acceleration in the modern city, with its bustling crowds, ceaseless change, and shallow "cosmopolitan chatter" (200), "the social counterpart of a motor-car" (71). This prompts Margaret to pray for a "civilization that won't be movement, because it will rest on the earth" (200).

This longing for "earth and its emotions" that stay still and resonate with an unbroken, preindustrial past is the direct opposite of the tradition-smashing and temporal-spatial compression of Marinetti's explosive speed. In his work on motor speed record-setting in Edwardian Britain and its links with the construction of a British idea of masculinity and the nation, Ian Boutle points out that the British public discourses on the motoring heroes differ from continental modernist interpretations of motor racing as a fundamentally violent technological spectacle (451). While the continental discourses celebrate speed and a revolutionary future of new "ways of perceiving and conceptualizing time and space" (451), the British response nurtures the comforting certainties of a specifically British past by stressing the motorist's gentlemanly virtue and mental and physical supremacy, in line with a venerable British tradition. This difference further surfaces in a conversation between the English Vorticist Wyndham Lewis and Marinetti, which Lewis records in his autobiography *Blasting and Bombardiering*. To the speed-embracing Marinetti who relishes the "*ivresse* of travelling at a kilometer a minute," "[i]t is *only* when [something] goes quickly that it *is* there!" (qtd. in Zurbrugg 11). Lewis, though famed for his own valorization of explosive energy and volcanic intensity, is more resistant about speed, responding that he "cannot see a thing that is going too quickly" (11). When Marinetti replies excitedly—"See it—see it! ... But you do see it. You see it multiplied a thousand times. You see a thousand things instead of one thing," Lewis again retorts "That's just what I don't want to see. I am not a futurist ... I prefer *one* thing" (11).

Many British writers of the modern period may be less than enthusiastic about modern speed culture, but H. G. Wells provides some of the most sensitive readings of the importance of speed and all its sociocultural manifestations (Schenkel 735). This seems to be in line with Wells's interest in science and technology in general and their social impact. In his prose work *Anticipations*, Wells argues, like Virilio after him, that the pursuit of ever-faster speed has led to the invention of the railway steam engine, which is the most fundamental "symbol" of the nineteenth century (4). Wells goes on to forecast that this same pursuit of speed will lead to the domination in the twentieth century of automobile culture, which will be centered round "private roads of a new sort, upon which their vehicles will be free to travel to the limit of their very highest possible speed" (19).

Wells wrote this in 1901, before the days of no-limit highways, and this prophetic insight is also extended to his astute observations of the importance of speed for military and political power. Wells sees mechanized speed as having revolutionized modern warfare and weaponry: "I believe invincibly that the side that can go fastest and hit hardest will always win, with or without or in spite of massive defences" (209). In *Outline of History*, he further argues that Western powers have prevailed over older, more ancient cultures because they have better utilized "the modern need for simple, swift, exact" technologies (200).

Wells's appreciation of the importance of speed comes side by side with an awareness of the complicated roles speed plays in modern society, including its function as a new marker of status and class privilege, as is demonstrated in his literary portrayals of the New Woman cyclist. Wells is not the only modern writer to duly register this new modern force. In the literary and journalistic writings of the *fin-de-siécle* period which foreground the day-to-day life of the modern woman in the city, particularly the New Woman cyclist and typist, we have seen how these writings cast their subjects and characters as increasingly entangled with and structured by technologies of speed, and how such interaction enables the construction of a new type of modern femininity. The New Woman is new precisely because she is fast. Many of the complicated and often conflicting feelings voiced over the New Woman's unconventionality and her disruption of gender norms are, to a large extent, responses to the "fastness" that results from her use of the bicycle and the typewriter.

While these two are indeed machines of emancipation for middle-class women, they are also technologies of speed that exert new pressures on their body and psyche. Traditionally linked with organic nature and the private, sheltered home, women have long been perceived as alien to the values of industrial mechanization and machine-accelerated speed. But, as this book has demonstrated, these women's en masse usage of the typewriter and the bicycle thrusts them into the foreground of modern speed culture and challenges their long exclusion from speed. As these women respond to the shocks of techno-aided speed and are asked to be faster and more efficient, their frustrations and triumphs constitute an integral part of the experience of urban modernity, and add richness and nuance to its meaning.

In Mitton's *A Bachelor Girl in London*, Judith the typewriter girl credits typewriting with allowing her to be a "strong-handed, capable woman of thick boots and short skirts, whose life was a burden to no one," and who could claim "the supreme content, the glorious freedom of looking at the world squarely and owing no one for the bread she ate" (171). But the New Woman's typewriting body in the modern Taylorite office exposes her to the tolls of disciplinary speed, and signals her status as a representative modern worker in a society increasingly structured by the imperative for efficiency and profit-making. This experience aligns the typewriter girl with the industrial worker on the factory floor, for both are somatically and mentally disciplined and "brought up to speed" (Daly 20). The New Woman's cycling body in her leisure time outside the workplace further reveals the infiltration of speed beyond the area of production into that of consumption, when speed takes on a new role as commodity and conspicuous display. In the mid-1890s "bicycle craze," the modern, fashionable New Woman cyclist starts out as transgressive and iconoclastic, but is quickly subsumed under a new consumerist framework wherein her cycling body becomes the best advertisement for an elegant, glamorous, and safely middle-class femininity.

But beyond these roles for tightened discipline and conspicuous display, speed also offers a more positive, enabling potential for middle-class women. This book has examined the dialectical nature of women's interaction with the typewriter and the bicycle and their mutual structuring and articulation. The New Woman typist and cyclist offers a prime site to study questions of technological prosthesis and human agency—questions complicated by the addition of gender. But it also shows the mutual shaping of technology and the human body, in a way that reveals that human interiority is itself predicated upon and composed with prosthetic tools and technics. Modern machine-accelerated speed demands from women a constant adjustment and alertness to its mechanical exigencies, but it also offers a source of rejuvenation and excitement whereby women users, sped up and enlivened by the combined energies of the organic and the mechanical, could eventually construct a transformed, energized, modern subjectivity.

In an 1894 report on an annual typewriter parade in London, *Cycling: An Illustrated Weekly* writes that one participant stands out with her unusual skills. She is a cyclist-cum-typist who has mounted a typewriter on the handle-bar of her Safety bicycle and is typing with one hand while skillfully riding the bicycle. Called "An Office on Wheels," the report singles out this cyclist-typist because of her ability to pull off this seemingly impossible balancing act (247). In the *fin-de-siècle* period when tens of thousands of middle-class women ride a bicycle and work as typists, they similarly manage to perform a balancing act, trying to adapt to the disciplines of modern speed while also seeking expanded knowledge and skills. This balancing act is precarious and laden with pitfalls and dangers, but it also helps to engender a new type of multiskilled and speed-savvy women, a type retrained and "retooled" by her use of speed and better able to adjust to the shocks of industrial modernity (Daly 42). The New Woman, in this sense, is indeed a fast woman, staking a full claim to her place in progressive modernity.

Works Cited

Adams, Jad. *Decadent Women: Yellow Book Lives.* Chicago, IL: Chicago University Press, 2023.

Adburgham, Alison. *Shopping in Style: London from the Restoration to Edwardian Elegance.* London: Thames & Hudson Ltd., 1979.

Adler, Michael. *Antique Typewriters: From Creed to QWERTY.* Atglen: Schiffer, 1997.

"Ah!" *Illustrated Chips,* Jul. 24, 1897, p. 8.

Allen, Grant. "The Girl of the Future." *Universal Review,* no. 7, May 1890, pp. 49–64.

Allen, Grant. *Hilda Wade.* New York: G. P. Putnam's Sons, 1899.

Allen, Grant. *Miss Cayley's Adventures.* 1899. Richmond, VA: Valancourt Books, 2008.

Allen, Grant. "Personal Reminiscences of Herbert Spencer." *Forum,* no. 35, Apr. 1904, pp. 610–28.

Allen, Grant. *"Physiological Aesthetics and Philistia," My First Book.* London: Chatto & Windus, 1894.

Allen, Grant. "Plain Words on the Woman Question." *Fortnightly Review,* no. 46, 1889, pp. 448–58.

Allen, Grant. "The Trade of Author." *Fortnightly Review,* no. 45, 1889, pp. 267–68.

Allen, Grant. *The Type-Writer Girl.* 1897. Danvers: General Books, 2009.

Allen, Grant. *The Woman Who Did.* 1895. Oxford: Oxford University Press, 1995.

"Along the Brighton Road." *Lady Cyclist,* May 1895, p. 241.

Ang, Ien. *Living Room Wars: Rethinking Media Audience for a Postmodern World.* London: Routledge, 1996.

Anthony, Susan B. and Nellie Bly. "Champion of Her Sex," *New York Sunday World,* Feb. 2, 1896, p. 10.

Ardis, Ann. *New Women, New Novels: Feminism and Early Modernism.* New Brunswick: Rutgers University Press, 1990.

"The Arrival of Women in the Office." BBC News, Jul. 25, 2013, www.bbc.com/news/magazine-23432653. Accessed Mar. 2, 2021.

Atchison, Heather. *"Grant Allen, Spencer and Darwin." Grant Allen: Literature and Cultural Politics at the Fin-de-siècle,* edited by William Greenslade and Terence Rodgers. Aldershot: Ashgate, 2005, pp. 55–64.

"A Ballade of this Age." *The Wheelman,* no. 3, Oct. 1883, p. 100.

Banks, Elizabeth L. "New Paid Occupations for Women." *Cassell's Family Magazine,* Jul. 1894, p. 585.

Bateson, Margaret. *Professional Women upon Their Professions: Conversations Recorded by Margaret Bateson.* London: Horace Cox, 1895.

Bathurst, Bella. *The Bicycle Book.* New York: Harper Collins, 2011.

Beaven, Brad. *Leisure, Citizenship and Working-Class Men in Britain, 1850–1945.* Manchester: Manchester University Press, 2005.

Beeching, Wilfred A. *Century of the Typewriter.* London: Heinemann, 1974.

Beeley, Serena. *A History of Bicycles: From Hobby Horse to Mountain Bike.* Secaucus, NJ: Wellfleet Books, 1992.

Beetham, Margaret. *A Magazine of Her Own? Domesticity and Desire in the Woman's Magazine, 1800–1914.* London: Routledge, 1996.

Beetham, Margaret. and Kay Boardman, eds. *Victorian Women's Magazines: An Anthology.* Manchester: Manchester University Press, 2001.

Benjamin, Walter. "On Some Motifs in Baudelaire." *Illuminations,* edited by Hannah Arendt and translated by Harry Zohn. New York: Schocken Books, 1968, pp. 155–200.

"A Bicycle Story." *Bow Bells,* Oct. 9, 1896, p. 368.

Bijker, Wiebe E. *Of Bicycles, Bakelites, and Bulbs: Toward a Theory of Sociotechnical Change.* Cambridge, MA: The MIT Press, 1997.

Bird, M. Mostyn. *Women at Work: A Study of the Different Ways of Earning a Loving Open to Women.* London: Chapman & Hall, 1911.

Black, Clemetina. "Introduction" to Clemetina Black, ed., *Married Women's Work.* London: G. Bell, 1915, pp. 1–15.

Black, Clemetina. "The Organization of Working Women." *Fortnightly Review*, no. 52, 1889, pp. 695–704.

Bliven, Bruce. *The Wonderful Writing Machine.* New York: Random House, 1954.

"Books and Authors." *Hearth and Home*, May 5, 1898, p. 1060.

"A Borrowed Bicycle." *The Wheelwoman*, Nov. 13, 1897, p. 23.

Boutle, Ian. "'Speed lies in the lap of the English:' Motor Records, Masculinity and the Nation, 1907–14." *Twentieth-Century British History*, vol. 23, no. 4, 2012, pp. 449–72.

Braddon, Mary Elizabeth. *Lady Audley's Secret.* Edited by David Skilton. Oxford: Oxford University Press, 1987.

Bukatman, Scott. "Gibson's Typewriter." *South Atlantic Quarterly*, vol. 92, no. 4, 1993, pp. 627–45.

Bulley, Amy and Margaret Whitley. *Women's Work.* London: Methuen and Co., 1894.

Burgan, Mary. "Heroines at the Piano: Women and Music in Nineteenth-Century Fiction." *Victorian Studies*, vol. 30, no. 1, 1986, pp. 51–76.

Cameron, S. Brooke. "Sisters of the Type: The Feminist Collective in Grant Allen's The Type-Writer Girl." *Victorian Literature and Culture*, vol. 40, no. 1, 2012, pp. 229–44.

Campbell, Lady Colin. "The Tempestuous Petticoat." *Lady Cyclist*, Mar. 18, 1896, pp. 9–10.

Cane, Mike. "H. G. Wells Testimonial for a Typewriter." *Wordpress*, Dec. 28, 2012, https://mikecanepics.wordpress.com/2012/12/28/h-g-wells-testimonial-for-a-typewriter. Accessed Mar. 24, 2020.

Cassell's Family Magazine, May 1895, p. 456.

"Catastrophe." *Lady Cyclist*, Mar. 20, 1897, pp. 638–41.

"A Cause of Quarrel." *Windsor Magazine: An Illustrated Monthly for Men and Women*, Dec. 1897, pp. 254–58.

"Champion of Her Sex." *New York Sunday World*, Feb. 2, 1896, p. 10.

Chan, Winnie. *The Economy of the Short Story in British Periodicals of the 1890s.* London: Routledge, 2007.

Chase, Karen. "The Literal Heroine: A Study of Gissing's The Odd Women." *Criticism*, vol. 26, no. 3, 1984, pp. 231–44.

"Chats with Cyclists: Madame Sarah Grand." *Cycling World Illustrated*, vol. 1, no. 7, Apr. 29, 1896, p. 3.

Chopin, Kate. "The Unexpected." 1895. https://americanliterature.com/author/kate-chopin/short-story/the-unexpected. Accessed Oct. 20, 2021.

Clarke, Deborah. *Driving Women: Fiction and Automobile Culture in Twentieth-Century America.* Baltimore, MD: The Johns Hopkins University Press, 2007.

Clarsen, Georgine. *Eat My Dust: Early Women Motorists.* Baltimore, MD: The Johns Hopkins University Press, 2008.

Colby, Robin B. *"Some Appointed Work To Do": Women and Vocation in the Fiction of Elizabeth Gaskell.* Westport, Ct: Greenwood Press, 1995.

Collet, Clara. *Educated Working Women: Essays on the Economic Position of Women Workers in the Middle Classes.* London: P. S. King & Son, 1902.

Collet, Clara. "Prospects of Marriage for Women." *Nineteenth Century*, no. 31, 1892, pp. 537–52.

"Conversion of Ernest Warren." *Lady Cyclist*, Mar. 1895, pp. 40–43.

"Correspondence." *Boys' Own Paper*, Jul. 3, 1886, p. 639.

"Country Gentlemen." *Sporting Gazette*, May 23, 1891, p. 711.

"Country Ride." *Susan: The Badminton Magazine of Sports and Pastime*, Nov. 1896, pp. 579–93.

Coustillas, Pierre and Colin Partridge. *Gissing: The Critical Heritage.* London: Routledge & Kegan Paul, 1972.

Coutin, Talia S. *Bicycles, Advertising and the Limits of Heteronormativity: Will H. Bradley's Graphic Designs for Overman Wheel Co.* MA dissertation. University of Delaware, 2016.

Cowan, Ruth Schwartz. "The 'Industrial Revolution' in the Home: Household Technology and Social Change in the Twentieth Century." *The Routledge Companion to Modernity, Space and Gender,* edited by Alexandra Staub. London: Routledge 2018, pp. 69–86.

Craig, Patricia, and Mary Cadogan. *The Lady Investigates: Women Detectives and Spies in Fiction.* New York: St Martin's Press, 1981.

Cuming, E. D. "Domestic Helps and Hindrances." *Chambers's Journal,* vol. 3, no. 106, Dec. 1899, pp. 17–21.

Cunningham, A.R. "The New Woman Fiction of the 1890s." *Victorian Studies,* vol. 17, no. 2, 1973, pp. 177-86.

Cunningham, Gail. *The New Woman and the Victorian Novel.* London: Macmillan, 1978.

Cunningham, Hugh. *Leisure in the Industrial Revolution.* London: Croom Helm, 1980.

"Current News." *Women's Penny Paper,* Aug. 2, 1890, p. 483.

Current, Richard N. "The Original Typewriter Enterprise 1867–1873." *The Wisconsin Magazine of History,* vol. 32, no. 4, 1949, pp. 391–407.

Current, Richard N. *The Typewriter and the Men Who Made It.* Champaign, IL: University of Illinois Press, 1974.

Curry, Jane and Marjorie Binghman. "American Women and Sport." *OAH Magazine of History,* vol. 7, no. 1, 1992, pp. 39–49.

"The Cycle Trade and the Typewriter." *Cycling,* Oct. 3, 1891, p. 165.

Daly, Nicholas. *Literature, Technology, and Modernity, 1860-2000.* Cambridge: Cambridge University Press, 2004.

"The Dangers of Cycling." *Lancet,* no. 2, 1896, pp. 133–34.

Dauncey, Hugh. *French Cycling: A Social and Cultural History.* Liverpool: Liverpool University Press, 2012.

Davidson, Lillias Campbell. "Cycling for Ladies." *Cycles and Cycling,* by H. Hewitt Griffin. London: Frederick A. Stokes Company, 1890, pp. 87–97.

Davidson, Lillias Campbell. "A Few Cycling Dangers." *Cycle Magazine,* Jan. 1896, p. 206.

Davidson, Lillias Campbell. *Handbook for Lady Cyclists.* London: Hay Nisbet, 1896.

Davies, Margery W. "Women Clerical Workers and the Typewriting Machine." *Technology and Women's Voices,* edited by Cheris Kramarae. London: Routledge and Kegan Paul, 1988, pp. 29–40.

Davies, Margery W. "Women's Place Is at the Typewriter: The Feminization of the Clerical Force." *Radical America,* vol. 8, no. 4, 1974, pp. 1–28.

"Death of the Rev. J. G. Wood." *Boys' Own Paper,* May 4, 1889, p. 494.

"Degrees of Genius." *The Dart: A Journal of Sense and Satire,* Nov. 19, 1897, p. 15.

Dickens, Charles. *Hard Times,* 1854, Penguin, 2003.

Dickens, Charles. *The Old Curiosity Shop,* 1841. London: Penguin, 1998.

"Discord and Harmony: The Story of a Musical Ride." *Lady Cyclist,* May 1, 1897, pp. 900–05.

Doane, Mary Ann. "Technophilia: Technology, Representation, and the Feminine." *Cybersexualities: A Reader on Feminist Theory, Cyborgs and Cyberspace,* edited by Jenny Wolmark. Edinburgh: Edinburgh University Press, 1999, pp. 20–33.

"Double Marriage." *Lady Cyclist,* Jun. 19, 1897, pp. 194–96.

Doyle, Arthur Conan. "Cycle Notes." *Scientific American,* Jan. 18, 1896, p. 38.

Doyle, Arthur Conan. "The Solitary Cyclist." *The Strand,* vol. 27, no. 157, 1904, pp. 2–14.

Duffy, Enda. *The Speed Handbook: Velocity, Pleasure, Modernism.* Durham, NC: Duke University Press, 2009.

"Dunbar's First Lesson." *Windsor Magazine,* Jun. 1899, pp. 69–73.

"During the Hot Weather." *Illustrated Chips,* Sept. 2, 1899, pp. 4–5.

Edgeworth, Maria, and Richard Lovell Edgeworth. *Practical Education.* Boston: Wait, 1815.

Egerton, George. "Her Share." *Discords.* London: John Lane, 1894, pp. 67–81.

Ehrlich, Cyril. *The Piano: A History.* London: Dent, 1976.

"The Emancipation of Women from the Piano." *Music Opinion & Music Trade Journal*, Feb. 1, 1883, p. 181.

"Employment for Ladies." *Myra's Journal of Dress and Fashion*, Feb. 1, 1900, p. 15.

"The Employment of Women." *The Queen*, Sept. 22, 1883, 261.

"The End of a Club Run." *Lady Cyclist*, Apr. 1895, pp. 74–75.

"The English Typewriter." *Golf*, Feb. 20, 1891, p. 23.

Ernst, Sabine. "*The Woman Who Did* and 'The Girl Who Didn't': The Romance of Sexual Selection in Grant Allen and Ménie Muriel Dowie." *Grant Allen: Literature and Cultural Politics at the Fin-de-siècle*, edited by William Greenslade and Terence Rodgers. Aldershot: Ashgate, 2005, pp. 81–94.

"Events of the Quarter." *Englishwoman's Review*, Apr. 1873, pp. 160–61.

Faulkner, Wendy. "The Technology Question in Feminism: A View from Feminist Technology Studies." *Women's Studies International Forum*, vol. 24, no. 1, 2001, pp. 79–95.

Felski, Rita. *The Gender of Modernity*. Cambridge, MA: Harvard University Press, 1995.

"The Female Bachelor." *Saturday Review*, Jun. 2, 1894, p. 582.

"50,000!" *Cycling: An Illustrated Weekly*, Nov. 26, 1898, p. 425.

Fishpool, Mike. "Lady Racers: The Origins of Women's Cycling Racing." *Playing Past: The Online Magazine for Sport and Leisure History*, Jun. 25, 2018, www.playingpasts.co.uk/articles/gender-and-sport/lady-racers-the-origins-of-womens-cycle-racing/. Accessed May 2, 2023.

Fleissner, Jennifer L. "Dictation Anxiety: The Stenographer's Stake in *Dracula*." *Literary Secretaries/Secretarial Culture*, edited by Leah Price and Pamela Thurschwell. Ashgate, 2005, pp. 63–90.

Flint, Kate. "Introduction." *The Story of a Modern Woman*. By Ella Hepworth Dixon. London: Merlin, 1990, pp. iv–xi.

Forster, E. M. *Howards End*. London: Penguin Classics, 2000.

"Found in the Fog." *Pick-Me-Up*, Dec. 1, 1900, p. 14.

Foxwell, Elizabeth. Introduction. *Miss Cayley's Adventures*, by Grant Allen. Richmond, VA: Valancourt Books, 2008, pp. vii–xvi.

Fraser, Hilary, Stephanie Green, and Judith Johnston. *Gender and the Victorian Periodical*. Cambridge: Cambridge University Press, 2003

"From a Man's Point of View: A Latter-Day Comedy." *Lady Cyclist*, Mar. 1895, pp. 15–16.

"Fun's' Philosophy." *Fun*, Feb. 16, 1897, p. 60.

Galsworthy, John. *On Forsyte Change*. 1930. https://gutenberg.net.au/ebooks03/0300111h.html#c15. Accessed Jan. 21, 2022.

Garvey, Ellen Gruber. "Reframing the Bicycle: Advertising-Supported Magazines and Scorching Women." *American Quarterly*, vol. 47, no. 1, 1995, pp. 66–101.

Gaskel, Peter. *Artisans and Machinery: The Moral and Physical Condition of the Manufacturing Population Considered with Reference to Mechanical Substitutes for Human Labor*. London: John W. Parker, 1836.

Gaskell, Elizabeth. *Mary Barton*. 1848. Ware: Wordsworth Classics, 2012.

Gaskell, Elizabeth. *North and South*. 1854. London: Penguin, 1996.

Gissing, George. *The Collected Letters of George Gissing, Vol. 4: 1889–1891*, edited by Paul F. Matthiesen, Arthur C. Young, and Pierre Coustillas. Athens, OH: Ohio University Press, 1993.

Gissing, George. *The Collected Letters of George Gissing, Vol. 5: 1892–1895*, edited by Paul F. Mattheisen, Arthur C. Young, and Pierre Coustillas. Athens, OH: Ohio University Press, 1994.

Gissing, George. "A Daughter of the Lodge." *The Day of Silence and Other Stories*, edited by Pierre Coustillas. London: Dent, 1993, pp. 167–78.

Gissing, George. *Eve's Ransom*. 1895. New York: Dover, 1980.

Gissing, George. *In the Year of Jubilee*. 1894. New York: Dover, 1982.

Gissing, George. "Letter to Ellen, 29 September 1889." *Collected Letters, Vol. 4*, pp. 115–16.

Gissing, George. *New Grub Street*. 1891. Ware: Wordsworth Books, 1996.

Gissing, George. *The Odd Women*. 1893. London: Virago, 1980.

Gissing, George. "The Schoolmaster's Vision." *A Victim of Circumstances and Other Stories*. New York: Houghton Mifflin Company, 1927, pp. 130–44.

Gissing, George. *The Whirlpool*. 1897. Harvester, 1977.

"Gloom." The Dart: A Journal of Sense and Satire, Apr. 15, 1897, p. 15.

"Good-Looking Young Man." *Windsor Magazine: An Illustrated Monthly*, Jun. 1987, pp. 682–97.

"Gossip about Novels and Novelists." *Novel Review*, Mar. 1892, pp. 354–61.

Grand, Sarah. "The New Woman and the Old." 1898. *Sex, Social Purity and Sarah Grand: Journalistic Writings and Contemporary Reception*, edited by Ann Heilmann and Stephanie Forward. London: Routledge, 2000, pp. 69–78.

Gray, Jessica. "Typewriter Girls in Turn-of-the-Century Fiction: Feminism, Labor and Modernity." *English Literature in Transition*, vol. 58, no. 4, 2015, pp. 486–501.

"A Great Advantage." *The Dart: A Journal of Sense and Satire*, 25 Jun. 1897, p. 14.

Greenslade, William and Terence Rodgers, editors. *Grant Allen: Literature and Cultural Politics at the Fin-de-Siècle*. Aldershot: Ashgate, 2005.

Greville, Watson. "A New Leaf." *The New London Journal*, Jan. 18, 1908, pp. 269–71.

Guroff, Margaret. *The Mechanical Horse: How the Bicycle Reshaped American Life*. Austin, TX: University of Texas Press, 2016.

"The Hall Type-Writer." *Sporting Times*, Jan. 24, 1885, p. 8.

Hallenbeck, Sarah. *Claiming the Bicycle: Women, Rhetoric, and Technology in Nineteenth-Century America*. Carbondale, IL: Southern Illinois University Press, 2016.

Hammond, John. *A Preface to H. G. Wells*. London: Routledge, 2001.

Hanlon, Sheila. *The Lady Cyclist: A Gender Analysis of Women's Cycling Culture in 1890s London*. PhD diss. Toronto: York University, 2009.

Hardy, Thomas. *The Fiddler of the Reels and Other Stories*. New York: Dover Publications, 2016.

Hardy, Thomas. *Tess of the D'Urbervilles*. London: Penguin, 1994.

Harkness, Margaret. "Women as Civil Servants." *Nineteenth Century*, 10, 1881, pp. 369–81.

Haraway, Donna J. "A Manifesto for Cyborgs: Science, Technology, and Socialist Feminism in the 1980s." *Socialist Review*, vol. 15, no. 2, 1985, pp. 65–107.

Harman, Barbara Leah. "Going Public: Female Emancipation in George Gissing's *In the Year of Jubilee*." *Texas Studies in Literature and Language*, no. 34, 1992, pp. 347–74.

Harris, Frank. *Contemporary Portraits*. London: Grant Richards Ltd., 1924.

"The Hate That Changed." *Lady Cyclist*, Mar. 1895, pp. 28–33.

Hayles, N. Katherine. *How We Became Posthuman: Virtual Bodies in Cybernetics, Literature and Informatics*. Chicago, IL: Chicago University Press, 1999.

Headrick, Daniel. *Power Over Peoples: Technology, Environments, and Western Imperialism, 1400 to the Present*. Princeton University Press, 2010.

Heilmann, Ann. *New Woman Fiction: Women Writing First-Wave Feminism*. London: Macmillan, 2000.

Heilmann, Ann and Stephanie Forward, eds. *Sex, Social Purity and Sarah Grand. Vol. I. Journalistic Writings and Contemporary Reception*. London: Routledge, 2000.

Herkimer County Historical Society. *The Story of the Typewriter, 1873–1923*. Herkimer, 1923.

Herlihy, David V. *Bicycle: The History*. New Haven, CT: Yale University Press, 2006.

"History of Cycle Magazines, 1878–1900." *Cycling UK*. www.cyclinguk.org/cycle/history-cycling-uk-magazines-beginnings-victorian-golden-age-cycling-press-1878-1900. Accessed Jan. 20, 2017.

Hoke, Donald. "The Woman and the Typewriter: A Case Study in Technological Innovation and Social Change." *Business and Economic History*, vol. 8, 1979, pp. 76–88.

Hounshell, David A. "The Bicycle and Technology in Late Nineteenth Century America." *Transport Technology and Social Change*, edited by Per Sorbom. Stockholm: Tekniska Museet, 1980, pp. 173–85.

"How Dick Managed It." *Quiver*, Jan. 1888, pp. 23–27.

"How Ladies' Cycle Races Are Managed." *The Hub*, Sept. 23, 1896, p. 221.

"Humber Bicycle." *Lady Cyclist*, Jan. 2, 1897, pp. 278.

Hutchison, Hazel. "'An Embroidered Veil of Sound': The Word in the Machine in Henry Hames's *In the Cage*." *Henry James Review*, vol. 34, no. 2, 2013, pp. 147–62.

Huyssen, Andreas. *After the Great Divide: Modernism, Mass Culture, Postmodernism*. Blooming-ton, IN: Indiana University Press, 1986.

"The Ideal Lady Cyclist." *Lady Cyclist*, Oct. 1895, p. 283.

"Ideals of Womanhood." *Woman's Herald*, Sept. 24, 1892, pp. 3–4.

"In Chancery." *Funny Folks: A Weekly Budget of Funny Pictures, Funny Notes, Funny Jokes, and Funny Stories*, Apr. 14, 1894, p. 13.

"Is Type-writing a Successful Occupation for Educated Women?" *The Englishwoman's Review: A Journal of Woman's Work*, Apr. 15, 1891, p. 82.

Jackson, Sarah K. "Typewriters, Typing, Typists." *Technoculture: An Online Journal of Technology in Society*, vol. 3, 2013, pp. 1–23.

James, Simon J. *Maps of Utopia: H. G. Wells, Modernity and the End of Culture*. Oxford: Oxford University Press, 2012.

Jeffrey, Kieve. *The Electric Telegraph: A Social and Economic History*. Exeter: David & Charles, 1973.

"Just So." *Judy, or the London Serio-Comic Journal*. Dec. 13, 1899, p. 598.

Kenealy, Arabella. "Woman as an Athlete." *Nineteenth Century Review*, Apr. 1899, pp. 636–45.

Keep, Christopher. "Blinded by the Type: Gender and Information Technology at the Turn of the Century." *Nineteenth Century Contexts*, vol. 23, no. 1, 2001, pp. 149–73.

Keep, Christopher. "The Cultural Work of the Type-Writer Girl." *Victorian Studies*, vol. 40, no. 3, 1997, pp. 401–26.

Kennard, Mrs. Edward. *The Golf Lunatic and His Cycling Wife*. London: Hutchinson & Co., 1902.

Kennard, Mrs. Edward. *Guide Book for Lady Cyclists*. London: F. V. White & Co., 1896.

Kennard, Mrs. Edward. *The Motor Maniac*. London: Hutchinson & Co., 1903.

Kessler-Harris, Alice. *Out to Work: A History of Wage-Earning Women in the United States*. Oxford: Oxford University Press, 2003.

Kestner, Joseph A. *Sherlock's Men: Masculinity, Conan Doyle, and Cultural History*. Aldershot: Ashgate, 1997.

Ketabgian, Tamara. *The Lives of Machines: The Industrial Imaginary in Victorian Literature and Culture*. Ann Arbor, MI: Michigan University Press, 2011.

Kipling, Beatrice. "A Woman of Seasons." *The Paul Mall Magazine*, May 1893, pp. 397–416.

Kipling, Rudyard. *From Sea to Sea: Letters of Travel, Volume II*. New York: Charles Scribner, 1913.

Kipling, Rudyard. "In Partibus." 1889. www.kiplingsociety.co.uk/poem/poems_partibus.htm. Accessed Apr. 7, 2023.

Kipling, Rudyard. *The Letters of Rudyard Kipling Vol. 3: 1900–10*, edited by Thomas Pinney, London: Macmillan, 1996.

Kipling, Rudyard. "McAndrew's Hymn." 1894. https://rpo.library.utoronto.ca/poems/mcandrews-hymn. Accessed Apr. 7, 2023.

Kirby, Lynne. *Parallel Tracks: The Railroad and Silent Cinema*. Durham, NC: Duke University Press, 1997.

Kittler, Friedrich A. *Discourse Networks 1800/1900*, translated by Michael Metteer with Chris Cullens. Redwood City, CA: Stanford University Press, 1990.

Kittler, Friedrich A. *Gramophone, Film, Typewriter*. Trans., & Intro. Geoffrey Winthrop-Young and Michael Wutz. Redwood City, CA: Stanford University Press, 1999.

Kracauer, Siegfried. *Jacques Offenbach and the Paris of His Time*. 1937. Translated by Gwenda David and Eric Mosbacher. New York: Zone Books, 2002.

Kristeva, Julia, Alice Jardine, and Harry Blake. "Women's Time." *Signs*, vol. 7, no. 1,1981, pp. 13–35.

"The Ladies Type-Writing and General Copying." *Work and Leisure*, 1884, p. 421.

"The Lady Cyclist at Home." *Lady Cyclist*, Aug. 1895, p. 205.

Lady Jane. "To My Friends." *The London Journal and Weekly Record of Literature, Science and Art*. Feb. 6, 1904, p.117.

"Lady Shorthand Typist." *Women's Penny Paper*, Jun. 16, 1898 [page unknown].

Leach, William. *Land of Desire: Merchant, Power and the Rise of a New American Culture*. New York: Pantheon Books, 1993.

Ledger, Sally. *The New Woman: Fiction and Feminism at the Fin-de-Siècle*. Manchester: Manchester University Press, 1997.

"Letters of a Lady Cyclist." *Lady Cyclist*, Oct. 3, 1896, p. 633.

"Letting Her Down Easy." *Boys of England: A Magazine of Sport, Sensation, Fun, and Instruction*, Aug. 16, 1895, p. 208.

Lewis, Wyndham. *Blasting and Bombardiering*. 1937. London: John Calder, 1982.

Liggins, Emma. *George Gissing, the Working Woman, and Urban Culture*. London: Routledge, 2006.

Liggins, Emma. "The Life of a Bachelor Girl in the Big City": Selling the Single Lifestyle to Readers of *Woman* and the *Young Woman* in the 1890s." *Victorian Periodicals Review*, vol. 40, no. 3, 2007, pp. 216–38.

Lindsay, Mayne. "The Exception." *The Windsor Magazine: An Illustrated Monthly for Men and Women*, Jul. 1896, pp. 309–11.

London, Daniel. "Cycles of Fashion." *Narratively*. May 14, 2013. http://narrative.ly/stories/cycles-of-fashion. Accessed Jan. 20, 2018.

The London Phonographer, vol. 1, Jun. 1891.

Longworth, Deborah. "Perpetual Motion: Speed, Spectacle, and Cycle Racing." *Moving Modernisms: Motion, Technology, and Modernity*, edited by David Bradshaw, Laura Marcus, and Rebecca Roach. *Oxford Scholarship Online*, Aug. 2016. DOI:10.1093/acprof:oso/9780198714170.001.0001, accessed Mar. 11, 2021.

"Love and Lucre." *Pick-Me-Up*, Oct. 7, 1899, p. 30.

Lowe, Grahma S. "'The Enormous File': The Evolution of the Modern Office in Early Twentieth Century Canada." *Archrvarra*, no. 19, Winter 1984–85, pp. 137–51.

Mackintosh, Phillip Gordon and Glen Norcliffe. "Flâneurie on Bicycles: Acquiescence to Women in Public in the 1890s." *The Canadian Geographer*, vol. 50, no. 1, 2006, pp. 17–37.

Macy, Sue. *Wheels of Change: How Women Rode the Bicycle to Freedom*. Washington, D.C.: National Geographic Society, 2011.

Mangan, J. A. Introduction. *A Sport-Loving Society: Victorian and Edwardian Middle-class England at Play*, by J. A. Mangan. London: Routledge, 2006, pp. 1–10.

Marcus, Jane, ed. *The Young Rebecca: Writings of Rebecca West, 1911–1917*. London: Macmillan, 1982.

Marinetti, F. T. *Critical Writings: New Edition*, edited by Günter Berghaus. New York: Farrar, Strauss, and Giroux, 2006.

Marks, Patricia. *Bicycles, Bangs, and Bloomers: The New Woman in the Popular Press*. Lexington, KY: Kentucky University Press, 1990.

Marshall, Marian. "A Sketch. Type Writers. Marian Marshall." *Shafts*, Feb. 25, 1893, pp. 260–61.

Martin, M. Daniel. "Railway Fatigue and the Coming-of-Age Narrative in *Lady Audley's Secret*." *Victorian Review: An Interdisciplinary Journal of Victorian Studies*, vol. 34, no. 1, 2008, pp. 131–53.

Masterman, C. F. G., ed. *The Heart of the Empire*. London: Fisher Unwin, 1901, pp. 7–8.

McBratney, John. "India and Empire." *The Cambridge Companion to Rudyard Kipling*, edited by Howard J. Booth, Cambridge: Cambridge University Press, 2011 pp. 23–36.

McGurn, James. *On Your Bicycle*. New York: Facts on File, 1987.

Mecredy, R. J. and Gerald Stoney, eds. *The Art and Pastime of Cycling*. Dublin: Mecredy & Kyle, 1897.

"Meeting of Society of Typists." *Women's Penny Paper*, Jun. 8, 1889, p. 4.

"Methods of Practice." *Musical Standard*, Apr. 4, 1896, pp. 216–18.

Meynell, Alice. "A Woman in Grey." 1896. www.gutenberg.org/ebooks/1205. Accessed Oct. 1, 2021.

"Miscellaneous Jokes Section." *Boys of England: A Magazine of Sport, Sensation, Fun, and Instruction*, Jul. 28, 1892, p. 128.

"*Miss Cayley's Adventures* Review." *The Saturday Review*. May 13, 1899, p. 598.

Mitton, Geraldine Edith. *A Bachelor Girl in London*. London: Hutchinson & Co., 1898.

Modleski, Tania. *Loving with a Vengeance: Mass-Produced Fantasies for Women*. London: Routledge, 1982.

Mom, Gijs. *Atlantic Automobilism: Emergence and Persistence of the Car 1895–1940*, Oxford: Berghahn, 2015.

Morgan-Dockrell, Mrs. "Is the New Woman a Myth?" *Humanitarian*, no. 8, 1896, pp. 339–50.

Morton, Peter. *"The Busiest Man in England": Grant Allen and the Writing Trade, 1875–1900*. Palgrave Macmillan, 2005.

"The Motor Maniac Review." *The Graphic*, Jan. 24, 1903, p. 24.

"Mr. Edward Clodd and Grant Allen." Clement K. Shorter. *The Bookman*, Aug. 1900, pp. 151–53.

"Multiple News Items." *Funny Folks: A Weekly Budget of Funny Pictures, Funny Notes, Funny Jokes, and Funny Stories*. Oct. 26, 1889, p. 342.

"New Model 'Hammond' Typewriter." *Pick-Me-Up*, Feb. 13, 1892, p. 335.

"The New Woman: What She Really Is." *Lady Cyclist*, Feb. 20, 1897, p. 504.

Nord, Deborah, Epstein. *Walking the Victorian Streets: Women, Representation, and the City*. Ithaca, NY: Cornell University Press, 1995.

"Notes." *The Autocar*, Sep. 23, 1899, p. 835.

"No Title." *The Idler: An Illustrate Magazine*, Jan. 5, 1895, p. 427.

"Not Revealed by the Inquest." *Pick-Me-Up*, Jan. 5, 1895, p. 220.

"Occasional Notes." *Women's Penny Paper*, Aug. 17, 1893, p. 26.

Oddy, Nicholas. "The Flaneur on Wheels?" *Cycling and Society*, edited by Dave Horton, Paul Rosen, and Peter Cox. Aldershot: Ashgate, 2007, pp. 97–112.

"An Office on Wheels." *Cycling: An Illustrated Weekly*, Nov. 3, 1894, p. 247.

Olwell, Victoria. "The Body Types: Corporeal Documents and Body Politics Circa 1900." *Literary Secretaries/Secretarial Culture*, edited by Leah Price and Pamela Thurschwell. Aldershot: Ashgate, 2005, pp. 48–62.

Olwell, Victoria. "Typewriters and the Vote." *Signs*, vol. 29, no. 1, 2003, pp. 55–83.

"Our Pepper Box." *Pick-Me-Up*, Mar. 26, 1892, p. 418.

"Our Typewriter." *Fun*, Oct. 19, 1892, p. 168.

"Overlooked No More: Lillias Campbell Davidson, an Early Advocate for Women's Cycling." *New York Times*, Mar. 8, 2008, www.nytimes.com/2018/03/08/obituaries/overlooked-lillias-campbell-davidson.html. Accessed Apr. 6, 2022.

"Overthrown." *Lady Cyclist*, Apr. 10, 1897, pp. 745–46.

"Parisienne Cycling Modes." *Cycling World Illustrated*, Sept. 16, 1896, pp. 9–11.

"Parliamentary Nottings." *Women's Penny Paper*, Jul. 26, 1890, p. 475.

Parsons, Deborah L. *Streetwalking the Metropolis: Women, the City, and Modernity*. Oxford: Oxford University Press, 2000.

"Paul's Ring, or a Bicycle." *Lady Cyclist*, Apr. 17, 1897, pp. 815–17.

Petty, Ross D. "Peddling the Bicycle in the 1890s: Mass Marketing Shifts into High Gear." *Journal of Macromarketing*, vol. 15, no. 1, 1995, pp. 32–46.

Pflueger, Pennie. "The Piano and Female Subjectivity: Kate Chopin's The Awakening (1899) and Jane Campion's The Piano (1993)." *Women's Studies*, vol. 44, no. 4, 2015, pp. 468–98.

"Phoebe Strange." By Thomas Cobb. *The English Illustrated Magazine*, May 1897, pp. 125–33.

"Piano Playing without Practicing." *Musical Standard*, Nov. 30, 1895, pp. 350–51.

Pitman, Sir Issac. *Pitman's Typewriter Manual*. London: Pitman & Sons, 1897.

Price, Leah. "Grant Allen's Impersonal Secretaries: Rereading The Type-Writer Girl." *Grant Allen: Literature and Cultural Politics at the Fin-de-siècle*, edited by William Greenslade and Terence Rodgers. Aldershot: Ashgate, 2005, pp. 129–42.

Price, Leah. and Pamela Thurschwell, editors. *Literary Secretaries/Secretarial Culture*. Aldershot: Ashgate, 2005.

Price, Russell and Francesco Badoleto, "Social Subordination and Superiority in Gissing's A Daughter of the Lodge." *A Garland for Gissing*, edited by Bouwe Postmus. Amsterdam: Rodopi, 2001, pp. 237–46.

"Pros and Cons: Some Interesting Letters Addressed to the Editor." *Lady Cyclist*, May 1895, p. 118.

*The Queen.*Jan. 8, 1898, p. 92.

Rabinbach, Anson. *The Human Motor: Energy, Fatigue and the Origins of Modernity.* Berkeley: University of California Press, 1992.

"Rapid Review: Mrs. Edward Kennard *The Motor Maniac*." *St James's Gazette*, 6 Nov. 1902, p. 16.

Rappaport, Erika Diane. *Shopping for Pleasure: Women in the Making of London's West End.* Princeton, NJ: Princeton University Press, 2000.

"Rational Costume." *Punch*, Jun. 13, 1896. Repr. in Alison Adburgham, *A Punch History of Manners and Modes: 1841–1940.* London: Hutchinson, 1961, p. 157.

Rawlinson, Barbara. *A Man of Many Parts: Gissing's Short Stories, Essays and Other Works.* Amsterdam: Rodopi, 2006.

Re, Lucia. "Maria Ginanni vs. F. T. Marinetti: Women, Speed, and War in Futurist Italy." *Annali d'Italianistica*, vol. 27, 2009, pp. 103–24.

"The Reformation of Laurence Hope." *Lady Cyclist*, Feb. 20, 1897, pp. 508–10.

"Remington Standard Typewriter." *Horse and Hound*, Mar. 1, 1888, p. 180.

"The Result of an Accident." *Lady Cyclist*, Jun. 5, 1897, pp. 126–28.

"Review of *The Odd Women*." *The Athenaeum*, May 27, 1893, p. 667.

"Review of *The Type-Writer Girl*." *The Athenaeum*, Sept. 11, 1897, p. 348.

"Review of *The Typewriter Girl*." *The Birmingham Owl*, Dec. 23, 1897, p. 12.

"Review of *The Type-Writer Girl*." *Hearth and Home*, Oct. 7, 1897, p. 843.

Richards, Grant. "Mr. Grant Allen and His Work." *Novel Review*, Jun. 1892, pp. 261–68.

Richards, Thomas. *The Commodity Culture of Victorian England: Advertising and Spectacle 1851–1914.* Redwood City, CA: Stanford University Press, 1990.

Richardson, Angelique and Chris Willis, eds. *The New Woman in Fiction and in Fact: Fin-de-Siècle Feminisms.* London: Macmillan, 2002.

Richardson, Kenneth. *The British Motor Industry 1896–1939.* London: Macmillan, 1977.

Amy G. Richter. *Home on the Rails: Women, the Railroad, and the Rise of Public Domesticity.* Chapel Hill, NC: The University of North Carolina Press, 2005.

"Rising Stars." *The Windsor*, Dec. 1896, p. 383.

Ritchie, Andrew. *King of the Road: An Illustrated History of Cycling.* London: Wildwood House, 1975.

"Romance of a Bicycle." *Bow Bells: A Magazine of General Literature and Art for Family Reading*, Sept. 18, 1896, pp. 289–94.

"Romance of the Wheel." *Cycling: An Illustrated Weekly*, Apr. 25, 1896, pp. 18–22.

"Romance of Four Wheels." *Strand Magazine: An Illustrated Monthly*, Nov. 1897, pp. 497–506.

Rønning, Anne Holden. *Hidden and Visible Suffrage.* Bern: Peter Lang, 1995.

Rubinstein, David. "Cycling in the 1890s." *Victorian Studies*, vol. 21, no. 1, 1977, pp. 47–71.

"Rudyard Kipling, J. M. Barrie Talk About their Typewriters, 1902." https://oztypewriter.blogspot.com/2013/09/RUDYARD-KIPLING-JMBARRIE-TALK-ABOUT.HTML. Sept. 23, 2013. Accessed Jan. 12, 2021.

Rush, Anita. "The Bicycle Boom of the Gay Nineties: A Reassessment." *Material Culture Review*, no. 18, 1983, pp. 1–12.

Russo, Thomas A. *Mechanical Typewriters: Their History, Value, and Legacy.* Atglen, PA: Schiffer, 2002.

Schenkel, Elmar. "H. G. Wells and Speed." *Restoring the Mystery of the Rainbow: Literature's Refraction of Science*, edited by Valerie Tinkler-Villani and C. C. Barfoot. Amsterdam: Rodopi, 2011, pp. 729–41.

Schivelbusch, Wolfgang. *The Railway Journey: The Industrialization of Time and Space in the 19th Century.* Berkeley: University of California Press, 1977.

Scharff, Virginia. *Taking the Wheel: Women and the Coming of the Motor Age.* Albuquerque, NM:University of New Mexico Press, 1999.

Schnapp, Jeffrey T. "Crash (Speed as Engine of Individuation)." *Modernism/Modernity*, vol. 6, no. 1, 1999, pp. 1–49.

"Self-Supporting Women." *Practical Phonographer*, Sept. 1884, pp. 190–92.

Seltzer, Mark. *Bodies and Machines.* London: Routledge, 1992.

Seltzer, Mark. "Serial Killers (1)." *Differences*, vol. 5, no. 1,1993, pp. 92–128.

Sheffield, Suzanne Le-May. "The 'Empty-Headed Beauty' and the 'Sweet Girl Graduate': Women's Science Education in *Punch*, 1860–90." *Culture and Science in the Nineteenth-Century Media*, edited by Louise Henson, Geoffrey Cantor, Gowan Dawson, Richard Noakes, Sally Shuttleworth and Janthan R. Topham. Aldershot: Ashagate, 2004, pp. 15–28.

Shiach, Morag. *Modernism, Labor and Selfhood in British Literature and Culture 1890–1930*. Cambridge: Cambridge University Press, 2004.

Shiach, Morag. "Modernity, Labor and the Typewriter." *Modernist Sexualities*, edited by d. Hugh Stevens and Caroline Howlett. Manchester: Manchester University Press, 2000, pp. 114–29.

Showalter, Elaine. *Daughters of Decadence: Woman Writers of the Fin-de-Siècle*. London: Virago, 1993.

Showalter, Elaine. *Sexual Anarchy: Gender and Culture at the Fin-de-siècle*. London: Virago, 1992.

Sillars, Stuart. *Visualization in Popular Fiction 1860–1960: Graphic Narratives, Fictional Images*. London: Routledge, 1995.

Simpson, Clare S. "Capitalizing on Curiosity: Women's Professional Cycle Racing in the Late-Nineteenth Century." *Cycling and Society*, eds. Dave Horton, Paul Rosen, and Peter Cox. London: Routledge, 2007, pp. 47–66.

"The Skylight Room." *Idler*. Aug. 1910, pp. 1169–73.

"Sloane Gardens House." *Girl's Own Paper*, May 16, p. 526.

Smethurst, Paul. *The Bicycle: Towards a Global History*. London: Palgrave Macmillan, 2015.

Smith, Robert A. *A Social History of the Bicycle: Its Early Life and Times in America*. New York: McGraw-Hill, 1972.

Snyder, Carey. *The Iconoclasm of H. G. Wells and the Modernist Canon*. London: Routledge, 2019.

"Society of Typists." *Women's Penny Paper*, Aug. 3, 1889, p. 2.

"Society of Typists." *Women's Penny Paper*, Jul. 4, 1891, p. 584.

"Some Literary Typewriters." *The Idler: An Illustrate Magazine*, Jul. 5, 1894, pp. 321–37.

"The Song of the Wheel." *Outing*, Feb. 1897, p. 455.

"The Sorrows of Marie Corelli." *Wheelwoman*, Dec. 19, 1896, p. 7.

"Speed v. Pleasure." *Lady Cyclist*, May 1897, p. 211.

Spiers, John. *Gissing and the City: Cultural Crisis and the Making of Books in Late Victorian England*. London: Palgrave Macmillan, 2006.

"Sporting Notes." *Sporting Times*, Apr. 5, 1890, p. 1.

Srole, Carole. "'A Blessing to Mankind, and Especially to Womankind': The Typewriter and the Feminization of Clerical Work, Boston, 1860–1920." *Women, Work, and Technology: Transformations*, eds. Barbara Drygulski Wright et al. Ann Arbor, MI: University of Michigan Press, 1987, pp. 84–100.

Stevenson, Catherine Barnes. "The Working-Class Woman in North and South." *The Victorian Web: Literature, History & Culture in the Age of Victoria*. https://victorianweb.org/authors/gaskell/n_s4.html. Accessed Apr. 1, 2023.

Stiegler, Bernard. *Technics and Time: The Fault of Epimetheus. Vol. 1*. Trans. Richard Beardsworth and George Collins. Redwood City, CA: Stanford University Press, 1994.

Stiltner, Barry. "*Hard Times*: The Disciplinary City." *Dickens Studies Annual*, vol. 30, 2001, pp. 193–215.

Stubbs, Patricia. *Women and Fiction: Feminism and the Novel 1880–1920*. Hassocks: Harvester, 1979.

"The Stranger." *Cycling: An Illustrated Weekly*, Sept. 8, 1894, p. 128.

"The Strange Tale of a Type-Writer." *Harper's New Monthly Magazine*, Oct. 1890, pp. 679–80.

Sussman, Herbert. *Victorian Technology: Invention, Innovation and the Rise of the Machine*. Santa Barbara: Praeger Publishers, 2009.

Sykes, A. G. P. "The Evolution of the Sex." *Westminster Review*, no. 143, 1895, pp. 396–400.

"Table Talk." *The Literary World*, vol. 46, 1892, p. 13.

Thackeray, William Makepeace. *Vanity Fair*. 1848. Ware: Wordsworth Classics, 1998.

"Things Not to Dwell On." *Pick-Me-Up*, May 31, 1890, p. 136.

Thompson, F. *Over to Candelford*. Oxford: Oxford University Press, 1941.

"Tiffs and Tales." *Judy, or the London Serio-Comic Journal*, Jan. 24, 1900, p. 40.

"To My Friends." By Lady Jane. *The London Journal and Weekly Record of Literature, Science and Art*, Feb. 6, 1904, p. 117.

Tonna, Charlotte Elizabeth. "The Forsaken Home." *The Works of Charlotte Elizabeth Tonna, Vol. 3*, New York: M. W. Dodd, 1845, pp. 418–46.

"To Time: An Apostrophe." *Pick-Me-Up*, Oct. 1, 1892, p. 2.

Tooley, Sarah. "Women of Note in the Cycling World: A Chat with Mdme. Sarah Grand." *The Hub*, Oct. 17, 1896, p. 419.

"To the Girl Typewriter." *Women's Penny Paper*, Nov. 9, 1893, p. 608.

Travers, Timothy. *Samuel Smiles and the Victorian Work Ethic*. New York: Garland, 1987.

"Trespassers Will Be Prosecuted" *Lady Cyclist*, Jul. 31, 1897, pp. 388–92.

Twain, Mark. *Autobiography of Mark Twain*. Vol. 2. Berkeley: University of California Press, 2013.

Twain, Mark. "The First Writing-Machine." *The Complete Essays of Mark Twain*, ed. Charles Nieder. New York: Da Capo Press, 2000, pp. 324–26.

Twain, Mark. *A Connecticut Yankee in King Arthur's Court*. 1889. New York: Bantam Classics, 1983.

Twain, Mark. *Life on the Mississippi*. 1883. New York: Signet, 2009.

Twain, Mark. *The Adventures of Tom Sawyer*. 1876. New York: Signet, 2008.

"The Type-Writer and Type-Writing." *The Girl's Own Paper*, Aug. 18, 1888, p. 745.

"The Typewriter Girl." *Strand Magazine*, Aug. 1900, pp. 161–69.

"A Type-Writer's Romance." *Bow Bells: A Magazine of General Literature and Art for Family Reading*, Mar. 23, 1894, pp. 301–05.

"Typewriters v. Pianos." *Women's Penny Paper*, Aug. 24, 1893, p. 423.

"Typewriters' Stub Finger." *Pick-Me-Up*, Mar. 26, 1892, p. 418.

"Type Writing." *Englishwoman's Review*, Oct. 1884, p. 480.

"Typewriting and Touch." *Musical Standard*, May 23, 1896, pp. 327–28.

"Typewriting and the Typist." *Atalanta*, Oct. 1, 1897, p. 52.

"A Typewriting Episode." *The Leisure Hour*, Feb. 1900, pp. 348–54.

"Typewriting Has Become Quite a Fashionable Accomplishment." *Le Follet*, Aug. 1, 1890, p. 170.

"Type Writing Machine." *Scientific American*, Jul. 6, 1867, p. 3.

"Typewriting Notes." *The Phonetic Journal*, Jun. 4, 1892, p. 354.

"The Type-written Letter." By Robert Barr. *The Idler*, Jan. 1893, pp. 597–605.

"Typing like the Lightening: *Answers* Chats with the Champion Key-Tapper." *Answers*. Jan. 9, 1909, p. 237.

Tyrrell, Brenda. "Tracing Wells's New Woman through *The Wheels of Chance* and *The War of the Worlds*." *The Wellsian*, no. 39, 2016, pp. 48–64.

"Uncle Bob." *The Windsor Magazine: An Illustrated Monthly for Men and Women*, Dec. 1897, pp. 590–95.

"Vagaries of Fate." *Lady Cyclist*, Jul. 17, 1897, pp. 310–12.

Veblen, Thornstein. *The Theory of the Leisure Class*. New York: Random House, 2001.

Veeser, H. Aram. *The New Historicism*. London: Routledge, 1989.

"Vicar's Daughter." *The London Reader: Of Literature, Science, Art and General Information*, Jul. 28, 1883, pp. 301–10.

Virilio, Paul. *Speed and Politics: An Essay on Dromology*. Los Angeles, CA: Semiotext(e), 1986.

Virilio, Paul. *The Aesthetics of Disappearance*. Los Angeles, CA: Semiotext(e), 2009.

Wajcman, Judy. "Reflections on Gender and Technology Studies: In What State is the Art?" *Social Studies of Science*, vol. 30, no. 3, 2000, pp. 323–480.

Walkowitz, Judith R. *City of Dreadful Delight: Narratives of Sexual Danger in Late-Victorian London*. Chicago: University of Chicago Press, 1992.

Wainwright, David. *Broadwood by Appointment: A History*. London: Quiller, 1982.

Walters, Margaret. Introduction. *The Odd Women*, by George Gissing. 1893. London: Virago, 1980. pp. i–x.

Wånggren, Lena. *Gender, Technology and the New Woman*. Edinburgh: Edinburgh University Press, 2017.

"Wanted—A Bicycle." *Windsor Magazine: An Illustrate Monthly*, Jun. 1899, pp. 713–26.

"Wanted Common Sense." *Women's Penny Paper*, Oct. 11, 1890, p. 606.

Weber, Max. *Economy and Society. Vol. 1.* 1921. Transl. and ed. G. Roth and C. Wittich. New York: Bedminster Press, 1968.

Wells, H. G. *Ann Veronica: A Modern Love Story*. London: T. Fisher Unwin, 1913.

Wells, H. G. *Anticipations of the Reaction of Mechanical and Scientific Progress upon Human Life and Thought*. London: Chapman & Hall, 1902.

Wells, H. G. *Certain Personal Matters*. 1897. Tennessee: Nabu Public Domain Reprints, 2011.

Wells, H. G. *The Correspondence of H. G. Wells. Volume I. 1880–1903*, ed. David C. Smith. London: Pickering & Chatto, 1998.

Wells, H. G. *Experiment in Autobiography: Discoveries and Conclusions of a Very Ordinary Brain (Since 1866)*. London: Gollancz, 1934.

Wells, H. G. "The Novels of Mr. George Gissing." *George Gissing and H. G. Wells: Their Friendship and Correspondence*, ed. Royal A. Gettmann. Chicago: University of Illinois Press, 1961, pp. 242–59.

Wells, H. G. *The Outline of History: Being a Plain History of Life and Mankind*. New York: Doubleday, 1961.

Wells, H. G. "A Perfect Gentleman on Wheels." *H. G. Wells: Complete Short Story Omnibus*. London: Gollancz, 2011, pp. 783–92.

Wells, H. G. *The Wheels of Chance: A Bicycling Idyll*. 1896. San Bernardino, CA: Leeaf Classics, 2014.

Wells, H. G. "Preface." *The Wheels of Chance, Love and Mrs. Lewisham. The Works of H. G. Wells. Vol. 7.* Atlantic Edition. New York: T. Fisher Unwin, 1925, p. ix.

Wershler-Henry, Darren. *The Iron Whim: A Fragmented History of Typewriting*. Ithaca, NY: Cornell University Press, 2005.

"What a Typewriter Costs." *Pick-Me-Up*, Apr. 21 1894, p. 38.

"What is a Bicycle?" *Cycling World Illustrated*, Oct. 7 1896, p. 81.

"What Shall We Do with Our Daughters." *Women and Work: A Weekly Industrial, Educational, and Household Register for Women*, vol. 1, iss. 18, Oct. 3, 1874, p. 2.

"What to Do with Our Daughters." *Hearth and Home*, Oct. 27, 1892, p. 790.

"What to Do with Our Daughters." *Hearth and Home*, Feb. 9, 1893, p. 375.

"*The Wheels of Chance* Review." *The Athenaeum*, Nov. 28, 1893, p. 752.

"When in Doubt." *Lady Cyclist*, Mar. 1895, p. 42.

White, E. L. "The Powder Mutiny: A Clever, Complete Story." *Answers*, May 30, 1908, p. 80.

"Whitwell Roasted." *Cycling: An Illustrated Weekly*, Sept. 15 1894, p. 137.

Whorton, James C. "The Hygiene of the Wheel: An Episode in Victorian Sanitary Science." *Bulletin of History of Medicine*, vol. 52, no. 1, 1978, pp. 61–88.

"Why Lady Cyclists Should Dress Well." *Lady Cyclist*, Mar. 1896, p. 9.

"Whyte." *The Owl: A Journal of Wit and Wisdom*, Feb. 17, 1899, p. 4.

Willis, Chris. "The Detective's Doppelganger: Conflicting States of Female Consciousness in Grant Allen's Detective Fiction." *Grant Allen: Literature and Cultural Politics at the Fin-de-Siècle*, eds. William Greenslade and Terence Rodgers. Aldershot: Ashgate, 2005, pp. 143–55.

Willis, Chris. "'Heaven defend me from political or highly-educated women!': Packaging the New Woman for Mass Consumption." *The New Woman in Fiction and in Fact: Fin-de- Siècle Feminisms*, eds. Angelique Richardson and Chris Willis. London: Macmillan, 2002, pp. 53–65.

Wintle, Sarah. "Horse, Bikes and Automobiles: New Woman on the Move." *The New Woman in Fiction and in Fact: Fin-de- Siècle Feminisms*, eds. Angelique Richardson and Chris Willis. London: Macmillan, 2002, pp. 66–78.

Withers, Jeremy. *The War of the Wheels: H. G. Wells and the Bicycle*. Syracuse University Press, 2017.

"Woman of Today." *Lady Cyclist*, May 1895, pp. 104–7.

The Woman Worker. First issue (London), Sept. 1907.

"Women on Wheels." *The Victorian Cyclist: A History Blog on the Joys and Perils of Cycling in Victorian Britain.* WordPress. Jul. 26, 2015. https://thevictoriancyclist.wordpress.com. Accessed Jan. 20, 2018.

"Won't Wash." *Funny Folks: A Weekly Budget of Funny Pictures, Funny Notes, Funny Jokes, and Funny Stories,* Nov. 28, 1891, p. 406.

Wosk, Julie. *Women and the Machine: Representations from the Spinning Wheel to the Electronic Age.* Baltimore: Johns Hopkins University Press, 2001.

Young, Arlene. *From Spinster to Career Woman: Middle-Class Women and Work in Victorian England.* Montreal: McGill-Queen's University Press, 2019.

Zheutlin, Peter. *Around the World on Two Wheels: Annie Londonderry's Extraordinary Ride.* New York: Citadel Press, 2007.

Zimmeck, Meta. "The Mysteries of the Typewriter: Technology and Gender in the British Civil Service, 1870–1914." *Women Workers and Technological Change in Europe in the Nineteenth and Twentieth Centuries,* edited by Gertjan de Groot and Marlou Schrover. Milton Park: Taylor and Francis, 1995, pp. 67–98.

Zurbrugg, Nicholas. "'Oh What a Feeling!' – The Literatures of the Car." *The Motor Car and Popular Culture in the 20th Century,* edited by David Thomas, Len Holden and Time Claydon. Aldershot: Ashgate, 1998, pp. 9–27

Index